Praise for Sexy Witch

"What a terrific book! Exhilarating, smart, practical advice to getting excited and empowered by the wonderful gift that is a woman's body and her sexuality, fused with profound magickal wisdom anchored in the most vital and positive expression of spirituality in the modern world—Witchcraft.

"LaSara weaves a common thread of feminist pride in all women, but it is her encouragement of the individual to define their own expression of their femininity, i.e., their own unique definition of Feminism—that is the most powerful gift of this book. Read, play, experiment, enjoy, be free and meet the sexiest person in the world—you."

—FIONA HORNE, author of *Witch!* and
Magickal Sex: A Witch's Guide to Beds, Knobs and Broomsticks

"Wake up and smell the pussy! *Sexy Witch* is so much more than your typical book of love spells. It's the antidote to that pervasive cultural brainwashing that tries to turn us all into quiet, pretty, scentless Barbie dolls. People say that sex, religion, and politics are the three things you shouldn't discuss in polite company—well, fuck that! As FireFox shows, they are all incredibly important and intimately related, and need to get talked about. I wish every woman in the world would read this book and, more importantly, DO this book. *Sexy Witch* isn't meant to be theory sitting on a shelf. It's a tool for transformation."

—JENNIFER HUNTER, author of *21st Century Wicca* and *Rites of Pleasure*

"It's not so much a matter of 'where is the sensual?' as of 'where is it not?': the touch of the breeze like morning-soft lips, the rumble of traffic like the rolling of cloud on mossy mountainside, the burble of draining bathwater like the poignant last gasp—the blink and spittle and sigh and song of life which is also the blink and spittle and sigh and song of death (we are only the in between imagining itself to be the person we believe we are). Anything that draws us closer to that reality is worthwhile, and that is what I believe your book is attempting to do. We are so delicate, so soft, so bruisable, yet also we are the wings of the eagle and the jaws of the lion: everything and nothing. We awake and touch ourselves because we are alone, and if that is through another body, we are still alone. That is what I feel you are saying: a nod, a wink and a tear, and from that shadow rises the Phoenix of existence, for we have been nowhere until we have been to our deepest, darkest light-filled soul. Your book is a gift. Thank you."

—PENNY RIMBAUD, artist/musician CRASS, and author of
Shibboleth: My Revolting Life

"This witty and smart, well-researched gem of a book has the power to transform the feminist movement at the radical roots—women's bodies and their sexuality. For any woman who wants to understand, enhance, reclaim or heal her sexuality, this book is a must. Guaranteed to liberate your sisters as well as the men and women who love them."

—ANODEA JUDITH, PH.D., author of
Wheels of Life and *Eastern Body, Western Mind*

"As a serious spiritual pragmatist, I am extremely impressed by this volume's detailed command of 'what works'—what really works—when it comes to the deep core of spiritually turned-on women's sexuality. The best teacher is truth, and LaSara FireFox is one helluva Sexy Witch."

—JORDAN GRUBER, Founder & CEO, Enlightenment.com

I have known LaSara FireFox pretty much all her life—she was born and grew up on the land in the large Hippie homesteading community where I also lived for many years. In fact, she has been my favorite niece, and I her favorite uncle, for over three decades. And I can assure you that LaSara has always been a Sexy Witch! I cannot imagine anyone more dedicated to her Path, her family, her children, her calling, and the greater causes of social justice, feminism, and environmental stewardship. She has served as Priestess and President of the Pagan church I founded, as well as President of the communal Ranch.

"LaSara writes out of a lifelong commitment of deepest integrity, and in *Sexy Witch* she lays it all out in unsparing frankness and personal vulnerability. She is your longed-for sister, lover, and confidante girlfriend—and she really knows what she's talking about! LaSara offers you authentic magick to transform your life into one of empowered radiance and self-assured confidence, as she cuts to the heart of the deepest woundings, shames, and insecurities of all women with the laser scalpel of her insight, experience, and wisdom. This book will become your treasured companion on your journey towards full realization of your glorious sexiness!"

—OBERON ZELL-RAVENHEART, author of *Grimoire for the Apprentice Wizard*

"In my quarter century of mentoring with the Earthen Spirituality Project, I've seen that how we perceive and experience our selves shapes how we approach and affect everything and everyone around us. We are sublimely wild beings called to reawaken and heal . . . beginning with the vital reinhabitation of our native Earth, our intrinsic responsibilities, sacred sentient bodies and essential Gaian bliss. Through LaSara's potent stories, rituals and practices, women of all ages (and men as well!) can reclaim that which was always and truly ours: our magickal sexuality, our hope and power."

—JESSE WOLF HARDIN, author of
Gaia Eros: Reconnecting to the Magic & Spirit of Nature

"Just when it looked like activism for women's rights had faded, along comes LaSara FireFox to stoke up the fires of feminism. She challenges many of our hidebound assumptions and enthusiastically solicits our participation in righteous revolutionary responsibility for our own health and pleasure—and she does this in clear, accessible language that encourages magic and fun. Although such a guide didn't exist for women of my generation, I'm heartened that our daughters and granddaughters have such a wonderful resource."

—M. MACHA NIGHTMARE, author of *Pagan Pride: Honoring the Craft and Culture of Earth and Goddess,* and Chair of the Public Ministry Program at Cherry Hill Seminary: Professional Pagan Ministry Education

"Sturdy and loving advice, even for those of us constitutionally unable to keep a straight face during the high priestess's candle-lit invocations."

—Ayun Halliday, author of *Job Hopper: The Checkered Career of a Down-Market Dilettante*

"A radical and subversive text for transformation and empowerment. The practices in this book have the potential for deep healing and complete awakening. A must-read for all who wish to change the world."

—NOAH LEVINE, author of *Dharma Punx*

"From the sexiest Witch of them all comes this very personal guide to finding the magick in yourself and putting that magick to work in your life. This book reads as though LaSara FireFox is holding your hand as you move through a wondrous spiritual and sexual landscape. Brava and Blessed Be!"

—KAT SUNLOVE, Legislative Affairs Director, Free Speech Coalition

"*Sexy Witch* awakens the inner spiritual healer by cultivating the intuitive goddess within all women. In the true spirit of sensual and sexual liberation, LaSara teaches you how to conjure powerful inherent magic through fun, juicy, and provocative rituals. *Sexy Witch* offers a brilliant searchlight along this mysterious and mystical road of self-transformation and self-discovery. This is groundbreaking and visionary ritual magic for rebuilding women's self-esteem and for nurturing the sacred within. Thank you, LaSara, for touching my soul with your vibrant, empowering and visionary words of wisdom."

—WENDY-O MATIK, author of
Redefining Our Relationships: Guidelines for Responsible Open Relationships

"The sacred practical feminine in *Sexy Witch* is spellbinding. This no-nonsense funny hip book educates us in the finer arts of sex and witchcraft."

—SOPHIA, author of
Fortune Telling with Playing Cards and *Fortune in a Coffee Cup*

"A call to sexual, magickal and personal initiation sure to transform the reader—male, female or otherwise. Clear, creative, fun and empowering! I'll never look at my witch sisters the same way again. Thank you, LaSara."

—CHRISTOPHER PENCZAK, author of
Gay Witchcraft, The Outer Temple of Witchcraft, and *Sons of the Goddess*

"*Sexy Witch* is so many things wrapped into one fantastic book! It's a manual of magick, a manifesto for the self, a revealing mirror held up to an image-obsessed society and a tool for positive transformation. It's filled with insights into history, culture, gender, psychology, ritual and the nature of feminine power!"

—JOSH WETZEL, author of *The Paradigmal Pirate*

"This incredible Sexy Witch, LaSara W. FireFox, is a modern-day Emma Goldman, Dr. Susan Block and Flo Kennedy rolled into one. Her writings are sunshine in a dark era of repression and theocracy. The book *Sexy Witch* is a reminder of the beauty of sexuality and the humanity that is possible when people are not programmed by anti-freedom forces. I hope everyone in the nation has an opportunity to read it."

—REV. BOOKBURN, RadioVolta.org

LaSara FireFox is a writer, ritualist, sex-positive activist and educator, and designer/facilitator of a wide variety of interactive, exploration-based workshops. She lives in Northern California with her husband/best friend and their two amazing daughters. LaSara believes that the most revolutionary, and perhaps evolutionary, act we can engage in is to become healthy, strong, and empowered.

You can find out more about LaSara and her work at www.lasara.us, and can contact her at firefox@lasara.us. She welcomes well-thought-out commentary from her readers.

Note from the Publisher

The woman's image on the cover is only one representation of who a Sexy Witch may be. We chose it because we thought it was stunning, powerful, and a good illustration of the spirit of *Sexy Witch,* but we hope you, the reader, know that Sexy Witches come in all colors, sizes, shapes, and ages.

To Write to the Author

If you wish to contact the author or would like more information about this book, please write to the author in care of Llewellyn Worldwide and we will forward your request. Both the author and publisher appreciate hearing from you and learning of your enjoyment of this book and how it has helped you. Llewellyn Worldwide cannot guarantee that every letter written to the author can be answered, but all will be forwarded. Please write to:

LaSara FireFox
℅ Llewellyn Worldwide
2143 Wooddale Drive, Dept. 978-0-7387-0752-5
Woodbury, MN 55125-2989, U.S.A.
Please enclose a self-addressed stamped envelope for reply,
or $1.00 to cover costs. If outside U.S.A., enclose
international postal reply coupon.

Many of Llewellyn's authors have websites with additional information and resources. For more information, please visit our website at http://www.llewellyn.com.

Sexy Witch

LaSara FireFox

Llewellyn Publications
Woodbury, Minnesota

First Edition
Second Printing, 2010

Cover photograph © 2005 Susanne Walstrom/Photonica
Cover design by Lisa Novak
Edited by Andrea Neff
Interior illustrations © 2005 Mary Ann Zapalac
Llewellyn is a registered trademark of Llewellyn Worldwide, Ltd.

Cover model(s) used for illustrative purposes only and may not endorse or represent the book's subject.

Excerpt from "Blood in the Boardroom" by Ani DiFranco ©1993 Righteous Babe Records
    used by permission.

Excerpt from "Bata Motel" © Crass/Eve Libertine used by permission.

The websites listed are correct at the time of publication.

Cataloging-in-Publication Data is on file with the Library of Congress.
ISBN 13: 978-0-7387-0752-5
ISBN 10: 0-7387-0752-X

Llewellyn Worldwide does not participate in, endorse, or have any authority or responsibility concerning private business transactions between our authors and the public.
    All mail addressed to the author is forwarded but the publisher cannot, unless specifically instructed by the author, give out an address or phone number.
    Any Internet references contained in this work are current at publication time, but the publisher cannot guarantee that a specific location will continue to be maintained. Please refer to the publisher's website for links to authors' websites and other sources.

Llewellyn Publications
A Division of Llewellyn Worldwide, Ltd.
2143 Wooddale Drive, Dept. 978-0-7387-0752-5
Woodbury, MN 55125-2989, U.S.A.
www.llewellyn.com

Llewellyn is a registered trademark of Llewellyn Worldwide, Ltd.

Printed in the United States of America

This book is dedicated to
Freyja Olsen, who helped me conceive of this book,
Jonna Weidaw, who helped me birth it,
and Aurora and Solome O'Greenfield, who will watch it grow.

Contents

Figures

Acknowledgments

I offer huge amounts of gratitude to many who helped this book come into existence. Without the understanding and love of my daughters, Aurora and Solome, my life would lack meaning, grounding, and direction. You girls have been most gracious in allowing me time to work, and still loving me even when you miss me.

Without the sometimes merciless yet always understanding, unflagging support and help from my husband, Bobby Cochran, I would not be able to work, nor live or love, as I do. You are my committed, on-the-spot editor, my brainstorming partner, and my force of grounding when I get too crazy. The support you offer me is truly beyond expectation.

The love of those I love keeps me strong on my path. I thank each of you from the bottom of my heart.

Without my wonderful agent, Nancy Ellis-Bell, I would still be looking for a publisher. And without Jonna Weidaw, I would still be trying to finish this book! Jonna is my total s/hero! By performing the task of being my research assistant and data-compiler,

Jonna made it possible for me to meet my deadline for *Sexy Witch*. She also brought me food when she visited, made me laugh, helped me work, helped me play when I needed to, and kept me supplied with my favorites vices while I slaved at the machine. I can't thank her enough. Her husband, Ryan, was extremely generous in his sharing of her time and attention. Thanks to the both of them!

Thanks to Natalie, Alison, Andrea, Drew, and the whole crew at Llewellyn. I couldn't have been brought into the world of publishing by a better group of folks. Throughout the process of bringing this book to fruition, I felt heard and cared for, even if not always agreed with. Everyone has had incredible patience with me as I learned the ropes. So to each of you, thanks for breaking me in gently!

I had a test-reading crew that helped out massively with their comments and critiques. Huge thanks to Marylyn Motherbear Scott, Traci Burleigh, Chris Zephyr McBride, Kim Haines, Rebecca Wong, Sherry Blanchard, Jody Gehrman, Tawny Martin, Cynthia McClendon, Kami McCullough, and, again, Jonna Weidaw and Bobby Cochran (my one and only male test-reader).

I thank Freyja Olsen for her help and inspiration, Annie Sprinkle and Nina Hartley for their support and friendship, and my huge and wonderful extended family of friends for doing what they do best—living the life we are creating. Yolkai Scott, Ackshawn Anthony Catanzaro, Traci Burleigh, Travis Smith, Lauren Spieler, Renee Petry, Josh King, Jonna and Ryan Weidaw, and so many others, thank you all for being here at this time in my life. Thanks also to my siblings for sharing in this life: Yolkai and Emrys Scott, Patience Foster, Tryntje and Tobias Young, and Jutta, Traven, and Talon Brandon.

Last, but not least, I thank the parents, Alice and Jim Cochran, for helping so much in so many ways through this long trek toward the life we are building. And thanks to my mother, Marylyn Motherbear Scott, and my father, Troll Brandon, for their sacrifices, their teachings, their support, their pride in me, and their enduring love.

Foreword

by Annie Sprinkle

Dear *Sexy Witch* reader,

Congratulations! How fortuitous that *Sexy Witch* has made it into your hot little hands. Welcome, and come on in. Dive into these soft, smooth pages to enter a magical Universe filled with sensual delights, inspiration, beauty, heated passions, and adventures beyond your wildest nocturnal wet dreams.

You can dive into this magical Universe in a variety of ways. Simply relax and read what the pages tell you, take their wisdom inside you, and roll their abundant ideas around in your pretty head. Or you can enter like Alice entered Wonderland, by trying and experiencing things. Either way, don't hesitate, just go on in. A sensual, magical mystery tour into the magnificent land of the Sexy Witch is coming to take you away. You will absolutely love it and likely have a sense of coming Home, of belonging in this special land.

LaSara FireFox is the perfect guide for your pilgrimage. Besides being an absolutely knock 'em alive, babelicious beauty, with fiery red hair, dancing freckles, and the body of the ultimate Amazon queen, she is breathtakingly beautiful on the inside as well. Kind, understanding, and compassionate, she'll take good care of you, put you fully at ease. (Wait till you feel how!) She'll generously reveal and share her sexual experience and her magical-life experience with you. She's been there and done it, many glorious times. I know because I've seen her in sexy-witch action, and it was awe inspiring. Not only did she bring down the moon, but the entire solar system and more. Time stood absolutely still. The Goddess came through her every divinely scented pore. The woman is powerful and hot hot hot! They don't call her FireFox for nothin', believe you me.

Another wonderful thing about LaSara is that not only can she fly around effortlessly on a broomstick, she can be sturdily grounded, organized, and efficient, and she takes care of business. The exercises she created for you here are well thought out, and do the trick. The steps are carefully laid out before you, building a stairway to Sexy Witch Heaven, or to the Sexy Witch Underworld, depending on what you need and want. LaSara built this stairway of steps to accommodate your unique needs, whether you are experienced or just starting your ascent, or descent, as it were.

Well, this is where I will take my leave. Enjoy these sexy pages, and enjoy your life. Hey, it is *your* life. Why not live it on your own terms? Magically and fully, starting now. Put that in your cauldron and stir it.

Abracadabra, presto change-o, and with a great big, big O! Oh, oh, aaahhh. The spell is cast. Blessed be, sacred sexy witch sister. Have a great trip! And merry we meet again.

Orgasmically yours,
Annie Sprinkle
aka Anya

Foreword
by Nina Hartley

It's with great pleasure that I get to say a few words about a wonderful, unique, smart, funny, sexy-as-hell woman who also happens to be a friend of mine. LaSara is one of those only-a-few-to-a-world women who is destined to leave her mark on those who meet her, and I'm thrilled that she has written the book you're holding in your hands.

LaSara is a Seeker of truth, and rather fearless about it. She is her own best advertisement. She remembers meeting me at a conference in Los Angeles a number of years back, and what I recall as our first meeting was, in fact, our second. It was at a small convention in San Francisco. I was standing around, bored at how slow it was, when across the room I spied a fantastically sexy woman pushing a baby stroller. She just glowed with strength, power, sensuality, and good humor. Normally, the presence of a baby commands all of my attention. This time, however, the mother radiated such "oomph" that I couldn't help but notice her first. She was just damn fine and sexy, confident, smart, open, easygoing, and all the things any girl wants to be when she grows up, me included. The term "sexy mama" was coined for LaSara, I just know. She clearly was on to something, though I didn't know then what it might be. We hit it off immediately, and have been buddies ever since.

When people ask me, "Nina, how did you get to be the way you are?" or, "How can I be like you?" or say, "I could never be like you!" I have this to say to them: I don't want anyone to "be like me." I want people to develop the freedom to be themselves, to have the courage to find out what about them they want to express, especially in the realm of sexuality, and to have access to the information necessary to help them achieve that goal. I took the tools available to me during my younger years and, fueled by my own sexuality, got myself to where I am today, one mistake and one success at a time. Back then, the library available to sexually adventurous women was much smaller than it is now, and there were a lot of gaps in the literature. There was plenty of theory but few concrete, proven ways to put these radical, new, exciting views into practice.

In order for me to become "Nina," the first task I had to accomplish—which anyone has to accomplish, actually—was to become comfortable with my body, to fully inhabit my skin, as well as being able to welcome pleasure on my own terms. While this should be natural, and is our absolute birthright as humans, our culture does all it can—deliberately as well as incidentally—to instill shame and guilt in us. Particularly insidious is the creation of such deep-seated levels of sexual guilt and shame that people can no longer enjoy their bodies, feel at ease during lovemaking, or even accept gestures of love and affection from others.

When we have been shamed and guilt-tripped about our bodies, we are unable to fully inhabit them, and our lives are much poorer for it. Without being connected to our physical selves, we'll be forever insecure about the love of others, constantly wondering what's "wrong" with us, and generally being unhappy in life. Each of us must, as adults, fight our way back into our bodies, find an internal balance, and strive toward wholeness. To paraphrase an old book, we must "become as little children" again, able to feel completely at home in our naked skins, reveling in the sheer joy of living, open to pleasure without shame.

My journey back to my body was helped by the books of the time, but none of them, not even Betty Dodson's immensely important book *Sex For One,* was programmatic in any way, helping one systematically back into one's skin so that one could enjoy life and adult pleasures. They offered advice, certainly, and Betty's book taught us how to have orgasms, which is vitally important. But the women's movement had to mature enough for the second generation of strong, sexual women to come of age. All this brings us to LaSara and her hard-won wisdom.

Here's the book I wished I had either found back then or been able to write now. Now, when people say, "But Nina, how do I make friends with my body, as you say I should?" I can tell them to get this book! LaSara has done her homework, and done it well. When someone is ready to tackle her personal issues about sex, her body, power, pleasure, spirit, and self-actuation, this is the book to pick up. Step by step, week by week, she takes the reader through what she must do to reclaim her body and to feel confidence in it.

We hear a lot about our bodies being sacred, about them being temples and how we should honor them. This is all well and good, and even correct. What's been missing is a way to consecrate our bodies that isn't also anchored in Monotheism and Puritanism, "modesty" and "chastity," the patriarchy and the notion of "women's virtue." As the saying goes, "Women's virtue is man's greatest invention." Women's innate power has, for millennia, been a source of fear and awe for many men, who have done their best to subdue and contain it. Women and men alike labor today under the cultural/psychic effects of such efforts.

For you to have picked up this book you likely have had a stirring of something deep within you, some feeling of wanting there to be more to life than you are experiencing now. Take a moment to praise yourself for your bravery. Why is it brave to pick up this book? Because you don't know what will be revealed to you as you go through the exercises LaSara has developed. It will take bravery to keep going when the feelings get white-hot, or fear is coursing through your veins, when doubt rears its ugly head and tries to get you to abandon your journey.

The reader may very well have two sides to her. One will be frightened by the immensity of the task at hand and want to run from it, while the other will be pushing eagerly toward the Promised Land. That second self is the one to listen to here. The frightened side is the Conditioned self, the one that doesn't want to get better, for it will have to "die" in order for your authentic self to be revealed.

The "self" that wants to move forward with the program is more the "real" you, the one who wants to live fully. As best as you can, let that part of you be the leader here, as she knows what she needs. By paying attention to your body and its responses to the exercises, by being open to what you learn about yourself, the healing will take place at the right speed for you. Our bodies can't lie to us, but we all must learn how to listen to them.

So, LaSara, thank you very much for your offering to the world, and thanks for generously sharing what you've learned with the rest of us!

—Nina Hartley

Sexy Witch Intro and Study Guide

READ THIS FIRST!

★ If you read only one part of this section, read "How to Work This Book" on page 5.

What Sexy Witch *Is, and Why I Wrote It*

Sexy Witch is a personal mission with a cultural context. The path you will discover within these pages is unique to you. A combination workbook, spell book, and informational guide, each chapter of *Sexy Witch* offers you the opportunity to move deeper into the process of deconstruction and then reconstruction of your relationships with your body, your sexuality, your sense of self, and your sense of power and empowerment. *Sexy Witch* offers you a process by which to establish your intuitive understanding of how you work, and what works for you. Through working *Sexy Witch*, you will be initiated into the mysteries of your own body, psyche, and power. You are the Priestess here, and yours is the Temple. Build it. Honor it. Enjoy it!

★ ————————————

Deconstruction: To take apart, in this case for the sake of examination and to prepare for reconstruction. I am *not* referring specifically to literary Deconstructionist theory.

• • •

Matrix: Womb, starting point, context.

• • •

Androcentric: Male-centered.

———————————— ★

Within these pages I offer a cultural context for the experiences that, as women, we nearly universally face. From body shame to body acceptance, from genital shame to pussy pride, from overall sexual fear and disempowerment to creation of a healthy matrix for personal empowerment, the roots of our causes of wounding *and* our potential for healing are becoming more and more exposed.

In *Sexy Witch* you will learn about the underpinnings that create an atmosphere supportive of our continued shame, and you will learn how to break free from that atmosphere. You will learn how androcentric culture has historically created self-supporting belief systems designed to stabilize the status quo. You will learn how everything from fashion to medicine and medical theory have been used as part of a system designed to keep women "in their place." And, you will learn about the work that women have done throughout history to overcome this oppression.

Perhaps more importantly you will also learn, through exercises, journaling, and ritual, how these cultural stories have shaped the person you are today. You will have the opportunity to explore where your early experiences (imprinting) and personal history (*your*story!) have created more personalized complexes of emotion and behavior. You will also see where these meet up with our cultural biases, and where they don't. You will have the opportunity to mine your own depths, and to transform coal into diamond. You will be offered the power to rebuild your worldview in ways that work specifically for you, and you will emerge from this experience with the ability to move beyond any limitations that you do not choose to maintain.

While *Sexy Witch* includes elements of cultural and feminist theory, this book is not about blame, and it is not designed to get you angry and leave you that way. My hope is that through offering a metaperspective of cultural influence, we can begin to release our feelings of responsibility for the multitude of conditions that allow our wounding while also claiming the power to heal those wounds.

Through claiming our wounds, we also claim our power to heal. Freed from our attachments to titles like "victim" and "survivor," we may find empowerment based in a healthy sense of personal awareness, power, and self-actualization rather than empowerment based in victimization.

It is important to recognize that all of us—woman, man, boy, and girl—are trapped in this cultural game. The experience varies from vantage point to vantage point, but we all have our programs. Or rather, the program has us.

As we begin to see this cultural fabric, we may become more able to recognize how some of our wounds are founded in it, and how the wounds of others arise from these same sources. At that point perhaps, at least to an extent, we can globalize those wounds. In doing so, we may see how healing ourselves can be a radical, magickal, and revolutionary act. Becoming healthy, strong, and empowered may be the most revolutionary, and perhaps evolutionary, act we can engage in.

So, I wrote *Sexy Witch* for me, for you, and in the hope of leaving this world a better place for the children (yours, mine, ours), and their children, and their children's children. May we all grow strong, resourceful, and healthy.

Some Words About Words

Words are powerful. We must recognize this in order to be truly effective in our goals and manifestation. Words and how we use them—or don't use them—also have an amazing ability to shape thought, culture, and our personal realities.

I feel that the roots of words are interesting and important, but truly, a whole book could be written on the origins and evolution of just a handful of the words you will see within these pages. However, for the sake of clarity and understanding, I feel

Metaperspective:
A massive overview that takes the whole picture into account.

. . .

Manifestation:
To bring into existence, or that which has been brought into existence.

★ ──────────────────

Wiccan:
A widely practiced
denomination of
Witchcrafting.

────────────────── ★

the need to define at least a couple of words you'll be seeing a bit of here: *sexy* and *Witch*.

When operating from a healthy and self-defined space, it is possible to know that the word sexy is about a feeling, an attitude. Throughout this book you will have many opportunities to find out what sexy means to you, and in the knowing of it, you will gain more power to claim your own desire and the personal power of sensuality and sexiness.

This book is not focused on "how to get your man" or "becoming a Goddess in the bedroom," though these may be pleasant side effects of the work you do here. Instead, the magick you will work chapter by chapter is designed to bring you into your power as an individual, as a woman, as a sensual and sexual being, and as a Witch.

The word Witch is a word that is often misunderstood, so I want to make very clear my intended meaning. The word Witch may come from any number of root words. Many linguistic historians believe the word Witch has Indo-European roots, and came from words meaning anything from "pliant branches" to "village" to "sorcerer."[1] At this moment, my main desire is to clarify how I use the word Witch, not to create a map of why.

I am not Wiccan, though many of my teachers along the way have been. My magickal practices are infused with a Wiccan flavor, but are also influenced by many other traditions. My spiritual orientation is very eclectic, and *Sexy Witch* draws upon all the teachings that have formed my magickal relationship with reality. My style of magick-working—and my relationship with magick in general—is what I term "intuitive." The magick you will work in this book is primarily intuitive magick.

When I use the word Witch, I mean magick-worker, magickian, mage, Priest/ess, God/dess, mother, sacred whore. (Whore is another interesting and magickal word, which I delve into in Appendix II: A Compendium of S/heroes.) I mean a worker of magick so attuned to her intuitive relationship with herself that she does bend and shape reality, whether she consciously decides to or not. (And I do hope that through this work we will all gain some ground on being more capable of consciously deciding to create our lives.)

The title Witch is not, in my opinion, one that is conferred, but one that is claimed. I claim it, and I offer you the freedom to do the same.

While we're on the subject of words, I may as well address the "magick" versus "magic" spelling choice. The magick spelling first came into use during the 1940s or so. This new spelling was used to delineate between "real" magick and parlor magic, as in magic tricks. For many practitioners, the spelling has stuck. The magick spelling is most commonly used in the Ceremonial Magick and Thelemic communities, but is widely used throughout the whole magickal community.

How to Work This Book

Sexy Witch can be worked alone, or you can create a group focused on sharing the process of self-discovery. If you want to share this process with your best girlfriends, you will find a series of rituals in part 2 titled "Rituals II: Rituals for Circles of Sexy Witches." This section will guide you and your crew in facilitating the rituals in a group setting.

If you prefer to work this transformation solo, part 2 also includes a section titled "Rituals I: Rituals for the Solo Sexy Witch." This is a ritual guide designed to facilitate you in honoring your own transitions in ritual space.

Before diving into the chapters and the work at hand, I suggest that you read the introductory sections of whichever ritual section you will be following (solo or group), and that you read through Appendix I: Recipes, Correspondences, and Other Details You Might Need to Know. If you find yourself wanting more information on any of the ideas or topics presented, check Appendix III: Informational Resources to find starting points for your additional research.

Also, while you may have performed some of the exercises included in this book in the past, I encourage you to do many, if not all, of the exercises included. With most magickal work, you will gain new information even from the same exercise if used in a different context.

Sexy Witch is modeled on the flow of initiation. Not all of it will be easy, though much of it will be fun, and all of it (even the frustrating parts) will deepen your understanding

★────────────

How to Free-Write:
Put pen to paper and
write. You can start with
a prompt word, or just
a topic. Do not stop
writing until your time
is up. If you get stuck,
start again with a new
prompt word, or with
the one you first started
with.

. . .

Mind Map:
A mind map is a map of
words on a page, with
lines connecting them to
one another (figure 1).
A mind map can be-
come a great visual rep-
resentation of how ideas
connect in your personal
view of reality.
    How-To: Write a
word in the center of
a piece of paper. As
you build off the center
word, you will create a
visual representation of
how your mind connects
concepts.

────────────★

of yourself. The first four chapters are dedicated to rendering the
structure that houses your assumptions. In so doing, you will
begin uncovering the roots of your discontent, and creating the
space to define the ideal relationship with yourself.

The last three chapters are dedicated to rebuilding a worldview that suits you. In the reconstruction-oriented chapters, you
will have opportunities to rebuild your relationship with your
senses, to adopt mentors (be they deities, cultural icons, or people
you know), and to allow yourself to fully accept, and to dedicate
yourself to, the responsibility and joy of living in your sensual,
sexual, self-loving, self-nurturing, self-adoring, and self-possessed
power.

Each chapter in *Sexy Witch* includes exercises, activities, and
journal pages designed to take you into, and through, your
process of transformation and empowerment. Throughout this
book you will also find sidebars full of fun facts, myth and lore,
illuminating quotes, and anecdotes that will deepen your experience of each subject covered.

You will need a journal to write in, writing implements that
you enjoy using, and some art supplies. All journaling prompts
should be completed in your journal so you can keep track of
your progress and so you will be able to look back over it later if
you feel the desire to do so. All art-related activities will have
complete lists of any supplies that are needed.

Journaling prompts are on-topic words or phrases that are
designed to be a starting point for your process of discovery
through writing. This writing is really just for you, unless you
want to share it with others. It's not about skill or readability, but
about mapping your own internal terrain regarding the personal
discoveries that may come up while working this book. Your
writing may be pages of prose, or it may be poetry, scrambled
scrawling, or even clusters of single words. It is not about the ap-

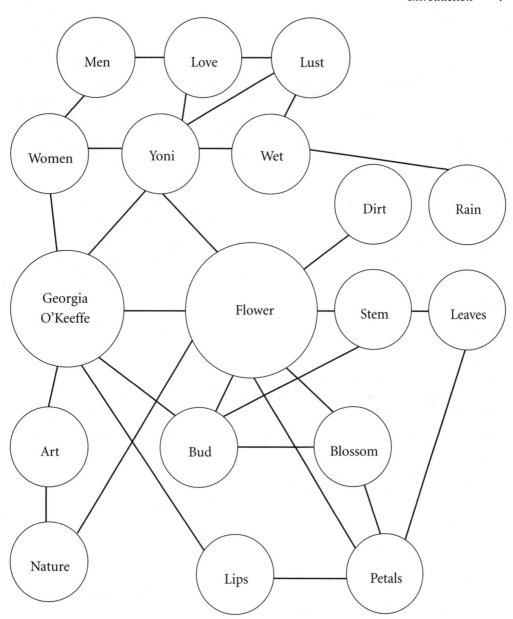

Figure 1: Mind Map

pearance of it, it's about getting at the depth we can reach when we begin to attempt to listen to our own inner voice.

The exercises and rituals for each chapter build on what was achieved in the previous one, so each chapter should be completed before moving on to the next. Each chapter is designed to be worked for one week. If you wish to take longer than a week in working a chapter, that is entirely up to you (and your crew, if you are working the book with others). However, I do suggest that you allow yourself at least seven days per chapter.

At the beginning of each week, I recommend that you read through the whole chapter. After you have read the chapter in full, go back and perform the exercises as the week progresses. Some will be assigned for the whole week, and those will be listed at the beginning of each chapter. If you don't get through all the reading on the first day of your new *Sexy Witch* week, you can hop ahead and begin your work immediately.

Now, Sexy Witch, read on, and enjoy the journey!

---

1. *Stav Academy Library,* http://www.stavacademy.co.uk/mimir/witch.htm.

PART ONE

The Chapters

CHAPTER ONE

Your Body Is a Temple

★ Daily Practice: Little Rituals Everywhere, page 20.

Your Body Is a Sacred Space

Your body is a sacred space. Maybe you've heard this sentiment before. Even if you have, chances are you have never quite believed it. But here it is: your body is the dwelling place of everything that makes you who you are. Your body is home to the amazing physiological and evolutionary alchemical magick that has created you, wholly unique and individual. Written in ancient code, our DNA carries secrets still undiscovered. Your body is a living ark, holding ancient stories encoded in your very cells.

More than merely a home to your heart and soul, your body *is* your heart and soul. And, your body is—in a profound way—your mind. The body and mind are not two things, separate and divisible, but one thing. The mind is a process, not an object. It is the amazing, synchronous magick of nerves, tissues, synapses, hormones, minerals, and molecules working in concert. Memory, desire, choice, and action are all born of the miraculous dance that is every cell in your body doing exactly what it is meant to do.

Alchemy:
A magickal process of transformation that can change the composition of elements.

. . .

Systemic:
Pertaining to a whole system. In this case, pertaining to your body as a system.

. . .

A Magickal Thought:
If you can change your mind, you can change anything.

. . .

Guided Visualization:
A technique that is used to great effect in counseling, sports, motivational speaking, and even medicine. Guided visualization is also a basic tool for ritual and magick.

Creating change in your body can create instantaneous change throughout the dynamic, living system that is your body/mind/spirit. Your entire being—your history, your potential, and your amazing ability to overcome adversity and create revolutions of evolution—may well be encapsulated in your very cells. And, changing the way you think may be the most effective way to create transformation immediately and effortlessly. Remember, thought is an adaptive physiological process replete with systemic feedback. It may be easier than you would think to create a new pattern to the flow.

Our bodies are the vehicles by which we manifest our Will on earth, and they are even more than that. Our bodies are the point of interface where the individual meets up with the rest of creation. In this chapter we will create ways to honor and sanctify this amazing, dynamic vessel that is our most unique and valuable temple.

Magickal Act: Visiting the Temple

This is a guided visualization. If you are not yet familiar with guided visualization, the exercise may take some getting used to. Or it may come naturally to you. Either way, as a Witch it is important to hone your skills of visualization, inner vision, creation, and exploration. The ability to journey inside yourself is a wonderful skill to have, and honing the ability to visualize is one of the most important things you can do to become effective in magick, and even in daily life.

During a guided visualization, you may see a series of images, or you may have the visualization run in your mind like a story line or dream, as one continuous flow. Cultivate nonattachment to how your visualization will present itself. Allow images to morph, flow, and change. If you find your mind blank for a moment, allow that blank spot in your journey to exist, and then to pass. Relax into the exercise, and allow yourself to just stay present with the process.

As with any exercise, the more you work on visualization, the more easily it will happen for you. If you feel less than satisfied with the results of a visualization the first time you try it, perform the exercise again. You could also record your voice reading the script, and use that recording.

What You Will Need

- Time. Visualization: five minutes; writing and art: twenty minutes, or as long as you want.
- Space where you will be uninterrupted.
- Your favorite art supplies.
- Journal.
- Writing implements.
- Pillow (optional).
- Blanket (optional).
- Incense (optional).
- Essential oils (optional).
- Fresh flowers (optional).

How-To

For this and other visualization exercises, you will need a space that is peaceful, quiet, and private. Create a time and space that's just for you, where you will be uninterrupted and able to focus. In this guided visualization, you will visit your temple. After this journey you will paint, draw, collage, sculpt, or otherwise craft an artifact representing your temple, or an image of it. Next you will journal about the visualization, and about creating the artifact, if you choose to. Prepare all the supplies you will need before you begin the exercise. Have paper, writing implements, and art supplies ready. As much as possible, stay in the visualization while you get it down on paper.

Some people prefer to perform guided visualizations lying down, while others prefer sitting up. Choose a position that allows you to relax, and at the same time keeps you alert. If you relax too much, you may lose focus or even drift off to sleep, not that that would be the worst thing. Sometimes it works out fine to sleep during the visualization, and then write down dream images. Staying awake has its benefits, though. A focused visualization is bound to be more fruitful. So, try for alert and relaxed as the ideal state for optimal performance of any guided visualization.

It may help to burn incense during the visualization (see "Blend Three: Inner Vision" in appendix I). It may also reinforce some prompts to have other scents present. Try a favorite essential oil or perfume, a freshly sliced orange, a chalice of wine, fresh flowers, or anything that makes you ready to enter your temple.

If you are not familiar with the concept of magickal tools, please read the section on magickal tools in appendix I and the sections on tools in part 2, Rituals I or II, before performing this visualization. The tools you encounter in this visualization may be the same ones listed, or they may be others. Allow them to be what they are, even if you do not understand immediately why they are there or what they represent for you. Do not become attached to finding tools that fit the correspondences in any conscious way. The tools you see in this visualization may be tools you use in everyday life, or they may be things you have never before seen. Remember them. Write down what they are, or create images of them, when you are done with the exercise. You may want to find or create representations of these tools for future use.

You will want to read aloud and record the visualization script beforehand.

Visualization Script

Close your eyes and relax. Focus on your breathing. Pulling each breath into your lungs, feel your lungs expand to their fullest capacity. Breathing out, release any tension you feel in your muscles. As you breathe in again, allow your lungs to become even fuller, pulling your breath deep into your abdomen. Allow your belly to relax, your ribs to expand, your mind to quiet. As thoughts come to the surface, allow them to gently pass.

As you continue breathing, feel yourself gently and slowly becoming present in your body. Feel the energy flowing through your muscles. Become aware of the rhythmic beating of your heart. Notice the steady, gentle rhythm of your breath.

Follow your breath, and the beating of your heart, deeper into a state of total relaxation. Become aware of the fluidity of your body. Allow your awareness to expand. Allow the boundaries of your body to become less defined. Continue breathing, gently and rhythmically, as your consciousness becomes more fluid.

Relaxed and present, allow yourself to see, in your mind's eye, a temple in the distance. This is your temple. This temple may be a building, or perhaps it has no walls. Is it a grove? A lake? A clearing with a river running through it? Perhaps it is a desert under the night sky. Maybe it's made of rock, or metal. Does it have walls of cloth? It may be a structure built entirely of thought.

Is your temple surrounded by land? By water? Are there plants growing? Your temple may be surrounded by a garden, or perhaps your temple is, itself, a garden.

Begin to approach your temple. As you move toward this sacred space, notice the air around you. Are there scents? Do you smell earth, or rain? Flowers, water, smoke? Perhaps you smell some ancient scent, copal or other resins, burning on the incense censer.

Keep walking, and enter your temple. Is there a door to pass through? Maybe there is a certain plant that lets you know that you are now inside your sanctuary.

As you continue moving forward, you are passing the threshold. This space is dedicated entirely to you. This is the passage into your own center, your inner sanctum. Breathe in the air of your own sacred space, and let it fill you with your own consecrated energies.

Look around you. What do you see? A throne? A bed? Books? Tools? What colors adorn your inner sanctum? How have the scents around you changed? Perhaps you smell the scent of flowers, or of soil, metal, warm wood, or sweat-misted skin. Is your temple warm, or is there a gentle, cooling breeze? Is it summer here? Spring? Winter? Autumn? Day, or night?

You see an altar, and walk toward it. Notice what is on your altar. You see tools before you, laid out and ready for use. These tools have been waiting for you to pick them up. You remember, perhaps, how these tools feel in your hands. Remember these tools, these artifacts, these adornments. They are yours. Kneel at your altar, and give thanks to your divine self for knowing exactly what these tools are, how to use them, and why they are essential to your manifestation of Love and Will.

Allow yourself to look around again, noticing the beauty, the depth, the mystery that surrounds you. Even you do not know everything that this temple holds. Some things are hidden from sight, your own secrets that will unfold for you at exactly the right time, in exactly the right place. You are safe here, even to face your deepest fears. But for now, you will relax and enjoy the amazing beauty and comfort of this place. This temple. Your temple.

Breathe, knowing that this temple is always here. You are always in it. This temple is you, and you are it.

Allow yourself to feel this temple settle into your flesh, your blood, your bones. Allow your breath to sustain it, your blood to nourish it. And follow your breath, your blood, the beating of your heart, slowly back to consciousness.

When you feel ready, gently open your eyes, and chronicle the story of this visit to your temple with words and images.

Honoring Our Bodies

There are many ways that we own, disown, honor, and ignore our bodies. We train ourselves to override our physical needs, communications, and impulses. We attempt to fit our bodies to a strict standard that doesn't work for all of us. We sometimes value appearance over function.

At times it can be helpful to be able to override physical needs (if you are being stalked by a tiger, or trying to outlive a famine), but for the most part, the ongoing battle against our bodies, against our desires, and against nature has lead us nowhere good.

Journaling Prompts: Honoring the Sacred Temple

- What are some of the ways that you dishonor or mistreat your body?
- What are some of the ways that you claim and honor your body?
- Of these self-honoring activities, which could you do more of?
- What other self-honoring activities could you claim as your own?

Magickal Act: Creating an Altar to You! Invoking Self-Love

Who better to love than yourself? Here is a great way to invest some time, energy, and devotion in the person most central to your experience of life—you! Make an altar to yourself. This altar will be a reminder to honor your body (the temple that you carry with you at all times) and your power and sensuality.

★ ──────────

Fasting as a Spiritual Practice: Fasting is a practice that has been employed as a component of spiritual seeking, ritual, and initiation cycles in most every culture. Fasting can be an amazing way to get in touch with the Divine, to create space in our lives for personal growth, and to reprogram our response cycles. (Note: Fasting is *not* recommended for anyone who has experienced eating disorders.)

────────── ★

Set up your altar someplace where you will see it often, but make sure the space is private enough that you will feel comfortable leaving it up when guests are over. Placing it on top of a dresser or any other surface in your bedroom is a good idea, but if that is too public, you can set it up in your closet. If you want to be reminded more often of your desire to honor yourself, put the altar where you will see it all day long, like in your living room. If you choose a more public place for your altar, make sure you are comfortable fielding the possible questions that might come from friends or family viewing it.

If setting up an altar in plain sight is not realistic for you because of safety concerns (judgmental roommates, friends, or parents, for example), you may want to create your altar in a temporary way just for the rituals. If so, get a container (a box or bin) that you can store and carry your altar items in.

Ideally, however, your altar will stay up for the duration of working this book, and you will add items to it as you go. Start out simple, with room to grow.

Spell Working: Sensing Meaning

This exercise can be used to improve your intuitive capabilities on any topic. You may find it useful for divining your relationship with anything. I present it here as a way to find a color that works as a base for what you are invoking through building your altar.

There are many color correspondences, and your relationship with color—or any other element, word, idea, or representation—supersedes all others. If you do not have a color that just automatically comes to mind for you as a good one for your altar cloth, I encourage you to take some time to explore what different colors represent to you.

To sense color meanings, close your eyes and visualize a color. See what thoughts and feelings come up for you regarding that color. When you open your eyes, write as many of the thoughts that you had about the color as you can remember. This is the beginning of your personal color correspondence chart.

Your relationship with certain colors may change over time. Perform this exercise anytime you feel that a shift may have occurred in your relationship with colors, or with any other element of magickal representation.

If you perform this exercise but still feel stuck, you can find my personal color correspondences in appendix I. Feel free to use them as a starting point.

How to Build Your Altar

Use whatever color of altar cloth that makes you feel like the Witchy, powerful Goddess you are. What colors represent the kind of self-devotion you are seeking? Perhaps you have a favorite color that makes it easy for you to drop right into your Witchy power.

Next, gather any things you can think of that make you feel Witchy, sensual, and self-loving. Here are some musts:

- A mirror. A hand mirror works well. Even better is a wall mirror, hung where you will see your face as you sit or stand before your altar.
- Flowers. Dried flowers are acceptable, but fresh are best.
- A chalice filled with fresh water.
- If you have found or created representations of the tools you found in your temple visualization, you may add those to the altar as well.

Depending upon the sort of self-love you are creating, building, growing, or invoking, you will want to use different items. Want smoldering sensuality? How about some musk oil, a red feather boa, and chocolate? Want to get more comfortable with your sexual anatomy? How about a vulva painting, puppet, or pillow? Want to conjure up some sweet, innocent self-love? Make yourself a Valentine card, and put it up there next to your mirror.

When setting up your personal love altar, you could find a statue or photo of Aphrodite, the Greek Goddess of love and beauty, or of Eros, the Greek God of love and sex (his name is the origin of the word *erotic*), and place her or him in the center of the montage. Even better, use a photo of your divinely sensual self, and put Aphrodite to one side of the picture of you and Eros to the other.

Now that you have your altar, here's what you can do with it. Every evening (the time of Venus) or at whatever time makes sense to you, spend some time with your altar. Refresh the water in the chalice. Breathe. Relax into your body. Take a sip of fresh water. Take in the images and talismans before you. Imagine the self-love that you are growing as a color. Visualize that color as a small orb in your heart chakra. (Your heart chakra is right around your sternum, in the middle of your chest. For more information on chakras, see appendix I.) Breathe. With each breath, visualize this orb of light expanding. Let it expand until it fills your physical body, and then allow it to move beyond your physical limits. As you continue breathing, let this energy fill the room, and then let it spill out all over the world. Let it expand throughout the universe, blessing all beings with your own unique flavor of love.

If that's not your style, use your altar as a reminder that self-love is good love, and use your time in front of your altar to masturbate. Remember, it's sex with someone you love!

Exercise Your Rights

We all know we're "supposed" to exercise, but it's great when it becomes an inspiration to take care of ourselves this way. Exercise is a very important aspect of self-nurturance. There are so many reasons that exercise is important, yet many of us have not yet successfully integrated regular exercise into our self-care routines. We get bored or busy, or let other things take precedence. But, a healthy body is key to a healthy being. Do it!

If you want reminders about why exercise is essential, here are some good ones:

- Exercise gives you a healthy glow.

- Exercise reduces stress.

- A healthy amount of exercise helps you maintain your body weight.

- Exercise decreases your risk of osteoporosis.[1]

- Recent studies show that exercise is a more effective treatment for depression than talk therapy.[2]

- Exercise helps diminish PMS symptoms.[3]

If you tend to get bored with a schedule or set routine, do like I do:

- Make a list of exercise options. Mine includes everything physical that I enjoy; for example, going out dancing, taking a walk or run, sex, Pilates, yoga, putting on a salsa

---

When you look good, you feel good. When you feel good, you look good. It's a positive-feedback loop!

• • •

Self-Esteem Boosters:
- Exercise!
- Notice things that you love about yourself.
- Accept compliments from others.
- Offer compliments to others.
- Create and recite self-adoration mantras.

• • •

Some Simple Rules for Creating a Self-Adoration Mantra:
- Always declare your desired state in the positive. Instead of saying, "I want to lose weight," (losing weight is a non-action,) say, "I am becoming even healthier."
- Declare your desired state in the present tense, with a sense of your spells already having done their magick.
- Make sure that when you say your mantra, you believe it with your whole body.

For more tips on mantra building, see appendix I.

Intention:
From the Latin *inten-dere*, "to stretch into the future."

• • •

A Magickal Thought:
Becoming healthy is a radical, (r)evolutionary, magickal act.

video and learning some new dance steps, and playing with my kids.

• Constantly expand your list of exercise options.

• Invest in some dance or exercise videotapes/DVDs to spice things up.

• Find places where you like to walk or run.

Creating a Daily Practice: Self-Honoring Rituals

The opportunity to create self-honoring in your life is available at any time. All it takes to create a ritual of honoring is intention. There are probably many self-nurturing activities you do on a daily basis. These might include putting on sunscreen, eating, dressing for your day, exercising, walking, or writing.

Your morning shower is a great place to start with honoring your body. As you wash, imagine the water cleansing you through and through. Let the water wash away not only the external funk, but the internal, too.

Many of us engage in little rituals throughout the day, though we may not be conscious of it. It's easy to become conscious of it, and to use that consciousness as a portal to the creation of a system of self-honoring that may change your life, and the lives of future generations of women. Every act of self-worship, self-care, and self-nurturance is a revolutionary act. Change begins with the individual. To change the world, take care of yourself!

Some of the daily rituals—or opportunities for ritual—are simple, and many of them are things we already do. The next time you are standing in front of your mirror and applying lotion, make a commitment to notice the things about your body that make you happy.

★ **Daily Practice: Little Rituals Everywhere**

Choose one activity that makes you feel great, and do it every day this week. As you perform your chosen activity, dedicate the time you have set aside to consciously honoring yourself. Whether you are going for a run, walking to work, taking a shower, or putting on your make-up, use this daily practice to really honor your self, your body, your health, your vitality, your sensuality, and your power. Even if this feels like a stretch to you, stick with it. I promise it will become easier, and soon you'll be absolutely bursting with self-adoration!

Self-esteem is the main topic of the next chapter, but being in our bodies, and LOVING being there, is a great starting point. Here is one more exercise in honor of the worship you so deserve.

Magickal Act: Picture This

Have you ever had naked photos of yourself taken? If you haven't, you have no idea what you are missing. So, it's time to find out. Okay, you don't *have* to be naked. You can be partially naked, or you can use a drape to cover the parts of your body that you aren't yet comfortable showing off.

These photos will be a testament to your beauty. At least one of them will be the perfect centerpiece for your self-love altar. You will be able to keep these images for your whole life, and if they're tastefully done, you may even want to pass them on to your kids or grandkids (if you plan on having any).

I recommend that you go to a professional photographer, if you can find one you like and if you can afford it. Those folks know how to work magic with the lighting, poses, props, and sets. And, the right photographer will really put you at ease.

You may feel more comfortable with a female photographer, or you may prefer a male. Either way, find out if the photographer does boudoir sets (that's code for slightly naughty pix), and if so, check out their portfolio. Meet them before the session, and make sure you like them, trust them, and feel comfortable with the idea of disrobing in front of them.

If you can't (or don't want to) find a professional photographer, have a girlfriend or boyfriend who's handy with a camera take the photos for you. (Make sure *you* end up with the negatives if you use a camera that takes film.) Maybe you can return the favor for your friend later. If you have access to a digital camera, that's the way to go. Then you won't have to worry about the film developers seeing you in the flesh, and you can just erase any photos you don't like.

With a photographer who is not a professional, you may need more than one session to get some pictures that make you just absolutely fall in love with your beautiful body. Play with the lighting, setting, make-up, and costuming. Pictures taken outside can be amazing, especially if shot on an overcast day. Sooner or later you will see a picture that makes your heart sing. That's the one to enlarge, frame, and place at the center of your altar.

Journaling Prompts: Naked Truth

- My body is . . .
- I am happy that my body . . .
- My body feels best when . . .

Onward and Inward!

Good work, Sexy Witch! You have completed chapter 1. Now, find your first ritual in part 2 of this book (Rituals I for solo Witches, or Rituals II for circles of Witches), and initiate yourself!

---

1. *The Mayo Clinic,* http://www.mayoclinic.com/invoke.cfm?id=HQ00643.
2. *Overcoming Depression,* http://www.overcoming-depression.com/depression-and-exercise.html.
3. *Free Beauty Tips and Samples,* http://www.free-beauty-tips.com/pms.html.

CHAPTER TWO

I Love Me, I Love Me Not, I Love Me

★ Magickal Act: Media Fast, page 31.
★ Daily Practice: Nurturing the Self, page 32.
★ Daily Practice: Another Measure of Water to Fill the Well, page 32.

This Is Me Coming Clean About My Self-Esteem Biases and Confusion

In researching this chapter, even after years of awareness and study, I found more data about how bad off women are in relation to body image, self-esteem, eating disorders, and the inability to age with grace and pride than I care to truly comprehend. Being overly image-conscious is a quicksand trap for our generation in ways that it never was for earlier generations of women.

The advent of "reality TV" programming, the ubiquitous—yet often subtle—influence of marketing, and the co-opting (and resulting corporate control) of themes from

★ —————————————

In Defense of the Doll—
The Barbie Revolution:
Barbie has gone from
being a vapid example
of how women are sup-
posed to be to being the
most successful female
in the United States.
Barbie has had 75+ ca-
reers and has busted
through the glass ceiling
in many frontiers.
"White House Barbie"
was launched in 2004!
With any luck, we mor-
tals will soon catch up
with this versatile, plas-
ticine character.

• • •

Self-Definition:
The creation of one's
own independent struc-
ture of ethics, dreams,
goals, worldview, and
self-image.

————————————— ★

"girl power" to "punk rock" have made a minefield of our sense of self-worth. We have had our identity as empowered women—feminists, in other words, as loath as many of us are to claim that title—put through a shredder, dried out, sterilized, made less dangerous, less unruly, and less effective, and reconstituted into a shrink-wrapped form that we are all supposed to comply with. This "made-for-TV" image of empowerment has been fed back to us by a corporate-controlled media. Is it really helping us reach our true goals to have the media defining those goals for us?

The glass ceiling has shifted up a few floors, but women still make cents on the male dollar. We can find feminist role models in just about any field, but even when we succeed in entering our chosen professions, we are constantly bombarded by the specter of discrimination based on age, gender, sexuality, and image. We are judged more often by how we look than how we think, let alone how we feel.

I don't have as many answers to the conundrums that are raised in this chapter as I have questions, but I believe that the questions raised here are extremely important for us all to examine. Issues related to body image, self-esteem, and radical empowerment are all part of our struggle toward the goal of self-love. These are arenas in which women are still in a defensive position, even in the very privileged Western world.

Women have steadily gained ground for generations, but in order to hold that ground we must remain vigilant, aware, and strong. We must continue to be self-defining in all the ways we know how, and we must continue to learn more about what it means to be self-defined. We must move forward with our power, our anger, *and* our love, to protect our self-respect, our dreams, our bodies, our souls, our goals, and our personal values.

It is also essential that we recognize that each of us must choose our own battles. I am not anti-image-consciousness, I am pro–critical thought. I encourage each of you to decide what the important elements of resistance and celebration are. Don't let anyone define your personal struggle for self-acceptance and self-definition for you—not me, not your parents, not your friends, not the media, not theorists, not the scientific community.

If make-up makes you feel good, wear it. If short skirts and heels make you feel unstoppable, go for it. If engineer boots and slacks are your idea of perfect, live in them. If cosmetic surgery is your answer to some nagging issue, get the work done.

Each of us is entitled—and, for our own health and sanity, possibly even required—to define our own goals and focal points in our process of redefinition. In allowing ourselves to create a very personalized worldview, the information presented in this chapter will be beyond helpful. This chapter will give you an overview of just how subtle the influences that define our daily concerns are, as well as give you some perspective on how we got where we are now.

One caution I offer you in embarking on this chapter is that looking around you and constantly seeing the Machiavellian workings of our culture is not sustainable in the long term. Seeing the vast underpinnings of our dysfunctional and disempowering culture can be depressing, disheartening, and even paralyzing. In reading this chapter, you may experience a sense of futility, or feel overwhelmed and, quite likely, angry. Remember, anger can be put to good use. Anger raises energy, and you can use that energy to fuel the fire of your own transformation.

Our empowerment lies in defining the boundaries of what is acceptable to each of us, what works, and doesn't work, for each of us personally. Our power lies in defining our allegiances, our boundaries, and our chosen battles. Out of all this we may find what it is necessary and healthy for each of us to defend, and with that clarity it will become easier to be effective in the work that each of us must do.

Machiavellianism:
The political doctrine of Machiavelli, which denies the relevance of morality in political affairs and holds that craft and deceit are justified in pursuing and maintaining political power.

—Source: *American Heritage Dictionary*, 4th ed.

★ —————————————

Subjugation:
To bring under control,
make subservient, to
enslave.

• • •

A Magickal Thought:
Loving your body is
a (r)evolutionary,
magickal act.

————————————★

In my own struggle with an overactive tendency toward a possibly inflated relationship with compassion, defining the edges of my ability to healthfully create change has been difficult. I have had to find the ability to say, "That's a good issue to defend. But it's not *my* issue." I encourage each of you to do the same. Let others define their struggles, and allow yourself the same quality of compassion in putting boundaries on your own areas of influence.

Self-forgiveness is a key component to this process. We may not be able to save everyone, but we can begin the process of healing humanity, and possibly the earth as a whole, by treating ourselves well. The realization that my own health and healing is as important as everyone else's has given me a new relationship with creating change in the world. I find that self-forgiveness comes more easily when I realize that I am part of the whole, and that my healing is an integral part of creating a sane world to live in, and to pass on to future generations. Self-forgiveness is also utterly important in getting from unwitting participation in our own subjugation to self-defined empowerment. In honoring our process of healing, and allowing ourselves the forgiveness we so need when we fall short of our own expectations, we offer others the skills and permission to do the same.

I am absolutely convinced that through living in our power, holding our dreams and our boundaries as sacred, and allowing ourselves to self-define, we can become the change we want to see in the world.[1] Self-defining and becoming healthy are revolutionary acts. By defining ourselves, we stand as proof that it is possible to create a new reality. By becoming healthy, we support others in finding health. Through empowering ourselves with choice, we make choice available to those we love.

Body/Image

Every day we encounter and consume images of women that defy any realistic expectation we could possibly have of ourselves, even while they define a cultural standard toward which we often (consciously or unconsciously) strive. Studies have shown that merely looking at pictures of fashion models causes a serious drop in self-image for many women.[2]

As advertising becomes more and more pervasive, we are bombarded by massive amounts of these images every day. We see stick-thin, 100-feet-tall women peering down at us from giant billboards; tiny, breakable women in compromising poses pleading with us from the pages of *Vanity Fair;* and big-breasted, perfectly coiffed, vacuous-looking girls staring at us from the pages of our *Victoria's Secret* catalogues.

We check our e-mail and get spammed with messages screaming "Lose 10 Pounds in 10 Days!", "Effortlessly Lose Weight!", "Secret Weight-Control Patch!" We are horrified by the specter of obesity—the almost ironic climax of our society's obsessive relationship with weight control,[3] and a direct result of our inability to listen to our body's signals.

Ten percent of eight-year-old girls in the United States have already dieted. Dieting is the most common trigger of all eating disorders.[4] People who diet are at risk for developing serious— sometimes fatal—eating disorders like anorexia and bulimia. One to three of every 100 Americans over the age of thirteen have been diagnosed with anorexia nervosa. About half of those treated for eating disorders achieve a healthy body weight in recovery, but 80 percent experience ongoing psychological issues.[5] Twenty percent of those who develop anorexia will die of it.[6] Ninety percent of people who develop eating disorders are women.[7]

"Fashion magazines promote such unrealistic images of beauty . . . women feel they can't live up to them. These are the same women . . . who turn out the lights during sex, and sometimes even while undressing. Self-esteem plays an important role in a woman's sexual function. If a woman doesn't feel good about her body or herself, or doesn't feel as in control or powerful, it's extremely hard for her to let go and sexually respond to a partner."

—Laura Berman, Ph.D., http://www.newshe.com.

Average American Woman	Barbie	Store Mannequin
Height: 5'4"	6'	6'
Weight: 145 lbs.	101 lbs.	Not available
Dress size: 11–14	4	6
Bust: 36–37"	39"	34"
Waist: 29–31"	19"	23"
Hips: 40–42"	33"	34"

Source: *Health* magazine, September 1997; and NEDIC, a Canadian eating disorders advocacy group.

★ ──────────────

Fat = Poor?
In his 2004 book *The Obesity Myth*, Paul Campos points out that poverty and obesity often go hand in hand. Is fat the new lower class demarcation? Campos claims that the "American elite," who value thinness over all else, may be projecting fears based in the realm of over-consumption (SUVs, environmental pillage, American imperialist tendencies) onto the easy target of over-consumption of food.

· · ·

Lookism:
A recently coined term that defines the fact that in this culture our looks have a lot to do with how we are treated. Studies have shown that people who fit the cultural ideal of beauty get hired more readily, taller men make more money on average than shorter men, and overall people treat those who are "attractive" with more kindness. Lookism relates to body type as well as facial features.

────────────── ★

The Great Weight Debate

There are many obesity skeptics coming out of the woodwork (or is that out of the closet?). Finally, some experts are stating a sane and viable truth: It's not about being skinny, it's about being healthy. Exercise is a must; dieting is not. Eating healthfully—getting adequate nutrition, avoiding processed sugars and empty calories, consuming diverse types of food—and maintaining a physically active lifestyle, *not* dieting, will improve your chances of living a long and healthy life.

Die Young and Leave a Beautiful Corpse

Not only are we afraid of getting fat,[8] we are mortified of getting, or at least of looking, old. Maybe getting old isn't a bowl full of cherries, but as they say, it sure beats the alternative, right? Wouldn't we really rather be old, alive, and well-worn than young and dead?

Well, apparently not all of us. Women are literally dying to look young and get thin. Cosmetic surgery is under-legislated and overhyped. We get wrinkles buffed, numbed, and even cut out. We dye our hair to cover the gray. We paint our skin to hide stretch marks. We tan even though we know it might end up killing us. If we can afford it, some of us get tummy tucks to hide the effects of aging or of having had children. We get breast lifts or implants to remove the inevitable sag.

And it's not even about just the aging or the weight. It's about having the "right" nose, eyes, lips, face, hair, and clothes. It's a prepackaged, pleasure droid–inspired, "new and improved" you!

It's a real challenge not to succumb to these social pressures. Even having all the information does not instantaneously transform us into healed and whole individuals who are not affected by our social conditioning. Though I can see the set-up that allows (encourages?) us to entertain the notion of cosmetic surgery, to diet, to fear aging, to mistreat our bodies—and creates the genesis of a mentality that is comprehensively prone to self-destruction—I am far from immune to the effects of this set-up. I have a pretty good perspective on how it all works and who's really in control of the cultural standard-setting, and I still can't say that I don't ever diet, that I have never thought about getting liposuction, or that I always treat myself fairly, kindly, or well.

As a matter of fact, I can't even say that I'm totally against cosmetic surgery. I know there's a chance that someday I will decide that microdermabrasion, or an eye lift, or breast implants are exactly what I need. Part of me believes that anything that makes a woman feel better about herself has got to be a positive thing.

Another part of me is aware that the statement I just made is an extreme oversimplification. I know that it doesn't take into account the whole structure that defines what makes us feel better (or worse, as the case may be) about ourselves. What I'm sure of is that I *am* against the infrastructure of self-hatred, image obsession, and imposed insecurity that makes us willing to spend our hard-earned cash on creating an outward image of "perfection," or willing to starve ourselves to death in an effort to fit an unrealistic mold.

What is feeding our willingness to starve, cut, and deny ourselves into this empty and illusive size-four fantasy? In a word, marketing. The diet industry was a 30-billion-dollar-a-year industry in 2004,[9] and the cosmetic surgery industry far outranks that, coming in at a whopping 136 billion in 1998.[10]

Big Business and Big Revenues

Annually, the buttock lift segments account for national revenues of $712 million. Total market billing for facelift procedures for the age group 51-64 was around $195 million in 1998, representing 39,000 procedures at an average price of $5,000. In 1998 the 19-34 age group spent over $91 million dollars in these categories. The total market demand for nose surgery yielded about $187 million in cosmetic and reconstructive surgery procedures. This fat injection market segment generates over $41 million in revenues for the cosmetic and reconstructive surgery industry. With nearly 37,000 customer-patients for this forehead lift procedure, the gross market segment value to plastic surgeons is around $111 million annually. The category of Retin-A treatment grew over 350% in the years 1992–1998. Approximately 107,000 procedures are undertaken annually. At an average price of $90, this market segment generates a modest $9.3 million in industry revenues, and is a high demand segment.

Source: *Cosmetic & Plastic Surgery Advice & Links,* http://www.cosmetic-surgery.us.com/cost-surgery.htm.

There's a war going on. It's a war of self-consciousness versus self-awareness. This war pits our minds against our bodies, and makes fighting for the "perfect" appearance the only game in town. This cultural battle against feeling good about ourselves is funded in the billions by markets that profit from our insecurities. This constant onslaught against self-fulfillment uses our fear of inadequacy as a most devastating weapon against us.

Spell Working: Building the Body Beautiful

Collage, draw, or paint an image of your body with as much love, admiration, compassion, desire, and hope as possible.

What You Will Need

- Paper or cardstock base.
- Images for collage.

Or:

- Paper or cardstock base.
- Paints, pastels, or pencils.

How-To

- Look at your naked body in the mirror with love and compassion. See the parts that you enjoy, and let them become your focal point.
- Collage, draw, or paint an image of your beautiful body.

Buying It

Even beyond the key marketing ploys that the fashion, dieting, entertainment, and cosmetic surgery industries use to play on our fears related to our image, weight, and age, marketing in general has one primary goal: to create a hunger, a deep need, that you will then ostensibly try to fill with the product that the marketer is attempting to sell you.[11] And it works. We buy the products in an attempt to fill our well of intentionally induced lack.

The more insidious, dangerous, and damaging side effects of marketing are that this well doesn't ever get filled, as it is being hollowed deeper and deeper into our psyches with every advertisement we see, every bad thought we have about our bodies, every movie we watch that shows us how women are "supposed" to act and look, every TV show that creates a desire for us to go out and purchase a $300 pair of Choo's or Blahniks just because we're having a bad hair day.

For the duration of working this chapter (and then the rest of the book, and the rest of our lives), let's make a vow to fill that marketing-inspired void with self-love, nurturance, understanding, and self-acceptance.

Magickal Act: Media Fast

For the duration of this chapter, abstain from looking at—or even leafing through—any mass-market mags, and I mean avoid even *Jane*. While *Jane* is head and shoulders above the rest of the market for edge and sexual empowerment, the models are still unrealistic and the advertising is still catering to our insecurities, because that's what advertising does. Avoid watching any movies or TV shows that have a consumeristic message or present a one-dimensional portrayal of female characters, and avoid dwelling on advertising displayed in public spaces.

Considering how pervasive and insidious negative messaging about women is in the media in general, it may be more realistic to do a complete media fast. If you feel up for this, I highly recommend it. This means avoiding all media for the duration of working this chapter—no newspapers, no books, no films, no advertisements, and no surfing of the internet, if you want to take it really seriously. Even though the internet is not totally controlled by the consumer market, advertising is very pervasive on the web.

One idea behind this exercise is that if looking at images of models has a negative effect on our self-esteem,[12] and marketing is built upon tearing us down, maybe we can slowly undo the damage done by giving our heads and hearts some time to heal. On a more mystical level, this is a rite of purification that may make it easier for you to work toward some stillness in the center of your world and yourself. This media fast is a magickal act that will begin the process of purification that leads to gaining the ability to hear your own inner voice.

Filling the Well That Lack Built

It's time to claim your right to enjoy life, on your own terms and in your own way. Now that you are beginning to have the space cleared in your mind to find out what things make you most profoundly happy and at home in your skin, it's time to act on them. What makes you feel good? What makes you happy? What makes you dance with joy, or sing your self-love at the top of your lungs? Put your joy into action, and make the time and space for celebration of the unique being you are.

★ Daily Practice: Nurturing the Self

I know that sometimes it's a challenge to do nice things for yourself, so maybe this advice will make you want to run for the door. You're probably thinking something like, "Oh, jeez . . . can't my self just nurture itself?" But, really taking care of yourself could be the beginning of a beautiful love affair! So at the risk of sounding indulgent, I'm going to command you to take time every day that you are working this chapter to give yourself some lovin'.

Don't get lazy or bored: each day, at whatever time is convenient, do a different thing that's good for you *and* makes you feel good. This exercise is similar to last week's daily practice, but this week, instead of doing the same thing every day, you will challenge yourself to find a new thing to savor and delight in every day of the week.

Take a long walk. Buy yourself flowers. Take yourself out to eat your favorite kind of food (mmmm, sushi!). Plan a date night with yourself. Masturbate. Take baths (see appendix I for a magickal bath mix). Create art. Write. Read. Make time to do what you love, because you deserve it.

★ Daily Practice: Another Measure of Water to Fill the Well

Many of us bond over our perceived imperfections. Think about it. Are you one of the millions of us who attempt to create common ground with female friends (and possibly win the endearment of the men in our lives) through self-deprecation? Have you ever caught yourself trying to create intimacy through revealing some embarrassing tidbit or talking badly about your body? I know I have. It seems to come easily and shockingly naturally to dish to our pals about our belly flab, silly habits, and sagging breasts, all in an effort to find something we hold in common.

Here and now, I give you permission to release the fear of your power and glory, and revel in your complete okay-ness. Positive thought begets positive thought, and positive thought turns easily into positive living. For this week, I challenge you to speak of yourself lovingly, to congratulate yourself on your successes, to own and honor your strengths, and to encourage your friends to do the same. Instead of diving into the pity party we all play at for acceptance, channel your inner diva and SHINE!

Fashioned into Submission

Beyond the consumeristic and marketing-driven aspect of our desire to fit into a soulless cultural ideal, there are other levels of programming and conditioning going on here. Fashion has been used to mold women into variations on the theme of the weak and helpless, vapid, dangerous, childish, and ultimately useless and burdensome creature that needs the men in her life, be they father, husband, brother, or son, to care for her. Why? Because it has been one of many useful tactics in keeping women unwilling and unable to step out of line, afraid to create a disturbance: owing, and owned by, the men in an androcentric paradigm.

This may seem to be an extreme view. I mean, fashion as a weapon against women? What? Fashion is our friend, right? Well, with enough research you find stories of the laws that kept women confined to "womanly dress," and stories about the women who broke those laws.

Dr. Mary E. Walker: A Hero of Dress Reform

In the American Civil War, more than 400 women are rumored to have dressed as men, and fought beside them. The second woman in the United States to graduate medical school, Mary E. Walker, M.D., was the first female doctor to serve in the military. She did not have to hide her gender, but adopted the male military uniform while in the service, and refused to go back to women's clothing after the war.

Dr. Walker was not the only woman thus inclined. Women continued dressing in men's clothes for many reasons. Some went so far as to disguise themselves as men to get work that paid often twice as much as the work available to women.

Women's clothes of this time period were uncomfortable, a threat to women's health and safety, and even carried the potential for death. Women died from corseting, and from their large, unruly skirts catching fire, tripping them and weighing them down.

Dr. Walker wrote two books, *Hit* and *Unmasked*. They both dealt with the dangers of women's dress, as well as tobacco and other vices. But Dr. Walker didn't confine her fight to the pages of her books. She campaigned in both word and deed against the confining and dangerous dress of her day. She and many others were arrested in the years after the war for dressing in men's garb.

Dr. Walker served time as a prisoner of war, and received the Congressional Medal of Honor in 1866 for her military service and stellar conduct as a physician and as a prisoner. She also served briefly as a spy. The medal was fairly earned.

In 1916, her right to a Medal was rescinded in the process of a government cleanup. It became illegal to wear the Medal without government consent, but Dr. Walker kept her medal, and wore it proudly until her death in 1919. After a lobbying effort by Dr. Walker's descendants, President Jimmy Carter restored Dr. Walker's Medal of Honor posthumously in 1977.

How Women Have Been "Formed to Perfection," and How It Has Injured Us

Then:

- Foot binding. In China, from the tenth century to the early 1900s. Adverse effects: severe limitation of mobility, lifelong pain, rot, death.
- Corseting. In Europe and the United States, 1700s to 1800s. Adverse results: organ damage and failure, broken ribs, expulsion of uterus from the vagina, fainting, death.
- Hoop skirts. Limited mobility. These skirts were also known to catch fire when women were cooking at campfires.
- Crinolines and petticoats. When paired with the corset, the yards of cloth, wire, wicker, bamboo, and other reinforcements made mobility nearly impossible.

Now:

- High heels. Habitual wearing of high heels can create lifelong problems with skeletal misalignment, knee problems, foot problems, and pain.[13] As anyone who has worn them knows, wearing heels also impedes mobility.
- Thong underwear. May cause an increased risk of vaginal and urinary tract infections.[14]

- Tight jeans. Wearing tight jeans can cause urinary tract infections, bladder problems, and low sperm count in men.[15]

- Hip-hugging pants. Can cause *paresthesia,* a nerve pinch that produces tingling in the thighs and legs.[16]

- Bras. Research is currently being performed on a possible link between wearing a bra and an increased risk of breast cancer. The theory is that compression of breast tissue restricts the effectiveness of the lymph system, leading to toxic congestion of breast tissue.[17, 18] There is also a lot of data out there on the link between badly fitting bras and nerve pinches, shoulder pain, and headaches.

How Free Are We?

It hasn't been so long that we have been permitted to dress in "men's clothing" without risk. And, sad but true, the laws against cross-dressing are still on the books. While applied with discretion, it's still illegal for men to dress in women's clothing, and often men cross-dress at huge risk to their personal safety. It is far less socially acceptable for a man to head out on the town in a skirt than for a woman to hit the street in slacks.

The fact that we are even aware that some men like to dress in women's attire and some women wear nothing but slacks and a tank top shows that we are moving away from such rigid rules of dress. But what are the bargains we are making now? We work hard and then spend more than we can afford on designer labels. We sometimes wear heels that make it hard (if not impossible) to run. We wear clothes that look good, but feel like crap. We rely on our uniforms to say something about us, as everyone does. What are we really trying to say through the image we present?

Excerpted from
"Bata Motel"
Album: *Penis Envy*
Band: Crass

I've got 54321,
I've got a red pair of high-heels on,
Tumble me over, it doesn't take much,
Tumble me over, tumble me, push . . .
These wounds leave furrows as they heal,
I've traveled them, they're red and real,
I know them well, they're part of me,
My birth, my sex, my history . . .
Will my tiny feet fit your desire?
Warped and tied I walk on fire.
Burn me out, twist my wrists,
I promise not to shout, beat me with your fists.
Squeeze me, squeeze me, make me feel,
In my red high-heels I'm an easy kill.

★ ———————————

Feral Cheryl: This eco-conscious, spunky retort to Barbie Culture is bound to improve your self-image *and* your sense of humor. Cheryl has tats, sports dark, natty dreads, and has natural-shaped feet that wouldn't even fit into Barbie's hobbling little heels. Lift her skirt, and you will see that Cheryl also has a healthy little bush covering her pantie-less snatch.

Feral Cheryl is crafted in Australia (no sweatshop labor here!), and is modeled after the Ferals of Down Under.

——————————— ★

Journaling Prompts: Fuck Fashion/Fashion Fuck

- When I hear the phrase "The clothes make the man," I think . . .
- My relationship with clothing . . .
- I like to wear . . .
- I feel most comfortable in . . .
- When I go out, I . . .
- Wearing _____ makes me feel . . .

Magickal Act: D.I.Y. Fashion Statement

What do you want your clothing to say about you? Well then, make it say it! It's easy, and fun, to make your clothes speak for you. Then you never even have to open your mouth if you don't want to, and you've still been heard loud and clear. Talk about magick!

What You Will Need

- Shirt, whatever cut and color you like to wear.
- Fabric pens, bedazzling kit, iron-on letters, fabric crayons, or fabric paint.
- Rhinestones, glitter pens, stars, or other creative additions (optional).
- Fabric glue (optional).

Or:

- Create a cardboard stencil.
- Spray paint your message on your shirt (and every other available surface, if you want to!).

How-To

What phrase do you want to wear emblazoned across your chest? Some possibilities: "I think, and I vote!" "Mother" on the front and "Whore" on the back. "Talk to the Face!" with an arrow pointing up. "Curvy and Loving It!" "This is What a Bi-Curious Femme Looks Like." "My Mother Said I Can Be Whatever I Want, So F**K You!" "Future Senator." "Like My Boobs? They Grew This Way." "Mine." Whatever you want to say, use this space to say it.

- If your shirt is new, wash and dry it before you do this project.
- Choose or create a slogan that says something you want people to hear.
- Set up your supplies.
- Stretch your shirt over cardboard.
- Paint, draw, write, or bedazzle your message onto your shirt. Follow the directions for whatever medium you are using.
- Make sure you do whatever is necessary to set the medium.
- Wash.
- Wear!

Gender Is a Construct

Gender awareness and gender identity are key components of self-esteem. Gender is a culture-specific, collective, subconscious set of agreements about how people of each sex are required to present themselves in order to be accepted. Gender is different than biological sex or sexual orientation. We all have ideas about what behaviors are appropriate to our gender, and some of those concepts may have held us back at times from acting in accordance with our desires.

Gender is a fluid concept, one that can change dramatically in a very short amount of time, on both the personal and the cultural levels. Looking back over less than a generation, we can see how rapidly changing a concept gender really is. In the past twenty-five years or so, we have seen enormous changes in gender-based expectations and assumptions in the United States. It wasn't long ago that in the Western world it was considered appropriately "ladylike" for a woman to vacuum in heels, fix all the meals, and surrender her career upon marriage.

★ ——————————

Sex and Gender:
Sex is a biological term meaning "the genetic or genital sex of an individual." Gender is a set of cultural and sociological identifiers. A person of the female sex may present as the male gender, or vice versa.

Sex is also more variable than the standard male-female duality system. There are numerous variations on the chromosomal make-up of sex.

· · ·

Zeitgeist:
A German word meaning "time spirit." The spirit of an era, age, or generation.

· · ·

Eugenics:
From the Greek *eugenes*, meaning "wellborn." Eugenics is the science of selective breeding, the method of "improving" the human race though socially controlled breeding.

Positive Eugenics:
Breeding to improve "quality."

Negative Eugenics:
Breeding out "defective stock."

—————————— ★

Science-based explanations have been both foe and ally in our ongoing effort to clarify just how gender works. Gender is different than sex, and it is different than sexual orientation. Gender is an idea, and, as one learns through any study of the topic, a very subjective one. Gender is a system of categorization. It is far from a valid excuse in support of keeping things the way they are or have been, though that is often how the concept is used. And, it is rare that the distinction between sex and gender is made.

Biological determinism is a scientific discipline that attempts to take gender behaviors and find scientific bases that are then used to support whatever the current ideas around sex-based capability are. Theories based in biological determinism have been used to support the notion that women are not fit for business, politics, or careers outside of the home. It has been used to justify men's "tendency" toward infidelity, and women's (assumed) desire for love over sex. Biological determinist theories were also used in attempts to maintain black slavery in the United States, and are still used to justify eugenics. These theories also come into play in discussions of homosexuality. Biological determinism is faulty science, to say the least. Don't buy the theories!

Gender-play has been a zeitgeist of sorts for years. Gender-bending cultural icons such as Prince, David Bowie, Annie Lennox, Laurie Andersen, Boy George, RuPaul, and many others have thrown their distinct flavors of gender-fuck into the mix. For more than a generation we have been publicly disassembling and reconstructing our cultural relationship with gender norms.

In working to create a realistic relationship with our sexual identity, it becomes necessary to disassemble our own gender-based assumptions. Gender concepts and gender-bending are fertile fields for discovery of our own concepts of how women and men are "supposed" to act and present themselves. How is it "different for a girl"? How do your dress, your self-image, and your relationship with and representation of gender affect your view of reality?

Journaling Prompts: Life Is a Many Gendered Thing

- My mother thought her body was . . .
- My father thought women were . . .
- When I was young, I thought women . . .
- I think women . . .
- I think I am . . .
- Men are . . .
- If I were a man, . . .
- If I had a cock, . . .

★ _____

Gender-fuck:
Messing with gender concepts, usually with the intention of challenging assumptions about gender.
_____ ★

Fun with Gender!

Gender-bending and a gender-fuck mentality have been hugely important facets of my process of self-discovery, and of my magickal growth. Gender-play has allowed me to accurately gauge my relationship with gender concepts, and to grow beyond these where that might have limited me before. I encourage you to play with gender, and see what occurs for you!

Five Reasons You Should Create Opportunities to Bend Gender

1. It's fun. People have the tendency to allow this sort of alchemy to change their default settings where human interaction is concerned, if only for the duration of the experiment.
2. It's challenging. Try to stay in character for a number of hours, or a number of days, and see how it changes your perceptions of gender-typed behavior.

3. Immediately, this experience will give you a deeper understanding of how you (and your peeps) perceive gender.

4. In the right circumstances, it will afford you (and your cohorts) an opportunity to transcend gender and gender identity.

5. Once you allow this tool to clarify your ideas of, and attitudes toward, the opposite gender and your own, you will be able, if you choose, to use this information to change your reality.

Where to Bend

Throw a theme party. Create a safe space for experimentation. Have a few of your closest (and most adventurous) friends over. Play dress up. Go on a cross-dressing shopping spree. Have a dinner party. Go out for cocktails. Attend a local drag king revue.

• An easy way to start out is a gender-bending Hallowe'en party. People know that just about anything goes around Hallowe'en.

• If you want to create an experience of ritualized gender-play, plan it on an equinox, the time of balance between day and night. Explore the balances of cross-gender experimentation. Design a ritual that mixes fe/male archetypes. Play with the tension, exciting and/or uncomfortable.

• Formalize the experience with a pre-party party where you invoke your alter egos. Trade clothing. Help each other with make-up.

• Or, dress and get into character alone. Come to the event (either cross-dress oriented or mixed), and see how long it takes people to figure out who you are!

• Once you get used to your persona, try going out in public. Go to a bar, a nightclub, a neighborhood party (but only if you have cool friends who won't trip on you as another gender), or a different city (if you don't want people to know who you are, or if you don't want to be "out" about your gender-play).

Please note: Use common sense when cross-dressing in public. Know the social climate of the locale where you choose to experiment. Sad as it is to say, we all know that many people have low (no?) tolerance for people who push boundaries, especially where gender (and therefore sex) is concerned.

Magickal Act: It's Good to Be King!

What You Will Need

- Drag (costuming).

- Make-up.

- Props.

How-To

- *The Clothes Make the Wo/man:* Get creative. What kind of guy/girl, boi, boy, drag king do you want to be? Exotic? Sophisticated? Silly? Slutty? Strong? Pick a theme, a hero to model yourself after, or just a set of clothes you like, and set to undertake the completion of your transformation. Remember to accessorize appropriately. Empty your purse into a wallet and pockets. Change your watch. Take off your jewelry. Cut your nails.

- *Breastless Wonder:* You may or may not want to bind your breasts. If you do, a heavy-duty back brace works well. If your breasts are on the larger side, try to find something reinforced. Ace bandages don't work too well if you are busty, but work with a smaller bust line. A size-too-small sports bra will also bind you pretty well. There are other methods, like plastic wrap or duct tape, for example, but how much are you willing to suffer for your transformation? In any case, wear a T-shirt or A-shirt under other clothes to hide your bindings. If all this seems like too much, you can also create a great illusion of breastlessness by rounding your shoulders and slouching slightly forward, hollowing your chest, and wearing a loose jacket. This technique works especially well if you have smaller breasts.

- *Packing:* Women, sooner or later you will probably want to pack. It's so much fun! Socks are not the best material. If you own a strap-on harness, there are great (and very lifelike) dildos on the market today. Another trick is to hang a substance-filled (hair gel, cornstarch and water, pudding, etc.) condom or balloon over a pair of thong underwear. This is a great technique, lending you lifelike, sort of squishy cock and balls. You may have to adjust your package from time to time, but that just makes it more convincing, right?

★ ————————————

Pass:
A term common in genderfluid, gender-transitioning, and transvestite circles, which means to pass as the gender you want to be perceived as in the moment.

———————————— ★

- *Give Good Face:* Make-up is the finishing touch. This is one of the best tools you have to help you pass. A five-o'-clock shadow can be created with a mix of eye-shadows, or with burnt cork or charcoal. Try to make the shade of your shadow just a bit darker than your hair. If you feel really inspired, go to your local costume shop and get a fake moustache or sideburns. Darkening the lines in your face will harden your look a bit, and you can accentuate certain features through the use of a dark blush. Bring out your jaw line with shadow, or set your eyes back a little by lining only the corners closest to your nose. Mess around for a while and see what works. Afford yourself plenty of time for this step. Forty-five minutes to an hour is not out of the question, depending on how involved you want to get.

- *Hair Play:* In the process of becoming a man, remember, less is more. Pomade, gel, or nothing at all are the traditional styling products that men use. Tie long hair back, leave it down, or hide it under a hat or your collar.

- *Fun Toys to Change Your Look:* Experiment with glasses, hats, shoes, jewelry (pinky ring, anyone? gold chains?), belts, scarves, ties, jackets, and bags.

Who are you in this new experience of gender? Stay present with your persona. S/he undoubtedly has something to teach you. Take some time to process your realizations post-bend. This experiment has the potential to bring up some issues as well as to shed light on your current mindset regarding gender and/or sexual orientation.

Be sure to enjoy this experience. Flirt, strut, primp, pimp, camp, vogue, and play. Have a wild ride! And don't forget to have a few pictures taken. These ones will go on your altar, too.

Journaling Prompts: Post-Gender-Bend

- Gender is . . .
- I am . . .
- Men are . . .
- Women are . . .
- Men have . . .
- Women have . . .
- If I were a man, . . .
- If I had a cock, . . .
- As a woman, I . . .

In the Stillness: Revisiting the Media Fast

So, you've gone for a week without media. How did it feel?

Journaling Prompts: Media Control

- When I don't consume mass media, . . .
- My ingestion of the media . . .
- My self-image has been [improved, deteriorated, not affected at all] by my media fast. That makes me . . .

Onward and Inward!

Now, find the ritual related to this chapter in the appropriate rituals section in part 2, and initiate yourself. You have made it through some challenging work here. Congratulations!

---

1. Mahatma Gandhi: "You should be the change that you want to see in the world," http://en.wikiquote. org/wiki/Mohandas_Gandhi.
2. *The Alliance for Eating Disorders Awareness,* http://www.eatingdisorderinfo.org/eating_disorders_statis-tics.htm.
3. *National Association to Advance Fat Acceptance,* http://www.naafa.org/documents/policies/dieting.html.

4. *The Alliance for Eating Disorders Awareness,* http://www.eatingdisorderinfo.org/eating_disorders_statistics.htm.

5. Ibid.

6. "Anorexia, Bulimia . . . and Obesity," *The PDR® Family Guide to Women's Health and Prescription Drugs,* http://www.healthsquare.com/fgwh/wh1ch34.htm.

7. "Mortality and Recovery Rates," *Breaking Free from Eating Disorders,* http://www.geocities.com/gina_rlp/mortal.html.

8. Robert Davis, "Teens' Cosmetic Dreams Don't Always Come True," *USA Today,* July 28, 2004, http://www.usatoday.com/life/lifestyle/2004-07-28-plastic-surgery_x.htm.

9. "Anorexia, Bulimia . . . and Obesity," *The PDR® Family Guide to Women's Health and Prescription Drugs,* http://www.healthsquare.com/fgwh/wh1ch34.htm.

10. Rosemary Church, host, "Plastic Surgery Becoming More Common," *CNN,* interview aired November 5, 2003, 17:00:00 ET, http://www.cnn.com/TRANSCRIPTS/0311/05/i_ins.01.html.

11. "Body Image and Advertising," *Mediascope* (Studio City, CA: Mediascope Press, 2000), http://www.mediascope.org/pubs/ibriefs/bia.htm.

12. "Super Heroes & Super Models," *Counselor: The Magazine for Addiction Professionals,* http://www.counselormagazine.com/display_article.asp?aid=Super_heroes_and_super_models.asp.

13. "High Heels Dangerous to Your Health," *Yale-New Haven Hospital,* http://www.ynhh.org/healthlink/womens/womens_6_01.html.

14. Laura and Jennifer Berman, hosts, "Trouble with Thongs," *Discovery Health Channel,* interview aired November 4, 2002, http://www.newshe.com/thongs1.shtml.

15. Victoria Stagg Elliott, "Health Risks Make Some Fashions 'Dont's,'" *American Medical News,* http://www.ama-assn.org/amednews/2002/08/05/hlsc0805.htm.

16. "Hip-Hugging Trousers 'Are Health Risk,'" BBC News, posted January 9, 2003, http://news.bbc.co.uk/2/hi/health/2643185.stm.

17. Ralph L. Reed, "Bras and Breast Cancer," *Natural Health and Longevity Resource Center,* http://www.all-natural.com/bras.html.

18. Nguyen Phawk Yu, M.D., "Bras and Breast Cancer," *Health2Us.com,* http://www.health2us.com/bra.htm.

CHAPTER THREE

Pussy Power!

★ Daily Practice: Quality Time, page 60.

This Is Your Pussy!

Have you explored your vulva lately? Have you ever explored it? Are you on a first-name basis with your hidden flower? Do you know what it likes, how it smells, how it tastes? If you don't, it's high time you did! In this chapter you will have the opportunity to begin to build a sweet, open, and loving relationship with the part that most emphatically marks you as a woman.

Why would we want to become more intimate with our intimate parts? The real question is why *not*? There's a good chance that increasing our overall awareness of our intimate parts may increase our self-esteem,[1] and there are also health-based reasons for having an intimate awareness of our nether regions.

★

A Magickal Thought: Pussy worship has been around forever. The Venus of Willendorf has a noticeable cleft between her luxuriant thighs, and may be the oldest piece of human-created sculpture. Sheila-na-Gigs (figure 3) grace lintels on ancient churches with lips held wildly agape. Food for thought: perhaps the desire that drives the porn industry stems from the same desire to worship at the altar of life and love?

Why It's a Good Idea to Foster a Positive Relationship with Our Genitals

I am woman, hear me roar . . . right? But if we aren't on speaking terms with our kittens, that roar might ring a little empty. How can we love ourselves without loving the cleft, canal, wild jungle that lies between our thighs? Our pussies, even more truly and extremely than our breasts—and in a much more hidden and intense manner—are the primary signifiers of our femaleness. They are the visible representation of the one thing that we have, and they don't. It is the pedestalized and denigrated origin of every worshipful and slanderous espousal you have ever heard about what it means to be a cunt.

When we think of body image, we usually think of our weight, our bellies, our overall level of perceived *externalized* attractiveness. What about our ideas and concepts relating to our secret spot? Is it a primal wound, or a primal wonder? Is it the seat of abuse, or a treasure chest?

Let's glorify our cootchies, and raise the banner of pussy power! Your garden may be no-man's land, or it may be common ground. But claim it for what it is: yours. And for what it does: it creates a map of the differences that exist. You are a woman, with the vulva to prove it.

Figure 2: Adoration of the Yoni

Figure 3: Sheila-na-Gig

Figure 4: East Indian Goddess with Vulva Revealed

★ ─────────────────────

───────────────── ★

Magickal Act: Drawing It

This exercise is about emotion and relationship, and how you view your vulva in a conceptual, abstract manner. Draw six sketches of your pussy. Each drawing will be a gesture drawing and will take sixty seconds to complete. It's not about accuracy, realism, or drawing skill, but about your emotional concept of your genital anatomy.

What You Will Need

- Six sheets of drawing paper, or at least unlined paper.
- Drawing pencils, colored pencils, or charcoal.
- At least ten minutes of uninterrupted time.

How-To

Don't think about what you will draw before you read the directions, or even before your drawing implement is on the page. Just read the drawing prompt, and then draw immediately!

- Drawing #1: Your vulva, as realistic as possible, from memory. (If you have never looked at it, draw what you think it *might* look like.)
- Drawing #2: A caricature of your vulva. What is your vulva's character?
- Drawing #3: If your vulva were a sign (an ad, a billboard, a road sign, a sign for a business), it would look like this . . .
- Drawing #4: If your vulva were an animal, it would be . . .
- Drawing #5: If your vulva were a plant, it would be . . .
- Drawing #6: Your vulva's personality.

Journaling Prompt

Take some notes about how this process was for you. Was it amusing? Entertaining? Revealing? Emotional? All of these? What do you think of the images that came up for you?

Sexual Comfort and Empowerment

If you don't feel at home "down there," how are you ever going to feel comfortable inviting a friend over? As our own comfort levels and intimacy with our genitals increases, it may become easier for us to share our sexual anatomy with our lovers. When we know how we look, smell, taste, and feel, it may become more comfortable to offer our sensual friends an invitation to venture south. And it's likely that you will gain an overall sense of sexual ease and comfort when you gain firsthand experience with your own genital anatomy.

Fact: The vast majority of women orgasm more easily through oral sex or other direct stimulation of the clitoris than through sexual intercourse alone.

Healthful Self-Awareness

Your gynecologist sees thousands of women's genital and reproductive organs. Yours may be the only female genitals you ever see, and you can see yours every day, if you'd like! This makes you the potential expert on your genital anatomy.

A lot can be said for taking a look at your cervix, but even short of that, just having an intimate awareness of how your external genitalia typically look is a good idea, just like performing a regular breast self-exam is a good idea. Your inner labia may change in color, texture, and sensitivity level according to where you are at in your menstrual cycle. They will most certainly—noticeably—change with pregnancy. As your hormones change, you may become more susceptible to yeast imbalances. The more awareness you gain about how your cycle works, and about how your genital and reproductive parts look, the more active a role you will be able to take in your own health care.

And yeah, look at your cervix! When your next annual exam rolls around, bring a mirror. When you are in the stirrups and the speculum is in place, ask your doc if she or he has a mirror you can use to look at your cervix. If s/he doesn't, say, "That's cool. I brought one, just in case." Pull out your mirror, and take a look at your magickal cavern. Ask questions. Get answers. After your appointment, take some notes. You will be able to remember with more accuracy what your interior looks like than your doc will. If you see changes from one appointment to the next, bring them up.

If you are truly curious, and really like taking an active part in your health care, get a speculum and do an exam on yourself in the privacy of your own home. As the Delphic Oracle said, "Know Thyself!"

A Rose by Any Other Name

There are a lot of names used to refer to the vulva. Each of us probably has a favorite or two, and most of us have one or two terms we've heard that make our blood boil! Many names of female-genital origin have become four-letter words, put-downs, insults. Many words for the vulva have come to define all that is ostensibly evil about women, our fatal flaw, our shame.

And there are many names that we are reclaiming, just like the word Witch. *Cunt* comes from the same root as "country," "knowing," and "kin."[2] *Snatch* is a word that some of us love and some of us hate. Cunt is a loaded word, and one that brings up feel-

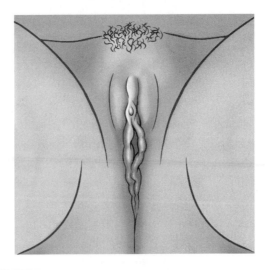

Figure 5: Vulva

ings for people that cover the gamut from shame to empowerment. Other words seem softer yet may carry with them a sense of belittlement.

All of these words have meaning at the cultural level as well as meanings that are relevant to each of us, individually. What words work for you? What words don't? And why?

What It's Called, Formally

- *Vulva* refers to the female external genital area. This word originates from the Latin *volvere,* and shares its root with *evolve, well, vault,* and *leaf of a door.*

- *Vagina* is the medical term for the canal that leads from the vulva to the cervix. Vagina is a Latin word that means "sheath for a sword."

- The *clitoris* covers a much larger area than most medical books credit it with. The clitoris is not just the nib somewhere near the apex of your vulva (which is actually the glans of the clitoris) but a whole structure of nerves and muscle that extends deep into your abdominal cavity and wraps around your vaginal canal. Your *inner labia* are also part of your clitoral structure.

Magickal Act: Names We Call It

This exercise has three parts.

What You Will Need

- A writing implement.
- Paper.
- At least twenty minutes of uninterrupted time.

How-To

- Give yourself three minutes to write down as many words as you can think of—positive or negative—that refer to the female genitals.

*What It's Called—
A Compendium of
Names for the Vulva:*
Animal, beast, bitch, boat, box, bush, cake, canyon, cat, cleft, cookie, cootch, crotch, cunt, down there, family jewels, fire box, fish, flaming lips, flower, fuck-hole, fuck-toy, garden, gash, girl, ground, hole, hope chest, it, jungle, kitty, meat, monkey, monster, mound, nappy dug-out, naughty, pie, poon, princess, privates, pussy, secret garden, she, shell, slit, snatch, south of the border, spicy tuna, spot, sushi, taco, toy, tuna, twat, well, window, wonder spot, wound, Y, yoni.

- Draw a line down the center of a piece of paper, and then create two mind maps (see the Introduction for details), one on each section of the paper. One side will be words you like, and the other, words you don't.

- Now, do a free-write for ten minutes. Each time you get to a stopping point in your flow, choose another word to start with, from the opposite side of your mind map.

Information: Clitical!

The word clitoris comes from the Greek *kleitoris,* meaning "incline" or "hill." Clitoris shares its linguistic roots with the words *climax* AND *bed.* How cool is that? The clit has 8,000 nerve endings, and averages—believe it or not—about the same length as the penis: somewhere around four inches in length.[3] More than three-quarters of the clitoris is hidden inside the abdominal cavity.

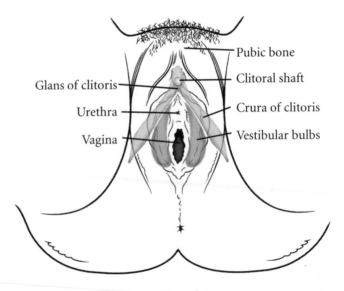

Pubic bone

Clitoral shaft

Glans of clitoris

Crura of clitoris

Urethra

Vagina

Vestibular bulbs

Figure 6: Clitoral Structure

The external part of the clitoris, which is called the *glans,* is on average about three-quarters of an inch long. Much of this tissue may be hidden by the *clitoral hood,* which is analogous to the foreskin of the penis. In fact, the clit (all of it, not just the part you can see) is made of the same kind of tissue as much of the penis: *corpora cavernosa.* Corpora cavernosa is an erectile tissue.

Female Ejaculation—How-To:
- Find your G-spot.
- Play with it.
- Allow yourself to relax and let go.
- Gush!

For more info, see the resources in appendix III.

Although some medical journals have included more or less accurate data and images regarding the structure of the clitoris since as early as the 1940s, all undergraduate-level textbooks still show only the glans of the clitoris. This appears as a peanut-shaped object at the apex of the *labia minora,* or "minor lips." (Labia minora seems a silly designation, too, as many women have much more pronounced inner lips than outer.)

These textbooks, and the even the posters of female sexual and reproductive anatomy on the walls of many women's clinics, do not show the overall structure of the clitoris. The clitoral structure includes the glans, the shaft, the crura, and the vestibules (figure 6). There is debate over whether the vestibules should be considered part of the structure of the clitoris or not.

The fact that we have historically had to work very hard to see images of the clitoris as a whole, unless we enter medical school, is unfortunate. But through the work of G-spot and women's sexuality pioneers like Deborah Sundahl, Annie Sprinkle, Nina Hartley, Susie Bright, Carol Queen, and now yours truly, we are remedying that, right? (For more info on these amazing women, see Appendix II: A Compendium of S/heroes, and Appendix III: Informational Resources.)

You've done the work, and you now have more info about how your sexual anatomy actually looks than most women who aren't doctors. Maybe this will help as you explore more thoroughly how it works!

The Goddess Spot

There are theories that the internal clitoral tissues are what make G-spot stimulation so amazing and intense for some women.

Other theories state that tissue in the urethral sponge, behind what is considered the G-spot, is analogous to the prostate, or rather that this *is* the female prostate. If you have had the opportunity to play with both the G-spot and the male prostate, you will be unable to deny that they seem to work pretty much the same way!

Male Names for Female Parts

In the tradition of imperialism, the one who "discovers" something gets to claim it. This has happened with many parts of the female body. *G-Spot* is short for the *Grafenberg Spot* and is named after Dr. Ernst Grafenberg, the male doctor who first wrote about the G-spot phenomenon.

If you want to claim your spot as your own, you could give it a name that works better for you. Some women call it the Goddess-spot (so as to keep the "G-"), some call it the spot, some call it the sacred gate, and some call it the ridge. Claim it! Use whatever word you like best.

Spell Working: Love This!

Write a love poem to your amazing anatomy of pleasure. Or, you could even write an anthem of Pussy Pride. Whatever form you choose, write something that makes you feel giggly, profoundly proud, wild, wanton, awestruck, defiant, delicious, or all of these.

What You Will Need

- Your journal.
- Writing implements.

Optional

- If you want to, you can write your piece on nice paper or cardstock, decorate it, and even frame it.

Geysers of Lovin'

Women can ejaculate. For some women, ejaculation occurs spontaneously, though some of us have to work at it if we want to see ourselves squirt. While ejaculating can be a disconcerting experience if it happens all by itself, it's nothing to be embarrassed about.

Unfortunately, many women who do not know that women can ejaculate become embarrassed by spontaneous ejaculation. Some assume that the ejaculate is urine, but it's not. Studies done on the chemical makeup of female ejaculate have found that the ejaculate is made up primarily of "prostate-specific antigen," or PSA. In other words, it's mostly prostate fluid, just like male ejaculate.

Tunnel of Love

There are so many parts of our wondrous anatomy to explore! Did you know that the vagina is not actually a tunnel? Your vaginal canal is not an actual space, but a potential space. When you are aroused, the walls of the vagina become engorged and pull out, making room for penetration.

In the images you have seen in textbooks, the opening of the vagina was almost certainly shown as a dark hole. If you were to look at your own vulva and vaginal opening, you would see tissue—layers upon layers of it.

Rose Bud

Okay, not everyone considers their anus part of their sexual anatomy. You may be cringing now as you read this. You may, at this very moment, feel shocked and embarrassed. Guess what? No one's watching you, so it's okay to let yourself get a little uncomfortable.

As with the rest of your anatomy, I really recommend getting intimate, in whatever ways are comfortable for you, with your bum. Visual awareness of what your anal area looks like when healthy is important.

★ ——————

What It's Called—
A Compendium of
Names for the Vagina:
Black hole, box, canal, cauldron, cave, cavern, closet, gate, hole, holy of holies, hungry hole, pit, sanctuary, scabbard, sheath, tunnel, tunnel of love, well.

• • •

What It's Called—
A Compendium of
Names for the Anus:
Ass, asshole, back door, brown eye, bum, bunghole, butt, crack, hole, pooper, rose bud, sphincter, starfish.

—————— ★

Many people (women and men both) really enjoy anal stimulation. If you have never journeyed down this path and are curious, there are some great books out there. Check appendix III for resources.

Right now we aren't going to push the issue of anal sex (pun intended). However, in preparation for the next exercise, I would like you to entertain the notion of bringing an objective eye to your anus.

Journaling Prompts: The Anus Monologues

- When I think of my anus, I feel . . .
- When I think of looking at my anus, I . . .
- When I think of anal sex, I . . .

Every Body Is Different

Most of us have no idea how vulvas look. FYI: Each one is different, like a snowflake! Coloring, shape, taste, scent, and sensation are individual, just like the lines on our palms and the sensitivity of our skins. Your vulva is another precious testament to your uniqueness.

In future chapters we will delve into sensation, taste, and scent. We begin here with the most ubiquitous of our senses—sight.

Journaling Prompts: I Spy, With My Eye . . .

- When I think about my vulva, . . .
- When I think of looking at my vulva, . . .
- My vulva is . . .
- Vulvas look . . .

Magickal Act: Pussy Gazing

What You Will Need

- A large, freestanding or wall-mounted mirror.
- Privacy.
- Uninterrupted time (at least an hour).

- A clock or timer.
- Pillows, a blanket, or your bed if you can set the mirror up to work there.
- Tissues, in case of tears.
- A glass of water, for thirst.
- Drawing, painting, and writing implements.
- Your journal.
- Your curiosity!

The goal of this exercise is to become familiar with your personal genital terrain, and to begin building up your sense of genital self-image and self-esteem. This is the starting point of creating an intimate relationship with your wonderful vulva.

This exercise may uncork some deep emotions, so be prepared for tears. It may feel ridiculous, so be prepared for embarrassed laughter. It may be uncomfortable on any number of levels, so be prepared to possibly feel a bit chagrined, or at least challenged. This exercise is sure to be interesting and revealing if you give it the time it needs, and if you open yourself up to the experience. Be prepared to see yourself in a whole new light.

Set up a comfortable area where you can relax while viewing your pussy in the mirror. Once your space is set up, remove your clothes (at least on the lower half of your body), spread your legs, and sit—or lie—back while looking at your vulva in the mirror. For at least ten minutes, visually explore your pussy.

Use your fingers to move your labia around. Pull back your clitoral hood, and look at the glans of your clitoris. Open the inner labia, and look at the opening of your canal. Notice the colors of the different types of tissue.

This is the region where you find the epicenters and culminations of physical passion. This area may, or may not—but *can,* nonetheless—stretch wide enough to allow a baby into this world. It's the spot that may have brought unwanted attention, or may have brought painfully desired interest. It's the nexus that is by turns the source of ridicule and worship. It is a place that is powerful in so many ways, and the sacred space that is hidden, occult.

This is an exercise in observation. This is not foreplay (unless you get so turned on looking at yourself that you just *must* have a go at it). It is an opportunity to know how you look, and ideally to find some awe in that.

★ ──────────

*Want to See Some Varia-
tions on the Theme?*

You can see all sorts
of different vulvas in
beautiful, intriguing,
and nonsexual photos at
www.the-clitoris.com.

────────── ★

Be open to whatever thoughts come up for you while doing this exercise. It may be emotional. You may feel shame or embarrassment. You may feel elation, or excitement. You may feel disgust, and you may feel awe. Maybe you will feel all of these things.

Notice the emotions you are experiencing, and let them pass. You will have the opportunity to write about them after you've had the time to sit with the experience for a little while.

After about ten to fifteen minutes of gazing, you can begin painting, drawing, or making a collage. Illustrate what you see and/or what you feel. Do this for at least five to ten minutes.

When you feel done drawing or painting, write about what you see and what you feel for at least five to fifteen minutes.

When you are done with this exercise, you may dress, take a break, drink some water, stretch. Once you feel ready, come back to your paper and writing implements, and write about the experience.

★ Daily Practice: Quality Time

Every day this week, spend some time with your vulva. Read your love poem to it. Take pictures of it. Dress it up. Dye its hair if it has any. (Manic Panic Hair Dye comes in wild colors, is mild, vegan, and is not tested on animals.) Anoint it with oils. Sing songs to it. Touch it. Play with it. Worship it.

Onward and Inward!

All right, sexy. It's time to go to the correct ritual section in part 2 and perform your third initiation. Enjoy!

---

1. Laura A. Berman and Jennifer R. Berman, "Viagra and Beyond: Where Sex Educators and Therapists Fit in from a Multidisciplinary Perspective," *Journal of Sex Education and Therapy* 25 (2000): 1.17-24.

2. *Take Our Word For It,* http://www.takeourword.com/pt.html.

3. *The-Clitoris.com,* http://www.the-clitoris.com/f_html/fr_index.htm.

CHAPTER FOUR

Carnal Knowledge: Masturbation, Menstruation, Matrices

★ Daily Practice: Sex Magick, page 71.

My *Body!*

It is not without reason that many of us are alienated from our genitals, our reproductive organs, our sexuality, or our power. These parts of us have all been used to hold us down, to keep us powerless, to tie us to an externally imposed "destiny." It's time for us to take ownership of ourselves, all in all. To that end, it is important that we know the tools of our oppression and repression, how they have been used, and how to recognize them so that we won't accept the old arguments as "fact" any longer.

★ ————————————

Malleus Maleficarum:
This book, written by
Heinrich Kramer and
James Sprenger, fanned
the flames of the Witch-
burning fires. It was first
published in 1486, and
was the reference by
which the Witch Hunts
were carried out. The
Witch Hunts lasted from
the late 1400s to the late
1700s. It was primarily
women who were ac-
cused, tried, convicted,
and executed. At the
height of the Witch
Hunts, some whole
towns in Europe were
left empty of women.

· · ·

Hysteria: A term coined
by Plato that meant
"wandering womb."
Hysteria was not re-
moved as a diagnosis
from the Diagnostic and
Statistical Manual of
Mental Disorders
(DSM) until 1994. The
term is still used to de-
scribe "overly emo-
tional" behavior.

———————————— ★

In an effort to give context to the shame and pain we may feel about our bodies and our sexuality, I will delve a little bit deeper than might be comfortable into some hidden terrain. This landscape may hold keys to the warp and weft of an invisible backdrop that is our collective angst.

Maybe This Explains Some of the Hating

During the Witch Hunts, which spanned over 300 years, expression of sexuality by females could be grounds for accusations of witchcraft.[1] The last execution in the name of the Witch Hunts was in 1782.[2] The last recorded Witch trial in the United States was in 1878.[3] In other words, your great grandmother could have been tried as a Witch.

The belief has been bandied about since the time of the ancient Greeks that "women's ailments" are caused by the womb.[4] With a more sophisticated awareness of anatomy, this belief grew to include the clitoris and ovaries.

In the United States alone, it was less than a hundred years ago that feminine sexuality was seen as something so downright *wrong* that a woman was likely to be put in a mental hospital if she dared indulge in sexual expression of any sort.[5] This included masturbation, expression of sexual desire, lesbianism, and everything between and around these actions and definitions.[6]

These "ailments" have been given different names and different diagnoses throughout the centuries, and ultimately meant anything deemed "improper" for a woman. For a very long time that has nearly universally included the expression of rage, emotionality, or sexual desire, regardless of the circumstances surrounding any of these emotions or responses.

In the United States we have a horrifying, hidden history that includes untold numbers of women treated for faddish diseases like nymphomania and hysteria. These women were put through unimaginable "treatments," the least of which was "genital manipulation" (manual stimulation of the clitoris by a doctor), enforced rest, and hospitalization. The more shocking, outrage-inducing treatments were hysterectomy, oophorectomy (removal of the ovaries—also known as female castration), clitoridectomy (surgical excision of the visible clitoral tissue), cauterization of the clitoris, cauterization of the cervix, and bloodletting by leeches, which were applied *inside* the vagina and directly to the neck of the cervix.

Other ailments that medically justified these treatments were suicidal behavior, eating disorders, and any "emotional" behavior. It looks like any complaint by a woman could have landed her in surgery, sans varied bits of her pretty pink parts when she walked out.

Astonishingly, as late as the 1950s, some doctors in the United States elected to "treat" masturbation with clitoridectomy. In 1936, clitoridectomy and cauterization of the clitoris were listed as viable treatments in the widely used *Holt Diseases of Infancy and Childhood,* which was published from 1897–1940.

Numbers of the women who suffered the knife in the United States for treatment of these imagined ills are hard to come by. Quite reasonably, the American medical industry is embarrassed by these stories of practices we now think of as utter barbarism, and have rewritten their story to create a kinder, gentler version. Only by picking through antique patient files, acquiring and reading old medical texts, and reading entries in personal journals have people been able to find accounts of these surgeries.[7]

Today, women's "diseases," like PMS, menstruation, menopause, pregnancy, and birth, are still being pathologized, and are treated mostly by male doctors, who rely on research done mostly by male researchers, sometimes performed on male research subjects![8] Yes, it's absurd, but many studies dealing with diseases that primarily affect women have been performed on male subjects, because the female system is more complicated. You have to take

In 1906, an estimated 150,000 American woman had received oophorectomies; removal of the ovaries, as treatment for "ailments" such as nymphomania, hysteria, and melancholia.

Source: *Men Who Control Women's Health: The Miseducation of Obstetrician-Gynecologists* by Diana Scully, 1980.

. . .

One doctor's rationale behind American female genital mutilation: "Why do we alter our colts and calves? Not that we expect to abate strength or endurance, nor yet to render them less intelligent: but that we may make them tractable and trustworthy, that we may convert them into faithful, well-disposed servants."

—Written in 1896 by Dr. David Gilliam, as quoted in Scully, 1980.

into account hormonal fluctuations and such, and the male system has less of that sort of "inconvenience." Does the hormonal component affect the course of some of these diseases? Yes. Heart disease in women has been under-tested, and many pharmaceutical companies have most drug testing performed on male subjects for the same reasons just stated.[9]

American women who are sure of themselves sexually are often made fun of, sometimes ridiculed, and are at times even at risk of harm or death for expressing themselves sexually.[10, 11]

In some cultures under Islamic rule, women can be legally stoned to death for adultery. This law has even been applied on occasion in the case of women having children out of wedlock.[12]

In many Muslim countries in Africa (and some other continents as well), the ritual practice of female genital mutilation (FGM) is often performed by older women on local girls and young women. FGM is a term that refers to the removal of part or all of the external female genitalia. The practice often includes clitoridectomy, and approximately 15 percent of the time it includes the more damaging practice of infibulation.[13]

The term *infibulation* comes from the Latin *fibula*, which means "to pin or clasp." With infibulation, varied amounts of the labia are cut away, and then the open wounds are joined together with sutures, bamboo slivers, or thorns. The wound heals with about a pencil-sized hole for menstrual blood and urine to escape from the girl's body.[14] Women who have somehow reached adulthood without having the ritual performed are often not considered marriageable.[15]

Religion, superstition, and medicine have all been used throughout our cultural memory in attempts to constrict women to a subservient role, to disallow us our sexual expression, and to keep us thinking of ourselves as crazy and thinking of our most pleasurable, creative (and procreative) parts of our bodies as the enemy.

We all carry vestiges of these cultural stories. From birth to death we are defined by our histories, both personal and pervasive, as well as our present circumstances. Knowing where our wounds come from can be the first step in healing them. How do the wounds that have been handed down, from generation to generation, manifest in your life?

Journaling Prompt: One Woman's Story

Write a story of one woman's experience of suppression, oppression, or depression. This can be your story, or your mother's, or your sister's, or your grandmother's. It can be personal, or it can be a cultural myth or history. Even if it happened to someone other than you, or may never even have happened at all on the physical plane, this is still your story.

Like the story of Eve and the apple, or the abduction of Persephone, or the story of how your grandmother lived her life, or the story of the rape of your best friend, this story rests in the deep spots of your psyche. It informs the way you present yourself, the way you interact with your surroundings, and what you see as safe, or right, or wrong, or permissible. It informs how you walk in this world.

Spell Working: Binding the Past

Binding our collective history is something that will help keep each of us in the place where we have the most power—firmly in the present. Only in the present do we have the power of choice. Only in the present do we have the ability to look forward and set a positive intention for our lives. In the present, we have the ability to create new answers to old questions.

What You Will Need to Bind

- Art or writing supplies.

- Scissors.

- Yarn or thread. I recommend black or white, but you may use whatever color you think is appropriate.

- A taper candle (for wax, to seal the binding).

Note: If you have a relationship with a deity that you think would be helpful in this binding, feel free to invoke it before you

---

Magick in Action— Binding: Binding is an act of sympathetic magick. You can bind energy, thoughts, spirits, or actions.

. . .

Intention: A stretching or bending of the mind toward an object; closeness of application; fixedness of attention; earnestness.

Source: *Webster's Revised Unabridged Dictionary,* 1998.

★ ——————————

Warding:
To keep something away,
to protect, to defend.

. . .

"When a woman has a
discharge of blood . . .
the uncleanness of her
monthly periods shall
last for seven days.

"Anyone who touches
her will be unclean until
evening.

"Any bed she lies on
in this state will be un-
clean; any seat she sits
on will be unclean. Any-
one who touches her bed
must wash his clothing
and wash himself and
will be unclean until
evening . . .

"If a man sleeps with
her, he will be affected
by the uncleanness of
her monthly periods. He
shall be unclean for
seven days. Any bed he
lies on will be unclean."
—Leviticus 15: 19-24

. . .

"They ask you about
menstruation: Say, it is
harmful; you shall avoid
sexual intercourse with
the women during men-
struation; do not ap-
proach them until they
are rid of it."
—The Quran, 2:222

——————————★

begin this ritual. Appropriate deities might be loving, like Inanna, Ishtar, or White Tara, or somewhat wrathful in aspect, like Kali, Babalon, or Red Tara. Any deities that you feel are pro- tective of you, or whom you see as being capable of warding, would be helpful. (See Appendix II: A Compendium of S/heroes for some info on these and other Goddesses. Better yet, research them yourself if you are not yet familiar with them. Google is an amazing tool!)

Also, you may wish to see the spell working titled "Blood Magick" in the menstruation section later in this chapter. Blood magick can intensify any magickal act, and if you perform this spell while you are menstruating, you may as well take advantage of that fact!

How-To

1. Create an artifact that represents one of these collective stories of betrayal, neglect, or deep injury. It can be a piece of writing, a drawing or painting, a sculpture, or anything you feel moved to create.

2. Once you are done creating your artifact, take a length of string or thread that is long enough to tie around it three times.

3. Wrap the string around the artifact, and as you do, think of the stories, the emotions, the images that you are binding. Imagine them becoming tied and bound, un- able to affect you anymore.

   a. If it helps you to speak while you work, you can say, "I bind you. I bind you. I bind you . . ." as many times as it feels right.

   b. If you have invoked a deity for this working, you may also choose to invoke the name of the deity to aid the binding. You may wish to say, "In the name of _____, I bind you."

4. Once you have performed the binding, place the bound artifact on the altar you built while working the first chapter. This artifact, this story, is a part of your history, and you can claim it. By so doing, you claim your wounds, and allow yourself permission to heal them. This bound artifact now represents a past that is contained, and a future that is wide open for growth and healing.

You may keep your binding, and add it to your altar. It is bound, after all. However, you may destroy it, if that feels more magickally complete to you. Burning is the best route for destruction of malignant forces. After you burn the artifact of binding, flush the ashes down the toilet, throw them in a running stream (but only if totally nontoxic items were used in its creation), or cast them to the wind in an open space.

Masturbation, Onanism . . . Can We Just Call It Sexual Self-Love?

Words, again! In researching the roots of the term *masturbation,* I found that there are two schools of thought as to the origins. One etymological theory says that the root is the Ancient Greek word for penis, *mezea,* and the Latin verb *turbare,* which means "to disturb." So, by that theory, to masturbate would mean to "disturb" the penis.[16] One more point for phallocentric language! The other etymological theory holds that the word masturbate comes from the Latin phrase *manus turbare,* which means "to disturb, defile, or dishonor [depending on the translation] with the hand."[17]

Onanism is the term that was used before the word masturbation was brought into play in the 1700s,[18] and it's even worse. Onan was a Biblical character who was put to death for "spilling his seed upon the ground." Not really accurate as far as our sexual relationships with our bodies, and really not nice!

So onanism is definitely out, and going by either of the etymologies, masturbation is not the most positive nor the most accurate word possible to describe what we're doing when we head downtown. The first etymology excludes women de facto, and the second is kind of ugly.

In an effort not to be overly sensitive, I will still use the word masturbation throughout this chapter. However, I encourage you, Ms. Sexy Witch, to adopt a word that works better for you. Who knows . . . if we had a word that actually meant what we mean by it, maybe we wouldn't feel so bad about doing it!

★ ————————

The Kinsey Report states that in studies conducted in 1948 and 1954, 92% of men and 62% of women reported that they masturbated.

In a 2003 study performed on-line by play-withyourself.co.uk, 99% of male respondents reported masturbating, while 96% of females did. Are we starting to catch up?

The frequency of masturbation that most of the female respondents reported was lower than that of most male respondents.

• • •

"I have a total love affair with my pussy. I thought everybody had done all that hippy stuff in *Our Bodies, Ourselves,* and that everyone was cool with their genitals.

"But I guess I was wrong. I have been hanging out with some women lately who are around my age, and there are three of them who swear they have never touched their pussies. I was amazed when I found out!"

Y. S., age 23

———————— ★

Masturbation is something girls (and "ladies," for that matter) just don't usually talk about. Blame it on negative word connotations, vestiges of puritanical thought, or plain embarrassment; it's an issue, whatever the origin. Our internalized, repressive fear of our sexuality is holding us back from really taking our needs into our own hands.

While this is beginning to change (see sidebar), it's still true that many men speak more openly about their solo sartorial pursuits.

So, do women really not masturbate as much, or are we just ashamed to admit that we do? Are we ashamed to admit we have sexual needs and desires, and ashamed that sometimes we take care of those needs *a mano?* Ashamed to say that we touch ourselves *down there?* Ashamed to say that we want sex more than we get it from our sexual partners? Ashamed to say we think about it at all, perhaps?

Journaling Prompt

• I (do/don't) masturbate because . . .

So . . . Why *Should I Pet the Kitty? If You Want Something Done Right, Sometimes You Gotta Do It Yourself!*

After all of this heavy stuff, the issue of masturbation may seem a frivolous topic. But what better way to claim ourselves, body and soul? Masturbation is an act that says, "This is mine, and I know how to use it!" It says, "I love myself . . . a lot!" It says, "Wow! I have this amazing, pleasure-giving, pleasure-making body!" And it says, "This is my sexuality. MINE!"

We have been without for far too long. Without the freedom to claim our bodies, our drives, or our needs. Without the security to go against convention and claim our desire for sex. Without the support to be out and proud as sexual beings. Without the benefit of being our own best bed-buddy.

Let "I wank!" be the new motto of the girl revolution! Let your own box be your newest musical instrument, and learn how to play it! Let your masturbation be a statement of sovereignty. Claim your body. Claim your pleasure. Claim your power.

And, for the practical among us, here are a few (mostly) pragmatic reasons to bang the box:

1. Masturbation allows you to teach yourself how to orgasm. And, if you learn how to get off on your own, it's going to be a lot easier to get off with others, too. Without the stress and pressure of making sure a partner isn't waiting for you to come, getting jealous of your toys, or feeling badly that he or she can't get you off, it will be much easier to focus on what really matters: you . . . getting off!

2. Orgasm is good for you for many, many reasons, including:

   a. Orgasm is a major stress reliever.

   b. Orgasm can help you get to sleep, and it doesn't have any side effects, like most sleeping pills do.

   c. Orgasm can relieve menstrual cramps and lower back pain.

   d. The hormones released when you orgasm can help combat depression.

   e. Masturbation and orgasm stimulate your immune system.

3. Masturbation encourages familiarity with your sexual anatomy. If you are familiar with your sexual anatomy, you will more likely be able to tell if something is wrong.

A Magickal Thought: Masturbation is a magickal, (r)evolutionary act!

. . .

Fun Toys You Can Buy Anywhere:
- Detachable showerheads—the more massager options, the better! ($10-?)
- Massagers ($10-60)
- Facial kits with pore cleaners ($30)

. . .

What It's Called— A Compendium of Names for Masturbation: Banging the box, beating the bush, doing your nails, feeding the cat, finger dipping, going downtown, going south, hitting the slit, jerking off, jilling off, kneading the dough, petting the kitty, petting the pussy, rocking the boat, she-bop, spending some quality time, taking a ride, tending the garden, two-finger tango, the two-finger salute, wanking.

4. If you are afraid of, or alienated by, your genitals, it is going to be uncomfortable to share them with a lover.

5. Masturbation feels good.

6. Masturbation can't get you pregnant.

7. Masturbation is *fun!*

8. Masturbation is revolutionary.

9. Masturbation is sex with someone you love.

If You've Never Ventured South

First, a word about orgasm. If you have never had one, you may not know what to expect. And, if you wonder if you have ever had an orgasm or not, you probably haven't. An orgasm generally consists of four to fifty contractions. You may feel them mainly in your genital region, or all through your body. You may have an emotional response, like laughing or crying.

As you go forth into the world of orgasm, you may want to play with breathing techniques. You may find that holding your breath, or breathing deeply, or rapid, shallow breathing makes your orgasm more pleasurable. Allowing yourself to make noise might be fun, or try forcing yourself to remain totally silent.

And here's a word about masturbation, in a general sense. If you find a producer, writer, actor, or product that you like, porn can be fun. Erotic reading materials, graphic novels, anime, videos, and good old "men's magazines" are used much more widely by women than you might think. If you have never tried using porn, you might want to. Your imagination is a great ally, too. Don't censor your fantasies. Follow your imagination where it wants to go, as long as it gets your pussy wet.

There is no one *right way* to orgasm. Just relax, do what feels good, and let yourself go.

How-To: Fingers

You will need a private space, some lotion or lubricant, some time, and maybe some porn (or erotica, if you prefer—wink, wink).

Relax into your space, and allow your fingers to explore your vulva, your clit, your entire genital region. Whatever feels good, do more of. Some women like direct clitoral stimulation, some like less direct. Figure out what *you* like.

With enough time, open-mindedness, and dedication, you are likely to find ways to make yourself orgasm.

How-To: Vibrator

You can pick up a vibrator at any drugstore. Your new best friend will be packaged as a "massager," and you can expect to spend as little as $10 to $50 for it. You will not find the quality or diversity at your corner drugstore that you will see somewhere at specialty sex stores like Good Vibrations in California (see sidebar), but you won't be dropping quite as much cash, either.

Once you have your new toy, find some private time and space, and play with it! Vary the speeds, and the intensity. If the intensity of the vibe on your bare skin is too extreme, put cloth between your clit and the head of the massager. Try it with lube, and without. Let your intuition be your guide.

Vibrators will tend to get you off quickly and simply. And take it from me—it's a real joy to be able to deliver a satisfying quickie to the one who matters most!

Journaling Prompt

- The first time I masturbated, . . .

★ Daily Practice: Sex Magick

Every day during the week that you work this chapter, "spend some quality time." Sexual energy is powerful, and you can use it to build joy in the world; not just with the intractable fact that it makes you feel good, and that feeling good tends to have a ripple effect (which is great in itself, and you may well become a beacon, emanating pulses of joy), but also the amount of energy that is released by your body when you orgasm (the activity of neurons, hormones, nerves, muscles, blood) is measurable. You can use this energy to power your prayers, intentions, spells, and wishes.

Sex Shops Where You Will Want to Shop!

- Good Vibrations, San Francisco, Berkeley, CA, http://www.good-vibes.com.

- Grand Opening!, Boston, Los Angeles

- Toys in Babeland, Seattle, WA, New York, http://www.babeland.com.

- It's My Pleasure, Portland, OR.

Good Vibes and Toys in Babeland, and many other sellers, sell great products on-line, too. But an in-person visit just can't be beat!

. . .

Fun Fact! A half hour of moderate sexual activity burns 144 calories in a 150-pound person.
    Source: http://www.clitical.com/sex-tutorials/sex-facts/sexercising.php
    (I include this fact only to show that sex produces energy. I am NOT suggesting that you need to lose weight.)

★

"When I get my period I get moody. But my moodiness isn't coming out of nowhere. The feelings just get bigger than they usually are. Sometimes it's a bit much, but I have learned to really pay attention when I am PMSing. I can learn a lot about what's really going on with me that way."

L. S., age 30

• • •

"I like getting my period. During the first few days, I get kind of spacey and feel a little bit high. It's kind of like time stretches out. And, I am really nice to myself when I'm bleeding. I take time to really take care of myself. That makes it a special time of the month for me."

A. C., age 23

★

With each orgasm that you rack up, say a prayer for those who went before, and give thanks for the liberties those libertines granted us. Every woman who ever lived outside the lines that her culture built around her made more room for you and me to be who we are today. And, you and I are doing the same for future generations.

While you are giving thanks, give thanks also for the miracle of muscle and flesh—our pleasure-making, sensual, sexy bodies; these amazing bodies that look exactly the way they look, feel exactly the way they feel, and work exactly the way they work.

Menstruation

Ever heard the saying "I just don't trust something that bleeds for days and doesn't die!"? Well, why the hell not trust? It is natural for a woman to bleed. This is yet another example of the sometimes supercilious denouncement of women that exemplifies our cultural construct of dismissal.

Of all the psychological areas in which misogyny has been internalized, our relationships with our menstrual cycles may well be where it is lodged the deepest.

Menstruation has been equated with uncleanliness by every major patriarchal or patrifocal culture in history, and is the most abundant example of the hatred and mistrust of the body in general, coupled with the hatred and mistrust of women.

Checking in with your own feelings about menstruation is probably all you need to do to see how true this is. If it's not, take as evidence the slew of products designed to hide the fact that you are bleeding, the pathologization of moodiness leading up to menses, and the mass of slanderous references to our periods: "Oh, don't mind her; she's on the rag!"

How can we own this most alienating aspect of our sex? There are lots of theories out there that may lend a bit of empowerment, like those that attempt to explain the concealed ovulation: the anomalous fact that women don't show outwardly—or sometimes even know—when they are ovulating. One theory regarding this evolutionary mystery is that human females can control their fertility by deciding when to invite sexual contact, and when not to.

There is also the lunar cycle theory, which postulates that our menstrual cycles are influenced by the cycles of the moon. This theory hasn't been proven, but perhaps our fertility cycle would mirror the cycle of the moon if we didn't intervene with hormones, electric light, alcohol, drugs, and stress. Perhaps it is true that women in a "natural" environment would share this cosmic link with *la luna*. But even so, it is not of much use to us in the culture we live in today, aside from being a possible reference point for a spiritual mythos.

Here is one true thing: Blood is powerful. Fear of blood is powerful, and reasonable. Fear of our own menstrual blood? Senseless. There is power in facing fears, and power in overcoming the fear of our own blood. Even the solitary act of facing the fears and shame may have a profound effect on your relationship with your body, your sex, and your concept of your gender.

Journaling Prompt

My blood, my moon, my period, my menses . . . What I call it, and how I feel about it.

Spell Working: Blood Magick

Next time you are bleeding, take a bath and relax. Once you are clean, comfortable, and dry, take some time to get familiar with your blood. It washes off, so don't be afraid to get some blood on you! Touch it. Smell it. If you are clean and fresh, your blood should smell fresh, too, if a bit metallic, and possibly pungent. Like vaginal fluid, your blood will have a smell that is unique to you. (If your blood smells bad in some way, something may be

The word *taboo* means "sacred" and "menstruating" in Polynesian and Siouan. In Dakotan, *wakan* means "spiritual," wonderful," and "menstrual."

Source: Penelope Shuttle and Peter Redgrove, *The Wise Wound*, New York: Grove Press, 1988.

• • •

Blood Art: A Compendium

• Karen Finley: http://www.karenfinley.net.

• Vanessa Tiegs: www.vanessatiegs.com.

• Tinet Emlgren: www.kommiekomiks.com/blood.htm.

• Saleena Ki': www.transformationalart.com/mohe/visuals/ajl/moong/moong.html.

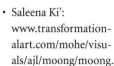

★ ──────────────
What It's Called:
Latin: Matrix
Greek: Hustera
Middle English: Womb
Middle English: Uterus
────────────── ★

amiss. It would be worth a visit to your doctor to make sure everything is fine.)

Once you've made friends with your blood, do some finger painting with it. (You don't have to show anyone if you don't want to!)

Using Blood to Charge Spells and Talismans

Blood of all sorts can be used to charge talismans and spells. Women are lucky to have an approximately monthly supply of life-blood that comes free of wounding. This blood is also special because it reminds us of our power to create.

Blood can be burnt over incense as an offering of your life force to the spirit world. It can also be dabbed on talismans, used to consecrate magickal and divinatory tools, and more.

Some practitioners of magick claim strict rules about when, and for what, blood magick should and should not be performed. I am not so sure that there are as many rules to it. Let your conscience be your guide. One thing to remember, though: dabbing your blood on a talisman will send some of you with it, so be choosy about where it goes.

Matrices: The Womb

Our wombs, center of the world. We all came from a womb. It is one of the few global predicates that exists; one thing we all have in common. Everyone has a mother, mater, matrix; a place to move forth from.

As women, we have myriad relationships with this inner sanctum, this yoke, this pit, this core, this center. This, more than any other place in our bodies, is our seat of creation. It is also the place where we can be fully owned by needs other than our own. It is our seat of power, and it is the place where we can feel the most hijacked. Our wombs can become a home of disruption, a resting place for intruders. Yet, this is also the home of our ability to "create breath," as Ani DiFranco says (see sidebar). It is the home of the future, the home of possibility, perhaps even the home of the possibility of the future of the whole human race.

This seat of creation that abides within us is the seat of responsibility and power. Where do you stand in this awareness? Do you find yourself in awe of creation, or fearing this magnificent muscle as the very yoke of our sex?

The womb, and the questions it raises with its mere (miraculous) existence, are not simple: To breed, or not to breed? If I choose not to, will I regret it later? If I choose to, will I regret it later? What is my worth as a woman, beyond my womb? Why can't I just be a person!?!

And then you start menstruating again, and are reminded that you are a woman, with a womb, and that you may as well get used to it.

Or perhaps you are on hormonal birth control, and your cycle has been force-fit to the mechanized cycle of the nonhormone-carrying pills in the pack. You never feel the pull anymore of the early flow, or the scare of late days. Or maybe you are one of the roughly 600,000 women who have had a hysterectomy performed in the past year, and you do not bleed, and you cannot breed, and you have no need for birth control.[19]

Seat of power, seat of choice. And with choice, again, comes responsibility. We are responsible, us and our wombs, for our fertility, for our control of it, for the ultimate choice should it come down to a question of shedding blood, or not.

The medical industry is still dominated by men, and medical textbooks are still written primarily by men. But this trend is changing. There has been a gradual yet somewhat steady increase of women going into medicine since 1848, the year in which an American woman named Elizabeth Blackwell was the first woman accepted into an American medical school. In the 2003–2004

Blood in the
Boardroom
by Ani DiFranco,
  Puddle Dive, Righteous
  Babe Records, 1993

. . . every woman learns
to bleed from the moon
    and we bleed to renew
life
    every time it's cut
down
    I got my vertebrae all
stacked up
    as high as they go
    but I still feel myself
sliding
    from the earth that I
know
    so I excuse myself and
leave the room
    say my period came
early
    but it's not a minute
too soon
    I go and find the only
other woman on the floor
. . .
    I ask her if she's got a
tampon I could use
    she says
    oh honey, what a has-
sle for you, sure I do, you
know I do
    I say, it ain't no hassle,
no, it ain't no mess
    right now it's the only
power
    that I possess
    these businessmen got
the money
    they got the instru-
ments of death
    But I can make life, I
can make breath . . .

★ ─────────────

Ovarian Illumination

Since 1912 it was thought that baby girls are born with all their eggs already developed, as opposed to men who produce more sperm than they could ever use throughout their lives.

In 2004, a study authored by Jonathan Tilly posited that the number of eggs may be renewed throughout adult life, and the scientific world is abuzz with the possibilities. This new look at women's reproductive realities is likely to revolutionize reproductive health.

—Source: http://focus.hms.harvard.edu/2004/March19_2004/reproductive_biology.html.

. . .

Fact: Hysterectomy's damage is lifelong. Among its most common consequences, in addition to operative injuries, are loss of sexual desire, arousal, and sensation; painful intercourse; profound fatigue; loss of short-term memory; despondency, irritability, anger, and suicidal thinking.

(continued)

───────────── ★

school year, 49.7 percent of those enrolled in medical school in the United States were women.[20] While there are still more male doctors than female in practice in nearly every field of medicine, there's a good chance that in the near future the numbers will be close to equal.

As a matter of fact, looking at the climb in the number of women choosing medicine as their profession over just the past few years, it's even possible that within the next decade or so there will be more women working in medicine than men.[21] And more good news: this is not only happening in the United States. There are women flooding into careers in health care in the United Kingdom and British Columbia, too.[22] And in 1998, a co-educational medical school opened in Afghanistan.[23]

How will this affect the future of our bones, our blood, our choice? What potential does this relative equality hold? How will things change when as many women as men are researching causes and cures, answering questions, and finding the right ones to ask?

Journaling Prompt

- My womb is . . .

Spell Working: The Womb Room

This is another guided visualization. The goal of this visualization is to claim the power of your womb. In this case, I am using the term *womb* to encompass the system that is made of the uterus, tubes, and ovaries. I know that's not literally accurate, but for the purpose of this exercise, please indulge me in this slightly quirky use of language.

Please note that if you have had a hysterectomy, you may choose to skip this exercise. Or you may want to use this exercise as an opportunity to create a magickal womb for yourself. This may be a challenging task, though. If you feel unsettled about your surgery, you may want to wait until you are more comfortable with your choice to create a magickal stand-in for the parts that were removed.

You may perform this practice by itself, or you may include it in this week's ritual (in part 2).

What You Will Need

- Time. Ten minutes for visualization, and ten minutes for journaling or drawing.
- Journal.
- Writing or drawing implements.

Again, you may want to read aloud and record the instructions for the visualization before doing this exercise.

Visualization Script

Sit in a comfortable position. Close your eyes and relax. Focus on breathing. Pull each breath into your lungs, allowing them to expand to their fullest capacity. Breathe out, and release any tension you feel in your muscles. As you breathe, let your lungs become even fuller, pulling your breath deep into your abdomen. Allow your belly to relax, your ribs to expand, your mind to quiet. When thoughts come to the surface, allow them to gently pass.

Once you feel relaxed and present, allow your consciousness to venture inside your body. Feel the temperature of your skin. Now, going inside your skin, notice the flesh, bones, and blood that are your body. Notice your heart beating, and your blood circulating.

Keep breathing, and notice your fingers, hands, toes, feet, and head. Keep breathing deeply, and slowly allow your consciousness to move inward toward the center of your body, through your arms, legs, neck, your thighs and chest, your sex and your belly.

Fact: Twice as many women in their twenties and thirties are hysterectomized as women in their fifties and sixties.

Fact: No drugs or other treatments can replace ovarian or uterine hormones or functions. The loss is permanent.

Fact: The uterus and ovaries function throughout life in women who have not been hysterectomized.

Fact: 98% of women HERS has referred to board-certified gynecologists after being told they needed hysterectomies discovered that, in fact, they did not need hysterectomies.

—Source: Adapted from a list posted at http://hersfoundation.com. HERS in the only independent, international organization dedicated to the issue of hysterectomy, and advocates for fully informed medical choices by women.

★ ───────────────

The New Eugenics—
Margaret Sanger,
Planned Parenthood,
Poverty, and Forced
Sterilization:
Margaret Sanger was re-
sponsible for much of
what we have in place in
the way of planned par-
enthood options. She
founded the first
Planned Parenthood or-
ganization, and deserves
hero status for that.

However, there is a
hidden side to the
Sanger story, which has
to do with her involve-
ment in the Eugenics
movement. While
Sanger was not racist,
she did believe in con-
trolling birthrates, by
force if necessary, of
"undesirable" elements
of society.

—Source:
http://www.plannedpar-
enthood.org/pp2/por-
tal/files/portal/medical-
info/birthcontrol/bio-ma
rgaret-sanger.xml.

─────────────── ★

Continue to breathe deeply, and then slowly, gently, allow your attention to focus on your womb. Notice that this is your temple, too. This is your inner sanctum. Here, you are child and mother. You are Goddess holding the power of creation and choice within you, Potential and Will. This space is yours. This space is.

Continue breathing, and sit with whatever emotions surface. Hold them with reverence and openness, and then release them as you see fit. Sigh, laugh, cry, smile. Notice how everything moves, how it all works. Notice the flow of hormones, so amazing, that engage with every thought and feeling you experience, and interface with the world around you in such subtle and miraculous ways.

Breathe, and allow yourself to become aware of the rhythm of your body. Notice how your uterus and ovaries comprise a system that interacts with the larger system of your body. This amazing system has an integrated relationship with your brain, your heart, your gut. More than just a tool for procreation, this system is an integral part of emotion, thought, sexuality.

Breathe deeply. Allow this breath to fill your core. Allow yourself to feel awe at the full awareness of what it means to have a womb. Now, claim this space. Claim the potential and the responsibility that sits at the center of woman. Claim the pain and the joy of it. Dedicate yourself to your right to decide what is best for you. Claim the power to heal the wounds, and the power to direct the energy that is cradled in this sacred sanctum.

Taste the power of your monthly blood. Feel the power of your right to decide to breed or not to breed. Allow yourself the enduring right to laugh when you want to laugh, and cry when you want to cry.

Breathe, and claim your womb as worthy, equal to your heart and your brain. As you claim the power of this amazing organ and the system, you claim the ability to wield that power wisely.

Allow yourself to feel gratitude for the gifts of choice and of awareness of choice. Allow yourself to feel gratitude for power and the awareness of power. Allow yourself to love this powerful place that defines the edges of being woman.

Keep breathing deeply, and slowly follow your breath back to consciousness. Allow your attention to move back out through flesh and bone, bringing you gently back to the space you're sitting in. When you are ready, slowly open your eyes, and journal or draw the story of this experience.

Onward and Inward!

Okay, you Sexy Witch, go to the proper section in part 2 and find your ritual. Oh, and by the way, congrats! You are more than halfway though your process of initiation.

1. Erwin J. Haeberle, "Sex and Psychiatry," *The Sex Atlas* (New York, 1981), http://www2.rz.hu-berlin.de/sexology/GESUND/ARCHIV/SDEV05.HTM#N27.

2. "Witch Hunts," *World History at KMLA,* http://www.zum.de/whkmla/period/absolut/witchhunt.html.

3. *Ask Yahoo!,* http://ask.yahoo.com/ask/20030430.html.

4. *The Perseus Digital Library,* http://www.perseus.tufts.edu/cgi-bin/ptext?doc=Perseus%3Atext%3A1999.01.0180&query=section%3D%23705&layout=&loc=Tim.%2091b.

5. Jeffrey L. Geller and Maxine Harris, *Women of the Asylum: Voices from Behind the Walls, 1840–1945* (New York: Anchor Books, 1994).

6. Dr. Stanley West, *Hysterectomy Hoax* (New York: Doubleday, 1994), http://www.rense.com/health3/hyster.htm.

7. Carol Groneman, *Nymphomania: A History* (New York: W. W. Norton, 2000).

8. Carol Tavris, *The Mismeasure of Woman* (New York: Simon & Schuster, 1992).

9. Ibid, pp. 99–100.

10. Bonnie S. Fisher, Francis T. Cullen, and Michael G. Turner, *The Sexual Victimization of College Women* (Washington, D.C.: U.S. Dept. of Justice, Office of Justice Programs, National Institute of Justice, 2000).

11. *ACLU Sports Hall of Shame,* http://www.nostatusquo.com/ACLU/SportsHallofShame/SportsList2.html.

12. "Shari'ah Law, Adultery and Rape," *International Society for Human Rights,* http://www.ishr.org/activities/campaigns/stoning/adultery.htm.

13. "What Is Female Genital Mutilation?" *Amnesty International,* http://www.amnesty.org/ailib/intcam/femgen/fgm1.htm#a1.

14. Guy Pieters, M.D., and Albert B. Lowenfels, M.D., F.A.C.S., "Infibulation in the Horn of Africa," *New York State Journal of Medicine* 77, no. 6 (April 1977): 729–31, http://www.cirp.org/pages/female/pieters1/.

15. Okumephuna Chinwe Celestine, "FGM: An Insult on the Dignity of Women," *The Female Genital Cutting Education and Networking Project,* http://www.fgmnetwork.org/countries/nigeria.htm.

16. *TheFreeDictionary.com,* http://encyclopedia.thefreedictionary.com/masturbation.

17. *Online Etymology Dictionary,* http://www.etymonline.com/index.php?term=masturbation.

18. Ibid.

19. Cynthia M. Farquhar, M.D., F.A.N.Z.C.O.G., and Claudia A. Steiner, M.D., M.P.H., "Hysterectomy Rates in the United States: 1990–1997," *Obstetrics and Gynecology* 99 (2002): 229–34, http://www.ahcpr.gov/news/press/pr2002/hysterpr.htm.

20. Debra Zelnio, "The Changing Face of Medicine," *MomMD,* http://www.mommd.com/changingface-healthcare.shtml.

21. Ibid.

22. Briefing on Women in Medicine," *Royal College of Physicians of London,* http://www.rcplondon.ac.uk/college/statements/briefing_womenmed.asp.

23. "Badakhshan Medical College, Faizabad," *Indiana University,* http://www.indiana.edu/~afghan/badakhshan_medical_college/Background%20&%20Description%20of%20Badakhshan%20Medical%20College.pdf.

CHAPTER FIVE

Coming to Our Senses

Sensing Our Power

In this chapter, you will begin rebuilding your worldview. You are done with the deconstruction, done with the limitations that may previously have disallowed you ownership of how and who you are in the world.

Now we get to create the world we choose to live and love in, with the awareness that we have choice and wisdom. We have moved through some blocks, and now have the freedom and tools to design and create a new template to build our lives upon.

In the remaining chapters of *Sexy Witch,* we will have the opportunity to integrate the work that we have done in the previous chapters in ways that work for each of us. We will have opportunities to envision and commit to ongoing practices that create a healthy and resourceful matrix for our lives.

★ ──────────────────

I Sing the Body Electric
by Walt Whitman

   . . . Womanhood, and
all that is a woman—and
the man that comes from
woman,
   The womb, the teats,
nipples, breast-milk,
tears, laughter, weeping,
love-looks, love-perturba-
tions and risings,
   The voice, articula-
tion, language, whisper-
ing, shouting aloud,
   Food, drink, pulse, di-
gestion, sweat, sleep,
walking, swimming,
   Poise on the hips,
leaping, reclining, em-
bracing, arm-curving and
tightening,
   The continual changes
of the flex of the mouth,
and around the eyes . . .
   O I say, these are not
the parts and poems of
the Body only, but of the
Soul,
   O I say now these are
the Soul!

──────────────────── ★

As a starting point for this new creation of our worlds, we will begin with the senses. Even reduced to a metaphor, the senses are a vital representational language. How we see is a metaphor for how we think, perceive, and put our worlds together. In the process of seeing, our eyes take in images, discard much of the data, and then leave it up to our brains to "fill in the blanks," so to speak.[1] In this way, seeing, like our other processes of perception, is subjective. We see, but we assume more of the image than we might think.

What if we could become aware of this process in our daily lives? What if we could notice where we are making these assumptions and leaps in logic, where we are filling in the unknown, unseen, unheard with our own shades and shapes? What will the world be like once we are aware of our powers of perception? What will it be like when we can truly receive the senses we experience, and take an interactive role in the process? What will it be like when we can listen *to* our whole bodies, and then *with* our whole bodies? What will it be like when we can allow ourselves to respond appropriately to signals from our nervous systems and limbic systems, instead of overriding or ignoring our needs and desires?

This is also the potential starting point for a whole new love affair with our bodies and our beings. How we work is nothing short of miraculous, and the inherent wisdom in the processes of perception, growth, and evolution is an ode to the place where we all come from. Following the path back to the single cell that was the starting point for all that we have become is a story imbued with mystery and magick.

This chapter, "Coming to Our Senses," is about creating a stronger relationship with our bodies, taking responsibility for our perceptions, and enjoying the experience of being present. It is about enjoying sensation, perception, and sensuality.

You are entering into new territory in your magickal journey. You are about to create a whole new world—one that makes sense!

Sensationale!

Our senses are a portal to discovery. Hearing, smell, sight, touch, and taste and our "extra" senses are the ways that we engage with the world that surrounds us. They are also keys to memories buried deep in the folds of our brain matter. Is it not true that sometimes you smell a scent on the breeze, and are transported to a long-forgotten memory? You hear a song on the radio, and are instantaneously awash with emotions from your eighth-grade dance or the first time you met a certain someone. You see an interesting shade of orange, and all of a sudden feel your hands in the pulp and seed of a pumpkin, cleaning it for carving. You taste a creamy sweetness, and feel some intense emotion, though you're not sure where it originates.

Our senses are constantly active, bringing us to the moment we are in, and sometimes simultaneously creating a portal to memories, distinct or indistinct. Our senses are a device of communication with the worlds, both inner and outer, present and past, concrete and perceived, "real" and imagined.

Coming to our senses means becoming aware. It also means owning our experience of reality, and deciding for ourselves what that means. It means getting in touch with how it all feels, looks, smells, tastes, and sounds. It means taking our experience of this momentary, fleeting, fidgeting reality, and owning it. Absorbing it. Ingesting it. Digesting it. It means staying present in our bodies/minds/spirits, and knowing exactly how that feels. It means claiming our experience of life. Of our bodies. Of the world.

Coming to our senses means being sensually, ecstatically even, aware and engaged with the world around us. It means being grounded in our bodies, having our feet stable and firm beneath us. It means connecting with the world that we create with every moment of conscious action.

The Heart of the Matter

Science is finally coming to the defense of those of us who are "feelers." If you have uttered the words, "It just doesn't feel right," or "My gut says . . .," then you may be a feeler. Science has begun studying the links between the heart, the gut, and the brain. And it

★ ──────────────

The heart is, in fact, a highly complex, self-organized information processing center with its own functional "brain" that communicates with and influences the cranial brain via the nervous system, hormonal system, and other pathways. These influences profoundly affect brain function and most of the body's major organs, and ultimately determine the quality of life.

—Source: *Science of the Heart: Exploring the Role of the Heart in Human Performance*, by Rollin McCraty, Mike Atkinson, and Dana Tomasino. HeartMath Research Center, Institute of HeartMath, Boulder Creek, CA, 2001, http://heartmath. org./research/science-of-the-heart.

• • •

Precognition:
The ability to sense something, or know that an event will occur, before it happens.

────────────── ★

has been found that there is neurological activity in the heart—making the heart almost like an independent brain. The heart and brain are constantly communicating. But the brain does not control the heart, and more than just the heart controls the brain. Either they work together, or they work at odds.[2]

The Seat of Extrasensory Perception?

While some edge-walkers in the scientific community have given the phenomenon of precognition some attention, overwhelmingly the scientific world is known for being skeptical of that which cannot be seen and formulaically proven. However, there are researchers looking at the power of prayer, and at the measurable communicative power of the heart. It is possible that we have a very real "sixth sense" based in a sort of physical communication that originates in our hearts. This amazing, wise, and muscular organ has a measurable magnetic pull, sends out electrical impulses, and controls sometimes subtle—yet comprehensive—signals such as the pulse.[3] These signals are received by every cell in our bodies, and each cell responds accordingly.

It is becoming apparent that not only do our bodies pick up on these signals, but that other bodies around us do as well.[4] We are communicating to and with our whole bodies, whether we are aware of it or not. Our bodies are also receptors of these communications from other bodies. Have you ever felt your anxiety level rise, and then realized you were in proximity to someone who was feeling anxious? Or felt pulled to turn your head, and locked eyes with some hottie staring you down?

Communication Is a Physical Process

Depending on the study cited, nonverbal communication accounts for anywhere from 74 to 99 percent of face-to-face communication. The category of nonverbal communication includes everything but the actual words said: tone and speed of voice, body language, facial expressions, involuntary actions or reactions such as flushing and shaking, chemical signals, and more. Some nonverbal communication is considered innate, or genetic, and other cues are assumed to be learned behaviors.

Awareness of nonverbal communication is utilized extensively in sales and marketing training as well as in some of the helping professions. However, awareness and mastery of nonverbal elements of communication are tools that will help any of us both receive and send out signals more accurately.

As each of us gains an awareness of these subtle elements of communication, we will be able to understand the worlds around and within us more easily. And the more acuity we develop in understanding these forces of communication, the more easily we will present ourselves in ways that are congruous to who we are, and who we are becoming.

Becoming Grateful

One of the most empowering things being learned about our hearts and how they should be treated is that gratitude is a key element to having a healthy heart. And I'm not speaking in metaphor, friends—this is for real! Science has proven that gratitude contributes to the health of your heart, and to your overall sense of joy and well-being.[5]

Gratitude can be a gift that gives twice. When we are truly thankful to others for the gifts they give us—support, help, a smile, or a shoulder to lean on at the right moment—we improve their day, and we improve our health. It's a true win-win situation!

The sticky wicket? We Gen-Xers and beyond are notorious for thinking that nihilism is cute and funny. Well, against the odds (and my cynicism), I started my family on a practice of gratitude about a year ago. Now at least once a day I get to voice my thanks for the little things, and to hear my partner and kids tell me about the *good* things that happened in their days. I will admit that the concept of gratitude is still a challenging one at times, but the more I learn about the gifts that the practice of gratitude offers, the more I realize the challenge is a worthy and fulfilling one.

So, at risk of offending your stylishly bleak sensibilities, here we go . . .

★ Daily Practice: Invoking Gratitude

There are many ways to practice gratitude. In my family, we practice gratitude at our dining room table during dinner. You may find that you like to practice gratitude first thing in the morning, or before or after yoga, or before bed, or whenever you feel sad or annoyed.

For now, we are going to practice gratitude in writing. Choose your favorite time of day for this practice, and then every day this week write down three to five things you are grateful for. These things don't have to be monumental, deep, or virtuous. You don't have to come up with grand gratitude themes. Sometimes it's the little stuff that really makes us feel good. Your journal may read like this:

- Today I am thankful that I noticed this amazing sale at my favorite little shop!
- I am thankful that I had five dollars to spend.
- I am thankful that I got a really hot new shirt.
- And, I'm thankful that I got to talk to my best friend.
- I am also thankful that my dog loves me.

As you begin listing the things you are grateful for, more of them may come to mind. If so, just keep listing them. Some days you will only be able to come up with three items, and they may be things like this:

- Today I am grateful that I got a seat on the subway.
- I am grateful I made time to eat lunch.
- I am grateful my dog is still around.

The only rule I will give for this practice is, as I have mentioned before, state it in the positive! Instead of saying, "I'm glad I'm not dead," say, "I'm glad I'm still living." Instead of saying, "I'm thankful I didn't have to sit in the rain for too long this morning," say, "I'm thankful the bus came on time." Instead of saying, "I'm thankful that I'm not ugly," say, "I'm thankful that I am a beautiful person, inside and out."

Okay, it might be a challenge, but give it a try. And when it starts working to improve your life, share the technology! Gratitude is a limitless and exponential force. If you share it, there's no saying how much more of it will come right back at you! Offer thanks when you feel grateful. Thank friends for caring. Thank your neighbor for watching your back.

★ **Daily Practices, Plural: Your Assignment, Should You Choose to Accept It . . .**

For the first five days of this week, you will focus on one of your senses per day, starting with hearing, then moving to sight, then smell, then touch, then taste. On the sixth day, you will pay attention to all five senses, and on the seventh day, the ritual day, you will indulge in them.

Magickal Act: Grounding Our Experience

You will want to use this exercise as needed or desired in learning to deeply receive your sensory information. Grounding is a great way to really quiet yourself and get ready to listen.

Grounding is about settling into our bodies, and becoming conscious there. This exercise is an important one. We can get a lot of information from our bodies through this sort of physical check-in, and we can also use grounding as a mini-meditation. We can use this exercise to release tension, to become present in the moment, and to relax.

You don't need anything to do this exercise but your body, and you can do it anywhere you feel safe closing your eyes for a few moments.

To begin, just close your eyes and draw in a deep breath. As you do so, check in with your body. If you find spots where tension may be resting in your body, release that tension. Visualize that tension as a color, if it helps, and imagine that color being released out of your mouth and dissipating into the air, becoming benign, or even beneficial, like the carbon monoxide we breathe out is beneficial to plants.

Breathe in again, and let the breath fill you all the way down to your gut. As you breathe, allow your attention to sit with your breath. Breathe out and relax. Breathe in again, and imagine letting the breath fill even more of your body. Keep breathing deeply, and visualize your body filling with breath, all the way out to your fingers, up to the crown of your head, and down to your toes.

You may open your eyes for the rest of the exercise, or leave them closed. Do whichever feels more comfortable to you.

Once your consciousness reaches your feet, feel how they are on the ground. Are your feet resting solidly on the surface beneath them? Is your weight distributed evenly? Bend your knees slightly and allow your center of gravity to drop down, weight evenly being supported. Allow your pelvis to rock gently forward, and your arms to become relaxed yet energized.

★ ───────────

A Magickal Thought:
Deep listening is a
(r)evolutionary and
healing act.

───────────── ★

You are now grounded in your body. You are present with your physical sensations. You are in the moment.

Listening to the Very Bone

Hearing. Listening. Voice. What do these things mean to us? What do they mean to you? Do you own your voice? Do you say it loud and say it often? Do you listen intently, hearing as many of the messages as possible? Do you listen to words spoken, and for those unspoken? Do you listen to your own words? Your own voice? Do you listen to the tapestry of sounds and silences that compose the backdrop of your life?

There is a form of listening beyond what we can hear with our ears. We can listen beyond words. We can listen with our whole bodies. We can hear messages sent without words. We can listen to the silences, to the spaces between our bodies and those of others. We can listen with our cells, with our blood, with our bones. We can listen with our guts and our hearts. We can listen with our souls and our spirits and our whole selves.

Listening is applying ourselves. Listening is being receptive. Listening is opening ourselves to the messages around and within us. Listening is claiming willingness to let some new truth in. Listening is a deep and magickal gift that allows for understanding. Listening is a healing, in and of itself, for those of us who may not often feel truly heard. Listening is a pathway to reconciliation, to a consensual truth, to peace between ourselves and others, and even to world peace.

Listening is one of those simple—yet not always easy—acts that allows for great change. Sometimes all we need is to be heard. Why not start with ourselves?

Journaling Prompts: Listening to the Core

- When I listen, . . .

- Listening is . . .

★ **Daily Practice, Day 1: Full-Body Listening**

For today, day 1 of this chapter, you will listen deeply to the world around you, and to the world within you. You will listen with your ears, but also with your body. You will listen to your gut, to your heart. You will listen with your nerves and your core.

Set your watch, clock alarm, or timer to go off once an hour. When the alarm alerts you, stop what you are doing for a few seconds, or longer if you can afford the time, and listen deeply. Write down what you hear, whether it's with your ears or some other part of your body.

Sight Beyond Sight

Seeing is believing, or so it's said. Seeing can be believing, but you can't believe everything you see. Can you believe things you don't see? Can you see things you don't believe? Our perception may very well be limited by our beliefs. And our beliefs may be expanded when we really open our eyes.

We can also see with our minds, with our brains. We can see memories and dreams. We can see worlds that exist only in the realm of our desires. We can see hopes, and we can see fears. Sight is not as reliable as some may think, and memory of sight can be even more faulty than the actual thing. But, we can see, and then believe. And sometimes we must believe before we can see.

Sight is an amazing thing. Our eyes, interacting with the world—amazing! But sight is also susceptible to smoke and mirrors, and to magic tricks and sleights of hand.

The process of seeing is a very intricate and mental process. As I said in the introduction to this chapter, much of what we "see" is the doing of our brains. We do not see in constant images, but in a basically seamless series of images that is a product of the flow of information between the eyes and the brain.[6]

How can we own our processes of seeing? We can engage with the process of sight, and we can decide to involve our brains more actively in the process of seeing.

Journaling Prompts

- Seeing is . . .
- Believing what I see means . . .
- Seeing what I believe means . . .

★ **Daily Practice, Day 2: Engaged Seeing**

As in the exercise for day 1, today you will again set an alarm to remind you to check in. When the chime alerts you, stop what you are doing. Take a moment to see what is happening around you. Jot down a few visual details. Do the things that you are seeing provoke emotions, questions, thoughts? If so, write these down, too.

You may wish to alternate between the outward vision and inward seeing. To do this, just close your eyes and allow images to come to mind. Write down some details and, again, any emotional responses that occur for you.

Smells Like Teen Spirit

Olfaction, otherwise known as smelling, is a sense that may well have its own very distinct relationship with memory.[7] Smell is what makes women cycle together when living in close quarters.[8] Our sense of smell is involved with mate selection, parent-child bonding, recognition of parents, siblings, and children,[9] and basic survival. Our ability to smell is key in figuring out which possible food sources are good and which are not.

Olfaction in relation to humans is the least-studied sense in the scientific community,[10] but there are many things that have been found to be true about our sense of smell. When offered breast pads (worn inside a lactating mother's bra to prevent milk leakage) from their mother's breast and from another's, babies will turn toward the one from their mother's breast, and are found to prefer the scent of an unwashed breast to that of one newly washed.[11] When women are exposed to the sweat of other women, their menstrual cycles synchronize.[12] Olfaction may be one of the factors (perhaps even the most natural and automatic factor) in mate selection. It is the main factor for animals, but whether this currently occurs in humans is a hot debate in scientific circles.[13]

★

Fun with Pheromones

- *T-Shirt Test:* In studies of t-shirts worn by men, women were most attracted to men who had a different genetics than their own.

  —Source: "Smell and Attraction," http://www.macalester.edu/~psych/whathap/UBNRP/Smell/attraction.html.

- *Snatch-Scented Goodness!* Some women swear by their own vaginal fluids as a sexual attractant, and dab a bit of their own scent on the spots usually reserved for a bit of eau de toilette.

- *Buying Beauty:* Many companies make a bundle on bottled pheromones. The jury is out on the effectiveness of these products, but that may be because most are made of nonhuman pheromones.

★

Aside from the biological power that scent has over us, and the way it can work as a tool, another aspect of olfaction is the link to memory and emotion. Often, smell-based memories are emotionally potent. This may be because the olfactory nerve is only two synapses away from the *amygdala,* which is a part of our brains that works to process and store emotional memories.[14]

Scent-based memory seems to work separately from other types of memory. In certain conditions, odor memory is not compromised even when other aspects are.[15] This makes sense, because we need to be able to remember not to drink sour milk or eat poison.

And, scent can be so sensual. How do certain smells make you feel? The smell of new rain, or of dry grasses. The scent of your body after making love. The incredible, gentle odor of an infant's head. The smell of your lover. The intense aroma of a good meal. The robust bouquet of a perfect cup of coffee.

Journaling Prompts

- When I smell _____, I feel . . .
- Smelling _____ reminds me of . . .
- Smell is . . .

★ Daily Practice, Day 3: Stop and Smell the Flowers

Set your alarm to remind you to pause once an hour. Stop whatever you are doing, and see what you smell. As you take in the scents around you, take note of whatever emotions come up. Jot down a few words about the smells you notice, and any emotional responses they bring to mind.

Skinship: A practice and concept that originated in Japan. It is the practice of nourishing a child with touch. That includes holding, family bed (child sleeping in parents' or sibling's bed), and bathing together.

The term skinship also includes the practice of bathing in communal baths, which was common until recently in Japan. Many felt that the opportunity to bath nude together was an opportunity to let rank, class, and social standing temporarily disappear.

Touch the Magick

Touch is actually many senses, not just one. Temperature perception, pain and pleasure, pressure, and spatial body awareness[16] are all contained in the general category of touch.

Many of us may take touch and physical sensation for granted, but touch is a constant part of our perceptive process. The need for interactive touch is also a basic human need. We know that failure to thrive in infants has been linked to a lack of touch,[17] but we can easily forget how important healing touch is for us throughout our lives. From birth to death, touch is a physical need, and we must feed it to be healthy, happy, and whole.[18]

It is easy to put all touch into the sexual category, thus making so many kinds of touch off-limits. We can fall into touch hunger, and not even realize that we are starving for contact.[19]

At other times in our lives, as moms especially, we may experience touch inundation. When being used as the jungle gym by wee ones, or breast feeding at all hours for years on end, we may just want to cry out, "Space! I need space!" Sometimes our relationships suffer from this, or our desire for all touch, including the sexual, may decrease for a time. This, just like learning to listen and respond appropriately to a hunger for food, is a boundary issue, and there are ways to healthfully work it out.

Touch is something that we can bring into our lives in healthy ways, and something we can set and own boundaries about. When you need a hug, ask for one. If you need a massage, make an appointment and get one. If you need to be left alone and abscond to the bathtub with a good read, do it! (If you have kids, and your partner won't take care of them for an hour—or if you are a single mama—get a sitter. If money is an issue, trade babysitting with a friend who has kids.)

If you need to prompt yourself for "me time," make "me dates": designate a weekly or monthly evening that is your time to do whatever you wish. The relief you will experience by getting a little self-time is more than worth it, and a healthy and happy YOU is the best gift you can give to your loved ones, not to mention yourself.

Touch is a sense that we often automatically associate with sensuality and sex. Make time for nonsexual touch. Cherish the physical affection you share with friends, family members, and even your pets. I encourage you to explore nonsexual touch as an experience worth indulging in. I also encourage you to explore touch in a sensual way. Where are the boundaries between sexual and sensual touch? Are they rigid, or fluid? In the exercises you will perform during this chapter, you will have opportunities to experience sexual, sensual, and nonsexual touch.

Journaling Prompts

- Touch is . . .

- Sensual touch is . . .

- Sexual touch is . . .

★ **Daily Practice, Day 4: Sensational Awareness**

Set your alarm to alert you once an hour. When you are re-minded, stop and sense with your skin and your flesh. How does your body feel right now? Notice temperature, pleasure, pain, tension, and pressure, within your body and outside of it. Write down the sensations you notice, and any emotions you feel along with them, or memories you encounter.

The Power-Hungry Brain: At birth, the human brain makes up 12–14% of body weight, and consumes more than 70% of the body's energy intake.

Taste This *Apple!*

Taste, ah taste, sweetly forbidden sense! Taste is a sense fraught with much emotion for many of us. If Chocolate Decadence didn't sound so sinful, would it sound so good? In the Biblical myth of the fall from the garden, the forbidden fruit is responsible for us getting a taste of shame. In *Snow White,* the Evil Stepmother tempts the darling Snow with a tainted apple as well.

In this denial-based culture, many of us are in a nearly con-stant war with our taste buds, and we have come to see self-denial as a virtue. (You know it's true. I'm sure you can think of at least one time recently where you bragged to someone about how little you eat, or how studiously you avoid ice cream. I know I can.) We eat the bland alternatives, eschewing the fat and sugars that have built us into the biological powerhouses we have become.[20]

We like the tastes of fats and sugars for good reasons. Fat is an easily stored energy source,[21] and sugars convert to immediate energy that allows us to elevate our mood and gain attention for the work at hand.

Yes, we can go overboard with fats and sugars. And when a can of cola has approximately ten teaspoons of sugar in it, that's not hard to do! But as with any substance, it's important to realize that creating a positive relationship with these sources of energy is necessary. The Omega-3 oils are integral to brain development and ongoing brain health,[22] and the heart needs a diet inclusive of "healthy" fats to maintain optimal health as well.[23] In addition, when used appropriately, fats can help us lose weight rather than gain it. Fat may allow for taste satiation to occur more rapidly, and including fats in our diets may even allow some of us to cut down on overall caloric consumption.[24]

Why disallow ourselves the pleasure of at least occasional indulgence? Even sporadic malnourishment can lead to permanent brain damage in those still developing, and hunger saps our energy and our mental focus. The desire for certain tastes is a message from our bodies. It can be part of an addictive cycle, but more often than not that craving is a cry for help from our tissues and cells.

We can rebuild our relationship with taste and satiation. We can allow ourselves to live in our bodies in pleasure, comfort, and health.

Journaling Prompts

- My relationship with taste is . . .
- The taste of _____ reminds me of . . .

★ Daily Practice, Day 5: Tasting the Fruit, No Longer Forbidden

The forbidden fruit is that which we desire but place outside of our realm of acceptance. For today, set your alarm for every hour, and when it chimes, listen to the hungers in your body. Listen to the desires for taste. If you are hungry for something sweet, have a bit of your favorite treat, be it chocolate, ice cream, or Red Hots. If you are hungry for fruit, eat a slice of apple, or a few seeds from a pomegranate. If you are hungry for fat, allow yourself a slice of bread dipped in olive oil and balsamic vinegar, a few onion rings, or a bit of cheese.

At the end of today, make yourself a meal with as wide a variety of flavors as possible. Taste each one completely and fully. Taste the saltiness of an umeboshi plum or salted fish, the sweetness of chocolate or pudding, the creaminess of a cream sauce, the bitterness of spring greens, the tartness of a lemon wedge.

Throughout the day, take notes on how the flavors affect you, and what emotions, memories, fears, or joys arise for you.

Sensing Home

Now that you have worked your way through the five recognized senses, you have a starting point for finding out which of your senses are most vibrant for you. Everyone has their favorite senses, the ones that make the most sense to them. What senses are the ones you rely on the most?

Journaling Prompts

- I am most disconnected from my sense of _____ because . . .
- I rely most on my sense of _____ because . . .

★ Daily Practice, Day 6: Integration and Recognition

When your chime rings today, take inventory. See what sense you rely on first. Write down which sense it is, and why it might be the one you are relying on in this moment.

At the end of the day, tally which sense you used most frequently. See which ones recurred, and take note if one or more of them never came up for you throughout today's exercise. If this happened, it may be a sign that you have trained yourself out of listening to one or more of your senses.

Magickal Act: Sensation Station Toy Box

What You Will Need

- A box to hold items for sensation play.
- Sensation play items: pieces of luxurious cloth that feel good to the touch, fur or faux fur, sound makers (rattles, a small drum, a tambourine), a hair brush to

play with on the skin, images you like to look at, a mirror, essential oils, tasty treats, a feather, candles, a mirror, a blindfold for playing with others, and anything else that makes you want to indulge in your sensual awareness.

How-To

Put all the sensation play items you have gathered in the box. Now, when you feel ready to explore your senses, you can draft a friend to play the Sensation Station game with you. This can be a sensual-yet-nonsexual experience, or it can be a sensual-leading-to-sexual game, depending on whom you play it with.

Playing with Others

Designate one player as the explorer and the other as the guide. The explorer gets blindfolded, and the guide takes the explorer on a guided experience of the explorer's senses. The last sense that is explored is sight, when the blindfold is removed. The explorer opens his or her eyes to his or her face reflected in the mirror. Then, trade roles. Explorer becomes guide, and guide becomes explorer. This can be gentle, sweet, and loving, or it can be more edgy if you are in a situation where there is enough trust in the relationship. After your sensual play, you may want to write about the experience.

Playing by Yourself

No blindfold here, but you can still indulge in each sense by turn. Lay out all your sensual play items on a surface near you. You may want to play on your bed, or anywhere else comfortable. As you play with all the items from your box, allow yourself to stay present with each of your senses. Once again, after your sensual play, you may want to write about the experience.

Feels Like the First Time

Now you have an idea of which sense come naturally to you, and you have an idea, conversely, of which ones might need more attention in your daily life. You know you can use them all, and you know through your daily-exercise notes which ones are challenging for you.

★ **Daily Practice, Day 7: Desire and Fulfillment**

Today you will indulge in all of your senses. You will listen to your body, and respond to your sensory desires. You will allow yourself music, art, and sensation, taste treats and flowers. Indulge yourself. Get a massage. Eat your favorite foods. Wear clothes that feel good. Stop what you are doing and smell the breeze blowing by. Today you can abandon your timed alarms, and settle into feeling and receiving the stimuli brought to you by your senses.

Magickal Act: Sexploration

This exercise builds on the work done in the pussy-gazing exercise from chapter 3. There is power in knowing what you look like, smell like, taste like. Now that you know where everything is *and* have a whole new relationship with your senses, it's time to really get to know your body.

Have you ever really made love to yourself? Have you ever approached your own body with the same zeal with which you approach a lover's? Allow yourself to be in awe of your magnificent self, and get down to it!

What You Will Need

- Uninterrupted time; the more, the better.
- A freestanding or wall-mounted mirror in a private space.
- A cozy, comfy space in front of the mirror in which to recline.

How-To

Take a bath and relax. Use only water. Do not use salts, soap, bubbles, or anything else. The purpose of this bath is to rinse off grime and stale scents as well as any artificial scents you wear. Do not replace those scents with other scents. The other purpose of this bath is to get your body into a state of relaxation.

After your bath, position yourself in front of the mirror in a way that is comfy and relaxed, and where you can get a good look at your body, including your vulva. Now, using every one of your senses, explore your body. Feel your muscles; tense them, and release. Smell your own scents. (Do you know what your armpits smell like? If not, why

★——————————

Fun Fact: Acidic fruits like pineapple can make vaginal secretions taste sweet.

——————————★

not find out now?) Look in the mirror and see your breasts, your belly, the cleft between your legs.

Be brave and bold. Take your time and really get to know the terrain of your physical self. Have you ever tried to lick your own nipple? Can you reach it? Do you know? Try it now.

When you feel sufficiently warmed up and sexplorational, look at your vulva in the mirror. Touch yourself. Get comfortable and explore the folds of your labia, the hood of your clit, the glans of your clit, your perineum, your anus, and the area surrounding these parts. Work your way toward your vaginal opening, and enter your cleft with your fingers. Feel the different textures of your vaginal walls. Try to locate your G-spot. It will feel ridged and sort of spongy.

Take your finger and smell it. Really sense what your scent is like. (Note: If your fluids smell strongly fishy, or "off" in some way, you may have an infection of some sort. A visit to your OB/GYN might be in order.) Touch your finger to your tongue, and taste the fluids on your finger. Allow yourself to relax into it.

Don't forget the rest of your body. Spend some "quality time" and really get into it.

When you are finished with this exercise, write about it.

Journaling Prompts: Pussy Prompts

- My body tastes . . .
- My pussy smells . . .
- My breasts are . . .
- When I think of sexing my own body, I . . .

Spell Working, Day 7: The Sensual Bath

Note: Take time to perform this exercise pre-ritual.

Making a sensual bath for yourself is an act of self-nurturance, and an opportunity to experience your senses on the sensual level. Indulging yourself in relaxation, sensual awareness, and enjoyment is a practice that may enrich your life, and make it so pleasant to be present in your body.

What You Will Need

- Candles, scented or unscented. See "Color Correspondences: A Primer" in appendix I. (Sight)
- Bath salts. See appendix I. (Touch)
- Essential oils. See the "Essential Oil Correspondence Chart" in appendix I. (Scent)
- Fresh rose petals. (Sight and Scent)
- Lavender flowers. (Sight and Scent)
- A mug of your favorite relaxation tea. (Taste and Touch)
- A glass of water. (Taste and Touch)
- A plate of tasty treats. (Taste)
- Silence, relaxation tape or CD, or music. (Hearing)
- Matches or a lighter for the candles.
- One small table to set by the bath, with the surface ideally at the same level as the rim of your tub.

Optional Items

- Music.
- Clay, milk, or other bath additions. See appendix I.

How-To

Allow yourself enough time to prepare and enjoy your bath. An hour is probably adequate, though I know lovely Witches who spend a lot more time in their tubs than that!

As you set the space for your bath, also set your intent on your desired goals: relaxation, honoring, sensual awareness, and quiet joy. The oils that you choose for your bath will also have attributes, as do the flowers and petals. So do the other optional additives. As you add each element, bring your intent to the gifts that each offers you.

Set the table by the tub. The table is functional, but it is also your temporary altar. If you want to place other items that represent or relate to your sense of your senses, please do. You may also want to place an altar cloth on the table.

Set the candles on the table, or on the edges of the tub if it's safe to do so. You may light them when you feel it is right. I often sense the lighting of the candles as a beginning point for a new phase of ritual. You may want to light them once you have set up your altar, or once you are ready to enter the bath.

Place the tea, water, treats, and essential oils on the table. If you will be playing a CD or tape, your player may go on the table as well.

Run bath water at a temperature that feels comfortable but on the warm side. The water will cool as the tub fills. Pour in the bath salts as the tub begins to fill. Remember to focus your intention. Next, add other ingredients, if you choose to (see appendix I for optional bath additions). Once the tub is full, turn off the water and add the oils, flowers, petals, and herbs.

If you are going to have sound, you may start your CD whenever you like, either after you set up your altar or before you get into your bath.

Disrobe, and step into your sensual bath. Relax. Enjoy. When you feel ready, indulge your senses in the treats you have gathered. Really take the time to taste, to hear, to be soothed and renewed. Sip at your tea. Listen to your thirst and your hunger, and respond by nurturing your body with nourishment.

Onward and Inward!

Good work! Now it's time for your fifth initiation ritual, in part 2. Enjoy!

---

1. "Tricks of the Eye, Wisdom of the Brain," *Serendip,* http://serendip.brynmawr.edu/bb/latinhib.html.

2. Doc Childre and Rollin McCraty, Ph.D., "Psychophysiological Correlates of Spiritual Experience," *Biofeedback* 29 (2001): 13–17, http://www.heartmath.org/research/research-papers/spiritual-experience.html.

3. Rollin McCraty, Ph.D., "The Energetic Heart," *Clinical Applications of Bioelectromagnetic Medicine* (2004): 541–562, http://www.heartmath.org/research/research-papers/energetic-heart.html.

4. Ibid.

5. "Gratitude and Health," *Mid-Columbia Medical Center,* http://www.mcmc.net/pdf/tyh0212.cfm.

6. "Seeing More Than Your Eye Does," *Serendip,* http://serendip.brynmawr.edu/bb/blindspot1.html.

7. "Olfaction and Memory," *Macalester College Neuroscience Page,* http://www.macalester.edu/~psych/whathap/UBNRP/Smell/memory.html.

8. Richard V. Lee, M.D., "Pleasure, Pain and Prophylaxis: Olfaction (The Neglected Sense)," *Baylor University Medical Center Proceedings* 13 (2000): 261–266, http://www.baylorhealth.edu/proceedings/13_3/13_3_lee.html.

9. Kelly Burgess, "Bonding from the Beginning," *Babies Today,* http://babiestoday.com/resources/articles/beginning.htm.

10. Dr. Leonardo Belluscio, "Visualizing Scent Networks in the Olfactory System," *Burroughs Welcome Fund,* http://www.bwfund.org/news/awardee_profiles/archive/leonardo_belluscio.html.

11. Heili Varendi, "Human Newborn Behavior During Exposure to Maternal and Other Odors," *Karolinska University Press,* http://diss.kib.ki.se/2001/91-628-4787-2/.

12. *The Straight Dope,* http://www.straightdope.com/classics/a2_306.html.

13. David Wolfgang-Kimball, "Pheromones in Humans: Myth or Reality?" *Melissa Kaplan's Herp Care Collection,* http://www.anapsid.org/pheromones.html.

14. "Olfaction and Memory," *Macalester College Neuroscience Page,* http://www.macalester.edu/~psych/whathap/UBNRP/Smell/memory.html.

15. Ibid.

16. *Wikipedia,* http://www.fact-index.com/s/se/sense.html.

17. Roger Shuler, "Techniques of Touch: New Knowledge About Nurturing Newborns," *Univ. of Alabama Magazine* 21:2 (Summer 2001), http://main.uab.edu/show.asp?durki=41209.

18. Kim Ballard, "Healing Touch, Massage & Alternative Therapies," *Vital Aging Network,* http://www.van.umn.edu/options/2g9_healingtouch.asp.

19. "Skin Hunger," *Extendicare,* http://www.extendicare.com/consumer/article35.htm.

20. S. Boyd Eaton, M.D., and Stanley B. Eaton, III, "Evolution, Diet and Health," *International Congress of Anthropological and Ethnological Sciences,* http://www.cast.uark.edu/local/icaes/conferences/wburg/posters/sboydeaton/eaton.htm; Michael Crawford and David Marsh, "Nutrition and Evolution," *NOHA News* 22, no. 3 (Summer 1997): 1–2, http://www.nutrition4health.org/NOHAnews/NNS97NutritionAndEvolution.htm.

21. Stefan Angheli, "Fat and Fats," *Health Fitness Newsletter,* http://healthfitness.com.au/diet/nutrition/fat-fats.htm.

22. Ann Gibbons, "Humans' Head Start: New Views of Brain Evolution," *Science* 296, no. 3 ((May 2002), http://66.102.7.104/search?q=cache:d9zOw2UJdjIJ:www.anakata.hack.se/papers/pdf/Science-296-835.pdf+lipids,+brain,+evolution&hl=en&ie=UTF-8.

23. Densie Webb, Ph.D., R.D., "The Heart-Healthy Fats," *Prevention,* http://www.prevention.com/article/0,5778,s1-3-61-93-2628-1,00.html.

24. Udo Erasmus, *Fats That Heal, Fats That Kill* (Burnaby, BC, Canada: Alive Books, 1993).

CHAPTER SIX

Myth Making and Mentors: Witch Power Rising!

★ Daily Practice: Speaking Words of Truth, Speaking Words of Love, page 114.

Creation and Re-Creation

In the beginning, there was the word. Or was it silence? A swirling mass of matter? A void? Chaos? The sun and the earth? God? Goddess? Goddess and God? Mother and Father? Raven? Whale? Spider Woman, weaving her web? The Big Bang?

Creation myths are important. They give us a sense of our beginnings, a sense of time and motion. They give us a starting point for our mythologies and a set of rules that govern our interface with reality.

Creation myths also place us within a rule structure. Myths that have some sense of wrongdoing or failure as a basis (or even as a component) set us up for a lifetime of trying to set things right. Conversely, myths that are based in empowerment give us a matrix for right action and self-definition.

If you are science-oriented, you may find it odd that I am putting the Big Bang in the same category as Genesis. My reasoning is that all creation stories are ideas that bind us to a certain interpretation of How Things Work. In addition, we don't know the whole story of our origins, nor of our eventual endings. We don't have the ability yet to measure the senses accurately, or to read, or comprehend, those stories encoded in our DNA.

For instance, once upon a time the world was flat. Every person knew this to be fact. To claim otherwise was lunacy—heresy! Above the earth was heaven, and beneath it was hell. And there were edges, off of which you would undoubtedly fall if you ventured too far.

What are the stories that shape our universe today? How accurate are these stories? As an experiment, I encourage you to allow your attachment to your belief structure to relax for this next set of exercises and spell working. Who knows what new information you may find?

Creation of Cosmos, Genesis of Life

What creation stories were you brought up with? The origin story of the scientific sort? The Big Bang, and the beginning of life on earth, born of fire and water meeting in furtive passion, the single cell dividing and slowly becoming all the variations on the theme of living beast? While this creation story is based in science, it is a story of our beginnings, and lends a flavor to how we view the world.

Genesis, of Biblical fame, is a creation myth that many of us are familiar with. It sets the stage for the inferiority of women, and makes a gold standard of the concept of sin. As women, with this creation myth as a building block of our worldview, we bare the burden of the Biblical concept of the fall from grace.

Many Native American tribes considered the world to be floating on the back of Turtle, and created by all the animals. However, the Hopi creation myth begins with *Tokpe-fla*, a term meaning "endless space."[1]

Egypt had many creation myths. One begins in darkness. Out of darkness comes Atum, who, out of loneliness, creates others to keep him company. In this creation myth, the earth is male: craggy, silent Geb. The sky is female: Nut, the arching, star-strewn vault of heaven.

The Greek myths start with Mist, out of which was born Chaos, envisioned as either a void or a complicated mass of energy. Some begin with chaos. In one Greek myth, out of Chaos came Nyx, the Underworld-dwelling Goddess of night. She was a black-winged, mysterious beauty. Nyx laid a golden egg from which, after eons, Eros emerged, with sparkling golden wings. Eros, God of love, was the bringer of life.

An Australian aboriginal myth begins with the Great Father of All Spirits and the Sun Mother. Another begins with the earth as a vast and empty plane that is changed through the emergence of the Dream Time. In the Dream Time, all the animals are human, and they sing, play, and dance everything else into form.

Other creation myths have other themes for our beginnings. What were you raised to believe?

Sympathetic Magick: Using one thing to stand in for another, often larger or more complicated thing. Working magick on the one thing affects the other, which in many cases is the final goal of the working.

Journaling Prompts: Creation of Belief

- What creation myth(s) were you taught as a child?
- How do these myths impact your worldview today?

Spell Working: Creating Creation

As we have been learning in the previous chapters, when something doesn't work for you, fix it! So, here is your opportunity to make a creation myth that works for you. Your myth may be about how the world or the universe was created, or how you, unique and singular you, came to be. It may start with the beginning of all that is, or it may begin with the meeting of your parents.

Re-creating the story of creation is a magickal act that will give you a starting point for creating your world of possibility, from the ground up. By re-creating creation, you are allowing yourself a clean slate, a new beginning, a revolutionized playing field that leaves you with all the advantages you deserve: a sense of purpose in being, a sense of equal opportunity, the right to live a life unapologetic and unfettered.

What You Will Need

- A writing implement.
- Paper.
- Your preferred set of art supplies: pens, collage supplies, paints, clay . . .
- Time and space where you will not be interrupted.

How-To

First, gather all your supplies. Then, sit in silent contemplation for a few minutes. Practice conscious, deep breathing. Allow images of the beginnings to come to you. Perhaps this will unfold as a story in your mind, or maybe it will be flashes of images, seemingly unconnected. Maybe you will hear a voice telling you the story of how you began, or you will feel this same story unfold in your bones, bowel, and blood.

Allow yourself to sit with the experience until it wanes in intensity. Slowly open your eyes, and write down the words, images, feelings, or sounds you encountered. This writing could be single words that you can use to jog your memory, or it could be a full account of what you experienced.

Once you have the words that will hold this experience in place for you written down, allow yourself to create some artifact that exemplifies your creation myth. This will be a talisman that reminds you of where you come from, and it will be an act of sympathetic magick. By creating, you become the Creator.

When you have finished your creation talisman, place it on your altar.

Mentors, Teachers, and Guides

Throughout our lives we find ourselves drawn to a variety of mentors, teachers, and guides. These may be living people, archetypes, saints canonized by our personal respect and admiration, or Gods, Goddesses, or spirit guides who find us in our moments of need or desire. In my experience, each relationship with these beings, in the flesh or extra-fleshorial (yes, I made that term up—do you like it?), is unique.

This revered type of relationship serves us for a moment, or a year, or a decade. And often, if they serve us boldly, intensely, shockingly, fundamentally, extremely, or comprehensively even for only a moment, they affect us for our entire lifetimes in some subtle way. These interfaces leave us imprinted, changed, deeper, wiser, and more willing to seek truth. These special—and often intense—bonds are not always easy, and our connections to those we admire, depend on, desire, and love can be painful and confusing, even while they carve our hearts deeper into our cores and create for us a most intense attachment to our truest manifestations of self.

Sometimes the loving and the hating go hand in hand. But, as an old boyfriend of mine said, "Hate is not the opposite of love. Indifference is." I don't know if that was his, or if he found the quote somewhere, but it has stuck with me, lo these many years.

I guess what I'm saying is that sometimes our greatest teachers are those whom we fear the most, love the most madly, want to change or be changed by, want to *be,* or want to kill, even. And in the wanting, wanting for all this, we find a deeper, truer sense of who we are.

Sometimes our mentors ask the most pertinent questions, causing us to stretch the limits of our own understanding. Sometimes they sit with us and hold our burning pain. Sometimes they become the nexus for our pain, or for our desire, or become a starting point for our Will by making us say, "No! No more. You don't own me."

Sometimes, though, our teachers are the shining examples of who we never thought we could be, or who we wanted to be so badly it hurt. Or sometimes it's our bestest friend . . . you know the one . . . the one who knew when to touch you, and when not to. Knew when to talk, when to listen, and when to let you sit in golden silence, waiting for the sunset to fade to black. The one who would fill your empty cocktails, even if they thought maybe you should give up the drink for a minute. The one who would drive you home after you'd weathered an abortion, and would ask only the easy questions, the right questions, the questions you needed to be asked, like, "Are you okay?" "Can I help with anything?" Or they asked nothing, and just said, "I love you," and held your hand as they steered the car.

Sometimes our mentors and guides laugh with our joy, and sometimes they make it possible for us to laugh at our own pain. Sometimes they mold us to their Wills, and sometimes they allow us to locate our own Wills, singing within our souls. Sometimes they stand on us, and sometimes they hold us up. And both are valid. And both cause us to grow. And both sides of this coin are equal.

Our mentors and guides may be male or female, or they may be beyond gender. They may be human, spirit, or animal. They may be old or young. They may be ageless. They may speak to us in words, or have an impact that is beyond words.

Journaling Prompts: My Mentors

Choose three mentors, from the three different times in your life listed below, to write about. Write about how each mentor came into your life, who they were, and why they were important to you.

- When I was a child, one of my mentors was . . .
- In my teens, one of my mentors was . . .
- Now, one of my mentors is . . .

Finding S/heroes

At different times in our lives, our needs will draw new mentors to us. Sometimes we need a mother figure we can rely on, or model ourselves after. Sometimes we need s/heroes who will stand as an example of who, or what, we want to become. Sometimes we need support, and sometimes we need the consternation that allows us to grow. All these mentors have their place in our personal evolutions.

Sometimes these mentors come automatically. Sometimes we need to find the right ones, and create an intentional relationship with them. To that end, I offer you Appendix II: A Compendium of S/heroes. Please create a list of your own personal s/heroes in your journal, if you feel inspired to do so.

It is important for many of us to have male mentors, teachers, heroes, and guides, too. However, you will have to make that list on your own. Here we are focusing on finding our power as women. While that may include finding men we can trust, admire, and love, this compendium is a devotional to our sisters, mothers, grandmothers, foremothers, Goddesses, guides, and saints who have created more room as women, for women to exist in the ways that fit us best. If you feel so inspired, your personal list may include your male mentors as well as the female ones.

Spell Working: Wisdom of the Web

As an exercise of faith and finding, go to your favorite search engine, type in the search values you seek, and hit return. (If you are looking for a s/hero in the arena of art, you might enter the words "female, artist, groundbreaking." If you are looking for a woman who was or is unafraid to love, you might enter "love, courage, woman.") This is a divination. Who knows what you might come up with? If you hit a book, read it. If you find a movie, watch it. If you get a name, research it. If you find a person, delve into her or his life story.

Magickal Act: My S/heroes

Using your personal list of s/heroes, Appendix II: A Compendium of S/heroes, and whatever you found in your web-based divinations, create a list of mentors who would have a positive, deepening, or growth-oriented influence on your life now.

What You Will Need

- Your journal.
- Writing implement.

How-To

Choose up to three categories in which mentoring would improve your current life. (See appendix II for categories to work from if you can't narrow them down.) Open your journal to a fresh page, and draw two lines lengthwise down the page, creating three columns. Then, list mentors for each category.

Making an Ally of Doubt

In seeking to build ourselves into more accurate representations of our core values, we may come up against some fear and excitement about who we are, who we are becoming, how we want to be perceived, or what is driving our desire to identify with a mentor or take on a new persona. With a newly open playing field, it is incumbent upon us to entertain a questioning process that allows us to decipher as many of our motivations as possible, uncover our own doubts and convictions, and find comfort with the gray areas.

Anchor: In Neuro-Linguistic Programming, there are two uses of the term anchor. In the usage I am employing in this section of the book, the anchor is a physical space (the pieces of paper on the floor) you will use to ground an experience. The other use of this term refers to a spot or circumstance that is used to contain or trigger an emotional response.

Giving ourselves permission to claim doubt as an ally can be overwhelmingly empowering. We may be drawn to things that scare us, or make us feel ashamed. What draws us? And, where does our fear or shame originate? We may have created rules that we think are right for our parents, and other rules that we feel are right for us (like the whole concept of being unwilling to think of our parents as sexual beings). We may want to speak more strongly, but be afraid of being heard. We may want to become more sexually open, and at the same time fear being hurt by our sexual desires.

Owning the areas where desire and disgust butt heads is a courageous act. Being able to admit to ourselves that we are of two (or more) minds about a given issue, and then presenting those different sides of our thought processes in conversation, allows us to grow through difficult transitions, to try things on and see how—or if—they fit, and to be honest about our occult shadows and our transparent light. It also frees us from the need to be right. We can be unsure, intimidated, and afraid, and do it anyway.

It is important to recognize, and develop gratitude for, the positive aspect of uncertainty. Often the genesis of insecurity is self-protection of some sort. To want to protect ourselves is a healthy thing, and we can all be thankful for the processes that allow us our self-preservation. This only becomes a liability when we are stuck in fear. So, let's get ourselves to the point where we can feel the fear, and do it anyway.

Spell Working: Angels and Devils; Allowing Permission for Doubt

So, you know the angel and the devil that pop out on the shoulders of cartoon characters and whisper in their ears? Here we will invoke these dualistic voices of our internal process and give each of them a place to speak from.

What You Will Need

- Writing implements. Two colors would be best.

- Your journal.

- Your mentor list.

- Space.

- A table.

- Two loose pieces of paper for "anchors."

How-To

This is a physical exercise. First, write in one color, on one piece of paper, the word "Angel." Then write on the other piece, in another color, "Devil." Or, if you prefer, you can draw a cute little angel and a cute little devil, instead.

Set the two pieces of paper, or anchors, on the floor about three feet away from each other. About three feet forward, and of equal distance from the two anchors, set up your table. You will have created a triangle, with each side measuring about three feet, with the table at the upper point and the anchors at the two lower points.

Open your journal to two totally fresh pages, and write "Angel" at the top of one and "Devil" at the top of the other. Next, choose one of the mentors who appeals to you, yet brings up mixed feelings. Write her name at the top of the page, somewhere between the words Angel and Devil. Set your journal, open to these pages, on the table.

Allow yourself to center and ground, and get a feel for this mentor, and for all the feelings that your bond with her brings up. Focus on your respect for her, and your lack thereof. Focus on your love and your fear.

When you feel centered in a sense of how this mentor affects you, walk to either the Angel anchor or the Devil anchor, and allow your internal Angel or Devil to voice her feelings. Actually speak the words aloud. Once your angel or devil has had her voice, walk to your journal and write down at least a few of the words. Then walk to the other anchor, and allow your other voice her rebuttal.

Continue this process for as long as you feel moved to. Remember this may be an emotional process. Allow yourself to go with it. Feel the excitement, the anger, the joy, the fear, the righteous indignation, the surrender. Cry if you have tears. Laugh if you feel inspired to do so.

You may do this with one mentor, or more. Once you are done with the active part of this exercise, journal a quick recap of the experience.

Journaling Prompts: Speaking in Tongues

- My devil is . . .
- My angel is . . .
- I claim my doubt as an ally, and in so doing I become free to . . .

Self as Mentor

In allowing ourselves this growth, and in allowing ourselves to claim our processes of self-discovery and self-definition, we sometimes become our own best mentors. So, in the upcoming exercises in this chapter, allow yourself to experience the possibility of envisioning yourself as one of your own mentors.

Spell Working: Communicating with Mentors

What You Will Need

- Writing implement.
- Journal.
- Time. About fifteen to thirty minutes.

How-To

- Choose three mentors from your lists. Remember, one may be *you!*
- One at a time, envision these mentors standing before you. With each one, allow yourself to ask them questions, and allow them to answer you.
- Write down your questions and their answers in your journal.

Magickal Act: Creating a Mentor Icon

This icon may be placed either on your self-love altar or wherever you feel the need. On your desk by your computer? In your bedroom? Your bathroom? Over your doorway? Put this icon in a place where you will see it when you need it the most.

Start this exercise by choosing one mentor whose influence you would like to have more of in your life right now.

What You Will Need

- An image of your chosen mentor.
- Collage supplies.
- Other art supplies, glue (stick, spray, and/or paste).
- A picture frame.
- A firm piece of cardstock cut to fit the frame.

How-To

Starting from an image:

- Cut or reduce the image to fit the cardstock.
- Paste the image to the cardstock.
- Paint, color, glitter, bedazzle the image to your heart's content (and in keeping with your mentor's temperament).
- Let dry.
- Fit to frame.
- Put on altar or hang. Voilà!

Collage:

- Create collage on cardstock.
- Fancy it up as you wish.
- Let dry.
- Fit to frame.
- Place.

Of course you can feel free to honor as many of your mentors this way as you'd like. What fun! You could do this all day! (I speak from experience here.)

★ ——————————

Personal Ecology:
Your system; body,
mind, and soul.

—————————— ★

Words of Power

Speaking the words that make us whole is a conscious act of magick. Learning these words is a process, the very one you have undertaken in working this book. As your awareness of your needs and desires and the consciousness of choice become pervasive, you are learning your own words of power and creation.

★ Daily Practice: Speaking Words of Truth, Speaking Words of Love

For this whole week, I encourage you to speak well of yourself and others. Speak in the positive. Encourage empowered thinking in yourself and others, and watch as it becomes empowered *doing!*

Spell Working: Creating an Empowerment Mantra

Out of the interactions you have experienced with your mentors, you have probably found some new wisdoms to explore and own. This is an opportunity to make them yours. If you need a refresher on creating a mantra, please visit appendix I and the last sidebar on page 19.

What You Will Need

- Writing implement.
- Journal.

How-To

Choose the most important quality you have uncovered in these exercises, and create an empowerment mantra. Remember: simple wording is most effective, always state your mantras in the positive, and be sure that the wording and the desired outcome fit with your personal ecology.

For example, when working with boundaries, you might say, "I own my space." When working to invoke a sexy attitude without compromising yourself, you might say, "I am safe in my sexual energy."

Go to it, grrl!

Self-Definition, Self-Determination

Self. Here we are at a new frontier. And you know what? It's all about you! I'm sure we've all heard the phrase "full of yourself" as a negative. An attack, a slur, a dis. But my question is this: If not full of our *selves,* what are we supposed to be full of? I encourage you to allow yourself to get full of the energy that is you. To get so full that you know exactly who you are, what you think, what you feel, and why you think or feel any given thing.

You are the center of the universe you call home. You are the creator, the actor, the magickian, the Witch. You define the reality that you live. Your thoughts and actions, conscious or not, create the stage that is your personal reality. The fuller of our own ideas, opinions, pleasures, fears, and desires that we become, the more we will know about where we want to get to next.

Self-definition is every person's right and responsibility. It can be a lot of work at times to be self-defining; to think for ourselves, claim our voices, stand up for our beliefs, or challenge our own assumptions. But what better work is there? By becoming self-defining, we are creating new ways of being, and we stand as examples to those who are looking for ways to claim their own power. We stand as examples to our children, our friends of all ages, our lovers, our families, and our communities. By allowing ourselves the room to define our own true desires and needs, to speak about them, to own them and be strong in that owning, we allow others the right to do the same.

"Our deepest fear is not that we are inadequate. Our deepest fear is that we are powerful beyond measure. It is our light, not our darkness, that most frightens us. We ask ourselves, Who am I to be brilliant, gorgeous, talented, fabulous? Actually, who are you not to be? . . . We are all meant to shine, as children do. We were born to make manifest the glory of God that is within us."

—Marianne Williamson, excerpted from *A Return to Love* (this quote is frequently attributed to Nelson Mandela)

Spell Working: Letters from the Self

It can be powerful to find the voices we have used, and the voices we will someday command. This exercise is designed to bring cognizance to the stages of our lives, and to find connection with past and future selves.

What You Will Need

- Your journal.
- Writing implements . . . pen, pencils, crayon. What did you write with as a child? What will you use as a crone?
- An artifact or belonging from your childhood.

How-To

In this exercise you will write two letters: one from your child self and one from your future self. Start each of the two letters with the salutation that feels right, and then: "I am _____ years old." Just let the age come to you. And go from there.

Child-Self Letter

Use the artifact from your childhood to pull you back to the time period it came from. Perhaps it sat on your dresser, or maybe it was your favorite blanket or stuffed toy, and you took it everywhere. Perhaps it is a picture you drew. Whatever it is, sit with it for a minute, and let it bring you, present and aware, back into your past. Write from this space.

Crone-Self Letter

Sit in quiet contemplation, and allow your consciousness to travel forward in time. Follow one of the many streams of possibility or probability, and become present in the future. Feel your bones, your muscle, your flesh. Allow your eyes to focus, and begin writing.

Always Becoming

Being sure of ourselves is obviously not about disallowing future growth; it's about claiming the awareness that we are always becoming more of who we are. Existentialism holds as one of its main tenets that existence precedes essence. We are, then we become. Working from this frame of thought, we are responsible for living the lives we want, and those lives become the reality we live. Act and outcome are inseparable. The means become the ends. The ends are defined by the means.

Self-definition is the "means" to self-determination. Self-determination, at the simplest reduction, means the ability to make your own choices, uninhibited by the ideas or ideals of others. It means the right to determine your own values, your own ethical structure, your own goals, dreams, and aspirations. It means being empowered to determine your own course in life, one based in your own desires and beliefs.

To live in this empowered space, it is necessary to realize that you determine the rules that define your reality. Ideally, these rules also allow you to interface with the realities of others. Your thoughts create your experience (or interpretation) of life, but there is also a space where the thoughts of others define the edges of your ability to define. The more aware you are of this process, and the more strongly you live within your own beliefs and act in accordance with your own rule structures, the more effective you will ultimately be in living the life you create.

Magickal Act: Making the Rules

When you become active in the process of making your own rules, it is no longer necessary to break the rules. You can be a rule maker instead of a rule breaker. Here are a few ideas to work with in creating rule structures that work in the long term:

- All rules are up for renegotiation if (when) they no longer serve you.
- Nothing is true; everything is permitted (chaos magick).
- Who and what you are now is exactly that—who and what you are now. You need not be defined by who or what you have been, or who or what you may become.
- Now is the only moment in which you have power of choice. However, the choice you have in the moment can be used to reinterpret past experiences and to project future intentions.

- Your thoughts, feelings, actions, and reactions are what define your experience, not the experience itself. Every experience can be interpreted any number of ways. It is your right, and your responsibility, to realize that you are defining your experiences constantly by way of your own personal interpretation.

- Your interpretations may be colored by your moods or your physical senses, but ultimately you may find that you control those systems (and your iterative responses to them) as well. Some of those systems are easier to learn to control than others, but it is possible that even the more difficult ones are sensitive to the power of thought.

How-To

This is an act of thought. From this moment on, you can work with the concept that *you* make the rules.

Spell Working: Breath of Life

In previous chapters, we touched upon how gratitude can help shape the life you live, and how becoming conscious of choice improves your chances of success. You have dreamed a new creation story as the nexus of your future growth and being. Here is where you will breathe life into the origin you have created. In this visualization you will return to your temple, and imbue your creation story with life.

What You Will Need

- Time. Ten minutes for visualization, and ten minutes for journaling or drawing.
- Journal.
- Writing or drawing implements.

You may want to read aloud and record the instructions for the visualization before doing this exercise.

How-To

Sit in a comfortable position. Close your eyes and relax. Focus on breathing. Pull each breath into your lungs, allowing them to expand to their fullest capacity. Breathe out, and release any tension you feel in your muscles. As you breathe, let your lungs become even fuller, pulling your breath deep into your abdomen. Allow your belly to relax, your ribs to expand, your mind to quiet. When thoughts come to the surface, allow them to gently pass.

Once you feel relaxed and present, allow yourself to see, once again, your temple in the distance. Begin moving toward this magnificent place. Does it look the same as last time you were here, or has it changed? Notice, and keep moving forward. Notice the scents that ride on the air. Feel the temperature of your skin. Keep breathing deeply, and continue moving.

Do you smell incense burning in the censers? Do you feel moisture on the air? Keep breathing deeply. Soon you will pass the threshold, and enter again into your glorious inner sanctum. Enjoy this time out of time, in this sacred, sweet space that is all yours.

Now you enter into your center, the center of this sacred temple. Is it the same as last time you were here? Has it changed? Can you feel now, more than before, the stillness present here? Can you almost see your mentors and guides protecting this space for you? Can you feel the presence of herstory, *your* story, filling the fabric of timelessness?

Walk toward the altar. See your tools. Are they the same? Have they changed? Are there new ones? Have you let any go? Recognize what is, give thanks for stability and for change, and kneel before your altar.

On this altar you see the artifact of creation that you brought into being. You crafted this beginning with your own hands, your own mind, you own emotions, dreams, and desires. Reach out and pick up this artifact. Hold it in your hands, and feel it. Look at it, and recognize the passion that is held in this ultimate act. Everything starts from here.

Let your emotions—desire, gratitude, passion, love, strength, and whatever else comes up for you in seeing this artifact—build within you. You have so much power. Let it fill you. Let it fill you all the way. Let it fill you until you are so full of your own being that you are about to burst.

Now, hold your artifact in front of your lips, and blow. Bring the breath of life to this creation story, the creation story that is yours. Allow your life-energy to fill this creation. Let this creation be born of your passion, your desire, your dreams, your breath.

Now release the artifact in a way that feels safe. Let it grow. Let it fill the space that is your body. Let it fill the space that is your temple. Let it expand and fill the space that is the earth. And the universe. And all that exists.

Breathe in, and know you are breathing breath that is yours. You created this breath. You created this life. You created the self that you are. You created this world. This universe. This existence.

Allow yourself to listen gently in this space. Give thanks for returning. Hold this sacred space in the stillness of eternity. Know that you have birthed a new world. Walk into that world now.

Keep breathing deeply, and follow your breath back to consciousness.

When you are ready, slowly open your eyes, and journal or draw the story of this visit to your temple.

Onward and Inward!

Only one more chapter to go. This initiation cycle is nearly complete. Now, go to part 2 and get ready for your sixth ritual! Remember, you have created a whole new world. You can do anything!

---

1. Harold Courlander, *The Fourth World of the Hopis* (New York: Crown Publishers, 1971).

CHAPTER SEVEN

The Seventh Initiation: The Mirror and the Path

★ Daily Practice: The Goddess in the Mirror, page 124.

You have reached the seventh, and final, gate. This is the last chapter of *Sexy Witch!* Yes, you are getting to the end of the book, but this is the beginning (as is every day, and every moment therein) of the rest of your life. At the end of this chapter you will experience your seventh initiation. You will walk forward from that moment in this new world, this new matrix, that you have created.

This chapter will focus on your final Sexy Witch initiation into your own power, but as you may have guessed by now, your work (and play) doesn't end here. This chapter offers you tools that will give the process you have worked in this book a more permanent home in your future life.

Initiation is not an ending, it's a threshold, a point of transition. To "initiate" means to begin. And thus, the mystery unfolds. Picture yourself before a large mirror, with a large mirror behind you as well. You look into the mirror in front, and see the mirror behind, and see that your back and front views replicate into eternity. You are in the moment that is present, with the past extending to all the "yous" you have been, and the future extending to all the "yous" you will be.

That is initiation: the moment between mirrors—doorways, thresholds—where you can see the future and past selves you will be and have been.

Initiation marks the ending of what's been before, and the beginning of what will be. Since time immemorial, initiation has held an honored place in the process of becoming who we are, who we're meant to be, who we're growing into being. Initiation is a doorway that we walk through, and in so doing gain awareness of the mystery of transformation.

In Western culture, we don't have many initiations that are recognized across the board. Some initiations we do recognize are graduations, birthdays (certain ones are seen as the Big Ones, but every birthday can be seen as a new year), getting a driver's license, marriages, childbirth, and even, if covertly, menstruation and menopause. However, we have no consensual reality that tells us how to honor these transitions in ways that truly mark these experiences as transformational. For many of us, the transformational aspect of these celebrations has been downplayed, if recognized at all.

The initiation you are encountering now is one wrought by your own hand, your own will, your own intention, and your own work. This initiation is an opportunity to allow yourself to grow into the being you have created through the work you have done over the past weeks. This initiation is an opportunity to honor your growth, the commitments you have made to self-definition and future growth, and the work you have done to create a new world to live in, one that allows you to present yourself as exactly who you are. This is an opportunity to have the work you have done in the past weeks recognized and honored.

This chapter is about ceremony. It is about the ritualization of your desire to be in integrity with what you have learned, how you have changed, and who you have become. This is a turning point that will create a new way for you to be in the world.

In this final chapter you will create vows of initiation, and charge a talisman that you can wear either all the time or just when you need extra strength or a reminder of who you have become through the work. You will have an opportunity to recognize yourself, who you are now, and to make commitments to this new you.

For the coming ritual, if you are working this book on the solitary path, I ask that you choose one or more witnesses, close and devoted friends, who will stand for you. If you are working this book with a group, your Sexy Witch sisters will be your witnesses, and you will be theirs. (You may decide as a group to invite other witnesses as well.) These witnesses will have the responsibility of reminding you of your vows. They will have the opportunity to see you honor the healing work you have done. For this reason, this person, or these people, must be people you love and trust.

Your witnesses may be male. If you have a partner, husband, or lover, I encourage you to think about whether you will invite your partner to witness your initiation. Even if you are working with a group, you may want to consider inviting witnesses who are not part of the group. Or maybe you want your mother, or sister, or brother, or best friend to be there. Bring this question to your group, and decide together.

Journaling Prompts: Witnessing

- Qualities that are important in my witnesses.

- My list of possible witnesses.

Self-Dedication, Self-Devotion

Past the concept of self-definition and self-determination lies the territory of your spiritual commitments to you. Self-dedication means being dedicated to your own relationship with you. It means recognizing the righteousness of your needs coming first in defining your dreams and boundaries. Self-devotion is the point at which you claim your relationship with yourself as a

Song of Myself
by Walt Whitman

  . . . *I have said that the soul is not more than the body,*

    And I have said that the body is not more than the soul,

    And nothing, not God, is greater to one than one's self is . . .

    I hear and behold God in every object, yet understand God not in the least,

    Nor do I understand who there can be more wonderful than myself . . .

    In the faces of men and women I see God, and in my own face in the glass . . .

. . .

A Magickal Thought:
Self-devotion is a (r)evolutionary, magickal act.

spiritual path. You can be dedicated to being a good mother, a conscious lover, a devoted follower of your teachers.

You can also claim your self-devotion as an ongoing spiritual path. Whom could it possibly be better to devote your study, worship, and faith to? You, unique and individual, deserve your faith and your worship. You raise yourself by your own worship. You become a beacon of self-ownership in the dark night of conformity. You build of yourself a temple that honors women everywhere.

Journaling Prompts: Devotion

- Self-devotion is . . .
- By devoting myself to me and my own growth, I . . .

★ Daily Practice: The Goddess in the Mirror

Every day this week, make time to meditate on the concept of self-devotion. Perform this meditation and mirror-gazing ritual. Answer for yourself this question: What does it mean to devote yourself to your own path?

What You Will Need

- Devotion oil. See appendix I for recipe.
- Time to sit at your altar, at least five minutes a day.
- A timer.
- Journal (optional).
- Writing implements (optional).

How-To

For the first three to five minutes:

- Sit before your altar in a position that is comfortable enough to not distract you, and with a posture that will encourage you to stay focused and breathe deeply.
- Position your mirror so you can see at least your face from your seated position.

- Use the anointing oil, and anoint yourself wherever you like. I always anoint at least my heart chakra and my third eye. If you wish, you can anoint all the major chakras, or wherever it feels important to do so.

- Close your eyes and breathe deeply.

You may wish to read aloud and record the following portion of guidance before doing this exercise.

Let the concept of self-devotion fill your mind, and let all other thoughts pass gently away. Allow words, phrases, and images of what self-devotion means to you to sit in your mind. Continue breathing, and allow these thoughts to fade and congeal, taking whatever form feels right.

If you get stuck, ask yourself the question "What does self-devotion mean to me?" and allow the answers to come. If you come up against blocks in your willingness or ability to allow self-devotion, give yourself permission to recognize those blocks, to feel them and know them, and then to let the blocks fade away. You do not need to hold on to them, and you don't need to force them away. Just let them gently dissipate.

Breathe into the concept of self-devotion as an aspect of your spiritual path. Now, continue breathing, deeply and rhythmically, and allow yourself to sit in silent contemplation of self-devotion until your timer chimes.

Next, for at least one minute, do the following:

Open your eyes, and look at yourself in the mirror. Allow love and gratitude to fill your heart. Offer this image of you the worship that she deserves.

Sit in worship of this Goddess who is you.

If you feel inspired to, journal about the experience each day when you are done with this meditation. The notes you take may prove valuable as you progress on your path of self-love.

Living an Empowered Life

You have worked to create a framework for your initiation into an empowered life. You have claimed your sensuality, your power, your right to define your own goals and desires. You have claimed your body and your spirit, your feelings and your thoughts. You have done exercises and worked magick to make all of this real. You have built your brave new world.

What actions are you willing to commit to for the long haul? What exercises are you willing to perform over and over again in order to continue your growth and self-definition? What days of the month are you willing to set aside for yourself? What points of the cycle are you willing to mark in pen on your planner pages as "me days"? How much of your time are you willing to gift yourself with, in order to continue this love affair you are building with the self that you are, and the self that you are becoming?

Making Magick of the Mundane

Contracts are seen as pretty mundane, but for many of us they are a huge part of what holds the world together: marriage contracts, employment contracts, loan contracts, ownership contracts. Contracts can be seen as nothing more than pieces of paper, yet those pieces of paper are loaded with tons of cultural significance.

Where the contract can become magickal is by what it does for us. It allows us boundaries, allows us expectations, allows us demarcation and, in many cases, even freedom.

Magickal Act: Empowerment Contract

As part of your initiation, you will now plan the future of your growth and self-commitment.

What You Will Need

- Your journal.
- Writing implement(s).
- Time.

How-To

- On two pages, preferably facing each other, write the names of the seven chapters, in the first person. Leave space under each title: 1. My body is a temple . . . , (space), 2. I love me, . . . (space), etc. On one page, in the space under each title, brainstorm the elements of that chapter that have really stuck with you. What exercises or spell workings stand out in your memory? What daily practices were totally rewarding? What new concepts have revolutionized your way of thinking, or of being in the world? For each chapter, write down phrases or words that remind you of what worked for you in working this book.

- Once you have some elements to work with, switch to the other page, and under each chapter title, write out what you are willing to commit to as your devotional or path. What exercises are you willing to continue working? What thought-forms do you want to integrate more fully? What mantras might help you hold on to the ways in which you have changed and the work you have done?

- Once you have done the first draft, rewrite the document, with a spot to sign and date it at the bottom. Don't sign it yet; you will sign this document in front of your witnesses at your initiation.

Word Crafting

Here is where we get to take the concepts that we have hammered down in creating our contracts, and turn them into art. Vows are an opportunity to let your commitment shine, to have it witnessed, to voice it out loud in front of God/dess, the universe, and everybody! It is a moment of speaking your words of power, the words that build your new world. Like marriage vows, these vows will become the backbone, the foundation, of your future relationship with yourself and your path of self-discovery; your growth, and your commitment to that growth.

These vows are where you get to define and claim your initiation. Who is this person that you are now? That you are continuing to become? What are the values that impassion you? What are the goals and intentions that give you the power to succeed? What are the future visions that inspire you? What is the past that you honor?

Spell Working: Vows of Initiation

This is your opportunity to create vows that will guide you, and hold you to your own path. In writing your vows, always use strong language. Instead of saying, "I want to . . .," say, "I will . . .," or "I vow to . . ." Use positive language. Instead of saying, "I will not . . .," find the positive intention behind the boundary, and state that instead.

What You Will Need

- Journal.
- Writing implements.
- Your empowerment contract (for reference, in case you get lost or overwhelmed.)

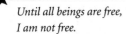

Until all beings are free, I am not free.

As one, we will penetrate the veils, we will pass beyond the bounds of suffering.

All paths to enlightenment are equal, and lead to the same destination. I will walk them.

May I awaken fully, for the benefit of all beings. May all beings attain enlightenment.

—An interfaith interpretation of the Vow of the Bodhisattva, written by the author.

For more information on the Vow of the Bodhisattva, see appendices I and III.

- Nice paper for your final rewrite.

- A frame for the final piece (optional).

How-To

You will take a vow, or a set of vows, based in the work you did in each chapter. You will have seven vows, or sets of vows. You may choose your own number of vows to have per section. If you have a favorite magickal number, use that number. Or you can use three for the three stages of life: Maiden, Mother/Whore, Crone. You may want to take vows for each of the directions according to your tradition: five in Wicca, seven in many Native American tribes, seven in many of the Faerie traditions. Or, perhaps you have another number that seems like the right number for you.

You may want to write your vows as a poem, or just in regular wording that feels good.

So, here we go.

1. Write down these headings:

   a. My Body as Temple

   b. Self-Esteem

   c. Pussy Pride

   d. Masturbation, Menstruation, Matrix

   e. Sensational Sensuality

   f. Mentors and Myth: My Guides and Creation

   g. Initiation: The Doorway

2. For each section, write out vows you will take to guide your future commitment and growth.

3. Once you are done, rewrite your vows on a nice piece of paper, one suitable for framing, if you'd like. This artifact will go on your altar, or somewhere else where you will see it often.

Wearing Your Heart on Your Sleeve

As with a wedding, you put on a ring to show the world that your status has changed. Here you will also have a wearable artifact that will be a testament to the work you have done and a reminder of the vows you have made. While no one but you and those you choose to tell will know what this represents, it will be a daily reminder that you get to see, feel, and wear in honor of your vows.

There is magick in wearing these talismans of commitment. This piece will be charged with all the promises you are making. In addition to being a reminder, this piece will be able to offer you strength when your convictions are challenged.

Spell Working: Creating an Initiation Talisman

This talisman will be a wearable artifact that holds the intentions of your initiation vows. This artifact can be a medicine pouch, a bracelet, a necklace, a ring, or whatever you think you will enjoy wearing on your body. It can be visible, or it can be something hidden.

If you are working with a group, consider gifting the women in your group with something. This may be wearable as well, or it may be an item that will go on your sisters' altars.

The talisman that is created from the consecrated beads you have gathered through the process of working this book will be made into a talisman in this week's ritual. But you may want to create or purchase other talismans as well.

What You Will Need

You will need whatever wearable talisman you choose. You will make the talisman with your beads in the ritual, but this talisman you may want to wear only in ritual space. Of course, maybe you'll want to wear it all the time! However, you may want, in addition, to purchase an item suitable to wear in everyday life, perhaps even an heirloom item that you may hand down to a daughter, apprentice, or protégée later in your life.

Maybe this is will be a ring—though if you get a diamond, please make sure it's provided by a humane, blood-free company. Better yet, have a local craftsperson make something unique to you, or use a hand-me-down ring your grandmother, mother, or aunt wore. You may instead want a necklace with your birthstone, a string of pearls, or a set of earrings.

If you choose both options, charge both items.

How-To

- Purchase or make your talisman.
- Charge this talisman. When charging magickal items, you may have your own methods. I usually do the following:
    a. I cleanse the talisman with salt water.
    b. Then I cleanse it with smoke from incense or a candle.
    c. Then I anoint the talisman with my own fluids: blood, pussy juice, saliva, or tears. The purpose of anointing the talisman with my own fluids is that this imparts a bit of my DNA to this magickal tool. It becomes related to me, joined to my body, through this act.

Spell Working: Walking into Your Future

The work you have done has created a future space built by intention. The future you have created is waiting for you to take the steps that will bring it present. Now is the time for you to walk boldly into a future where no one has gone before. This is your world. You built it from the foundation up. You own it. You have breathed life into this new world, and you have lovingly crafted the details of this place.

What You Will Need

- Time, about fifteen minutes.
- Water for drinking, after this working.
- Tissue or a hankie for tears, if they come.

How-To

You will want to record your own voice reciting these instructions before doing the exercise.

Stand, and center. Breathe deeply, and allow yourself to come present in this moment. Let thoughts flow through your mind, and then, as you keep focusing on your breathing, start noticing the elements of this future that feel like home; the most familiar ones. As you find these elements, let them begin building an image of this future in front of you. Some of these elements may be in the forefront. Some may be the back-drop. Let them organize of their own volition into a semi-static image in front of you.

Next, start noticing the elements of this future life that are a little bit more to the edges of your experience; the ones that are a little bit more intimidating, exciting, activating. Let these elements find their place within the original tapestry of safety and acceptance. Notice where these more challenging elements settle, and what they end up linked to. Notice, recognize, and allow, and then move on.

Now it is time to stretch yourself, and to allow your consciousness to sort for the things that might even scare you but that also empower you; those elements that truly challenge you, yet you still desire them. Allow these elements to find their place in this reflection of the world you are creating. What are these elements? Where do they fit in? What are these more intimidating—and possibly all the more intriguing for it—realities that you want to encompass as a building block to your new world? Where do they fit? What are they linked to? Notice, recognize, and accept, and ready yourself to enter into this image.

While this representation of the world you are building is currently at least a mostly static and stable image, once you enter into the image these elements are likely to shift, merge, divide, and create new totals that will almost certainly become more than the sum of their parts. You are the genesis of this creation. This is your world, your personal landscape, inscribed by your very own hand. Created by your own words of power. Built by your sweet sweat, your sweat tears, your sweat blood, and your sweat soul. This world is your Will, manifest.

You are ready now to enter this transformed world, this world created by your desires and your work. Breathe deeply. Remain conscious of this world in front of you, and of your body, and of the steps, few and short, between your body and this new world. And then, breathing deeply into the power of your solar plexus, your Will-center, and into your heart and your blood, slowly begin walking toward this world you have built.

Taking deliberate, conscious steps, begin to close the gap between you and your world. Walk gently, consciously, toward this sacred world, the one that is waiting for you. It may take three steps to arrive. It may take five, or even ten. Take each step with an awareness of the transition you are undertaking. You are walking into the world that fits you best; the world you have created, a world fit specifically to your very own needs, hopes, dreams, and desires.

Deliberately, you enter this world. Walking in consciousness, enter into this scared space, this place that is built of your own Will. For perhaps the first time in your life, you are truly coming home.

Let all those elements that create this space melt into an image surrounding you. Perhaps you are on a star-studded plane. Perhaps you see your guides here. Perhaps there are allies surrounding you. Perhaps you are alone, and comfortably so, in the very void of creation. You are the nexus. This is your matrix. You are the Creator, creating the world in which you now live.

If there are tears of relief and acceptance, cry them. If there is laughter at the wonderful ease you now possess, laugh it. If there is gratitude, feel it to your very blood and bone. You are home, and you have built this. You live here. This is yours.

Stay in this meditation for as long as you want to. When you feel ready, write in your journal about how it feels to have found your own world.

Spell Working: One More Letter to You

You have traveled far in this journey of self-discovery, and now, once again, you will set pen to paper and write yourself a letter. In this letter, you will talk about where you are now, how the process of working this book has been, and where you hope to be in a year. This letter will also include a copy of your vows of initiation, and a copy of your empowerment contract. Just like you did with the letter from the first chapter, you will give this letter to a trusted friend, who will mail it to you in a year. Make sure your friend will indeed send the letter.

In one year, you will receive this letter in the mail, and at that time you will be reminded of where you were a year ago, and what hopes you had in that moment for your future self. When you open this letter, you will have an opportunity to re-read your vows, your contract, and your hopes and accomplishments. You will have an opportunity to remember the changes you underwent while working this book, and you will have an opportunity to reflect on where those changes have lead.

Let this letter be partially a testament to your dedication, and partially a love letter from you to your future self.

Onward and Inward!

Congratulations! You have completed the work. Now it's time for your seventh and final *Sexy Witch* initiation, in part 2. Enjoy your new awareness, your new world, and the self-love you have built over recent weeks. Welcome home, and have a wonderful journey on the path that leads into your bright and beautiful future.

PART TWO

The Rituals

RITUALS I

Rituals for the Solo Sexy Witch

Building Ritual, in Theory

If you have been working magick for a while, you may already have a way that you perform ritual. If you have a form of banishing, casting, invocation, or other ways of creating sacred space that work for you, I encourage you to integrate those aspects into the ritual outlines in this section.

Ritual, ceremony, and magick are about consciousness. Our relationship with magickal consciousness can be highly intuitive. However, there are also strengths to formal practice as well. It is my desire to give you as many options as possible in this section so that you can find, build, or create the ritual format that works the best for you. It's your magick—modify at Will!

I have purposefully left the basic ritual outlines very minimal. From a minimalist Mindful Magick or Conscious Intuitive Magick perspective, the rituals work as they are presented. If you want to add more structure, you may. I have included many elements of ritual performance that can be added to the basic ritual outlines. If working with a more traditional approach is most effective for you, stick with it.

Building Ritual, Sexy-Witch Style

In this section I offer the tools to create rituals that are tailor-fit to your needs. I have included a description of Mindful/Conscious Intuitive Magick, a modified Lesser Banishing Ritual, some information on Wiccan circle casting, a few examples of ways to call the quarters, and then the more barebones, chapter-by-chapter ritual outlines. There are opportunities built into the flow of each ritual to read from journal entries and to consecrate artifacts created while working the chapters.

Sexy Witch Saturdays?

Try to allow enough time on your ritual days to really get into the material. You may wish to re-read your journal entries from the week, look at the artwork you have done, and reflect on how the work has been for you. You can also use this time to decide on which of your artifacts you will want to consecrate (see ritual outlines for directions), and which items you may want to add to your altar each week.

You may want to plan on having a ritual meal or a taking a magickal bath before the ritual. Each ritual will be an initiation, which is both an ending of one phase and a beginning of another. Give yourself the time to delve in and experience your transformations.

Doors of Perception

These weekly initiations, of which there will be seven—like the veils of Salome, or the gates that Inanna faced on her journey into the Underworld—are designed to be doorways between the chapters. You will move through the material in the chapters, find your depth, and then move ever deeper, toward the very core of your self. Each ritual will be a doorway that demarcates the transition from one chapter to the next, and also demarcates the spiraling journey in toward your center. It will be the pause between breaths, the transition point, the recognition and the act of transformation.

Tools: To Have, or Not to Have . . . That Is the Question

I have never felt a strong need for many magickal tools, though I have made some of my own, had some made, and been gifted with a few over the years. I have consecrated them and kept them on my altars. But I truly feel that anything that a wand can do in magickal space, a finger or hand can do as well. It's not the tool, it's how you use it!

I have my own superstitions about investing items with power, and feel most resourceful when my power is contained securely within my body. That is not to say that working with a wand doesn't make working certain magick easier for some Witches. If you have tools that make you feel strong, by all means, use them! Again, I am just reminding you of many possible options. It's your magick—own it!

Ritual Garb

I have more often than not been the Witch in street clothes. Or the Witch in a cocktail gown. Or the Witch in her birthday suit, if it's warm enough out. I almost never feel the need, and rarely have the desire, to dress in Renaissance-era garb for ritual, or wear a toga or a chitan, or a big, fancy cloak (unless it's performance ritual theatre, and costuming is required).

Yes, you wanna feel good. So, what does a Witch wear to perform ritual? Whatever she damn well pleases! You can wear your best dress or your nicest lingerie, or you can wear your pajamas if it's been that kind of week. The clothes *do not* make the Witch. Dress in whatever way makes you feel good. If that happens to be a ritual gown or cloak, more power to you. If it's not, more power to you as well. If there is certain dress that may assist you in any of the following rituals, it will be mentioned in that ritual's outline.

What to Bring to Rituals

This list is the main altar list. In the outline for each week's ritual you will find an additional list that is specific to each ritual. Please make sure you have all items from this list *and* from the week's more specific list.

- Your altar—an altar space integrating all the ritual items. (Make sure there is space for the artifacts that you will place on the altar every week.) This may be your self-love altar (chapter 1), or you may build a special altar for the rituals, which you may take down at the end of each ritual if you so choose.

- A "source" or "mother" candle—a seven-day jar votive. This candle will live on your altar throughout the seven weeks of your initiation process. It will be lit during every ritual, and extinguished afterward. Jar candles can be purchased in most supermarkets, in mercados mexicanos (Mexican markets), botanicas, and some carnecerias. Some of these jar votives will have the Catholic Saints, Jesus, or Mary on them, but you will also be able to find some without any decoration. Choose your color with intention. Of course, if you have an affinity for *the* Mary (see appendix II), feel free to choose the Mary candle. You may dress this candle, if you'd like. (For dressing instructions, see appendix I.)

- A smaller, individual candle. This is your candle. Tea lights or smaller votive candles are a good bet, and are available in most supermarkets. As the first one burns down, just replace it with another. You may dress these candles, if you'd like. (For dressing instructions, see appendix I.) You may want to provide personal candles for your witnesses who will be present at your seventh initiation. (See the section "A Few Final Words Before Diving In" later in this chapter, and Ritual Seven in part 2, for more details about witnesses and their roles in your final initiation.)

- A bead. The weekly outlines will state what each week's bead should represent.

- Candle holder for tea light or smaller votive (be conscious in choosing your color).

- Your copy of *Sexy Witch*.

- Your journal.

- Any works of art or writings created while working the chapters that you want to consecrate. One of these may become your weekly additional altarpiece for your altar.

- A small pouch to put beads in.

- A censer for the incense.

- Charcoal for the incense.

- Incense (see appendix I).

- A chalice for water.

- A chalice for wine, if desired.

- Wine, if desired (see appendix I).

- Water.

- Cookies, bread, or other edibles (see ritual outlines for details).

- Tissue or a hanky in case of tears.

- Any specific items mentioned in the ritual outlines.

- Don't forget things like matches or a lighter, a corkscrew (if needed), water, and a glass.

- Also, make sure you can tolerate scents and smoke in an enclosed space. Incense can be intense and can alter your senses in a good way, as long as it's not triggering an asthma attack or allergies.

Always read the ritual outline in advance so you have all the necessary items at hand when it comes time to perform your ritual.

Recording Prompts from Outlines

Before performing the rituals, you may wish to record the ritual prompts and visualizations so you don't have to read them while working the ritual. If you do record these, record—rather than read in circle—any prompts and directions that you think may distract you if you have to read them in ritual space.

Some words are for you to say out loud in ritual, and this direction is written into the outline. If you prefer not to read at all during ritual, you may use whatever words come to mind in place of the ones I have written, or you may say in the recording, "Repeat this out loud," before or after each piece that is preceded in the outline by "Say:".

Remember to build in a length of silence after each prompt so you have time to perform that section of the ritual without pressing the pause button.

A Few Final Words Before Diving In

In working *Sexy Witch,* you will have many choices to make. One of those is about how much time you want to dedicate to your ritual work over the next seven weeks. Another is how many aspects or layers of ritual you want to use in your ritual format. You will need to invite witnesses to the seventh initiation—who might these people be? (For more information on this aspect, see chapter 7 and Ritual Seven in part 2.) I encourage you to explore the extent to which you are able to make space in your life for the ritual aspect of *Sexy Witch,* and to create ritual outlines and weekly schedules accordingly.

In the ritual outlines, there are words to recite. Of course, as always, the words I have written down are optional. You can use mine, or you can make up your own if you'd like. You can make them rhyme, or not (I have not). Also relevant is that I have included a more stable liturgy in the solo rituals. The flow, words, and outline don't change as much from ritual to ritual, because with one person (you) performing all the rituals (instead of rotating facilitators—see Rituals II for more information), you may be able to memorize more and read from the page less. If you prefer to have the rituals be more specific from week to week (most notably in the bead consecration), please feel free to lift pieces for the group rituals in Rituals II.

The words I've put down on the page are not based on a secret formula. The magick that will be done in these rituals of initiation is you working ritual, and doing so with intention, focus, and growing skill. The magick is your intentional work toward growth and transformation. It's *your* magick. Work it!

Mindful Magick

In my magick working, I often take a minimalist approach to ritual. It's what currently works for me. I call it Mindful Magick, Mindfulness Magick, or Conscious Intuitive Magick. I do a lot of focusing inward, breathing, centering, sensing, and being.

Some of the concepts that I'm working with in creating ritual space at this time include recognizing space as sacred, rather than creating a space that is sacred. I focus on my body as a sacred space, and center in that. I focus on the world around me as a sacred space, and honor that. I encourage you to work with these concepts as well.

Use the outlines I have provided, but follow your intuition. Do what feels right. It's your magick. Create it. Shape it. Ride it. Follow it.

A Witch's Banishing Ritual,
Modified from the Ceremonial Lesser Banishing Ritual of the Pentagram

The Lesser Banishing is a simple and profoundly effective way to clear ritual space, cast the circle, and call on the guardians of the gates in one fell swoop. It is a beautiful piece of ritual when executed well, and can be modified to encompass your orientation.

This modification of the Lesser Banishing Ritual of the Pentagram was created by myself and assorted ritual partners over the years. Throughout the instructions I will give you options that will allow you to modify it even further yourself, and ideally to make it your own.

1. The practitioner enters the circle.

2. The Tree of Life, performed at the center of the circle.

    a. The practitioner points the index and middle fingers of her right hand, folding the other fingers.

    b. Touching her forehead with the extended fingers, she says:

    I am I,

    c. Pointing to the sky, she says:

    in harmony with the heavens,

    d. Pointing to the ground, she says:

    with the earth,

e. Touching her right shoulder, she says:

with the sun,

f. Circling to her left shoulder, she says:

and with the moon,

g. Bringing her hands to the prayer position, she says:

forever and ever.

h. Placing her left hand, palm down, on top of her right hand, palm up, she says:

So it is.

3. The banishing.

For the banishing, you can use whatever words make you feel that the guardian, entity, energy, or intention of a direction has been brought present. This can be done by assigning a Goddess to each quarter (e.g., Aurora in the east, Pele in the south, Oshun in the west, and Kali in the north); or by saying the name of the direction, or an idea that the direction represents (e.g., inspiration in the east, passion in the south, regeneration in the west, wisdom in the north); or you can use any of the words that have been used by any of the Ceremonial magickians. There are many formulas and phrases, and you can easily find them by doing a web search on the Lesser Banishing Ritual of the Pentagram.

a. The practitioner walks to the eastern edge of the circle and draws a pentagram in the air with her finger or her wand. In drawing the pentagram, start at the left lower point, and draw upward to the apex on the pentagram. This is the basic earth-invoking pentagram, but can be used at all quarters.

b. Starting with her arms at her sides, the practitioner slowly raises them, focusing intently on the pentagram she has drawn in front of her, and the word she will use to invoke the direction.

c. Once her arms are pointing out from her shoulders, parallel to the ground, the practitioner brings her hands to the sides of her face, palms facing back.

d. Next, she steps forward with her right foot, and while forcefully thrusting the energy with her hands towards the direction she is facing, she says the word out loud.

e. She will then step forward with her left foot meeting the right, and bring the index and middle fingers of her right hand to her lips in the sign of "shh…" (This is the sign of the initiate. For more information on the significance of this sign, do your research.)

f. Next, the practitioner will go to the south, and do the same, using whatever word she has chosen for the south.

g. The same in the west.

h. And in the north.

i. And she completes the circle at the east.

4. The center.

Again the practitioner stands in the center of the circle, facing east. She stands with her arms outstretched at her sides, parallel to the ground. She says:

Before me the rushing wind, behind me the raging sea, to my right hand the leaping fire, and to my left hand the cool and trembling earth. For about me is the omnipresence of Her body, and within me is the consciousness of the continuity of existence.

5. The Tree.

a. The practitioner performs the Tree again, as in step 3.

★ ——————

The Basics: To cast the circle, walk clockwise, also known as sun-wise, or *deosil.* To open (remove, dissolve) the circle, walk counterclockwise, otherwise known as *widdershins.* In many traditions, clockwise is the direction of building, and counterclockwise is the direction of dissolution.

—————— ★

The Basics: The calling of the quarters and deities or energy forms can be done in many different ways. Many traditions have their own script for callings. Another way to do it is just to focus on the representations that the entities hold for you, the practitioner. If you want some correspondences for the quarters, see "Correspondences: Quarters, Elements, Directions, and Other Entities" in appendix I.

Wiccan Circle Casting and Opening

Depending on your orientation, you may perform only this circle casting, and then move on to the rituals as I have written them for this book. Or, you may perform the circle casting and the calling of the quarters (see the next section), and then the ritual. Or, you may perform the banishing just described, then this circle casting, and the calling the quarters (and deities, if you'd like), and then the ritual.

You may also choose to do none of the above, and use just the simple format of the rituals written here. Remember, it's your magick! Perform it as you Will.

Many Witches use the *Rule of Three* as a basis for ritual and magick. The circle casting for most Witches relies on a three-time circumambulation. To cast a circle in the Wiccan, Dianic, Faerie, and many other traditions, you walk the perimeter of the circle three times clockwise to cast the circle, and three times counterclockwise to open it. Depending on the tradition, you will have different assignations for the three times around.

To cast a circle is to create a bubble, or sphere, of sacred space. Many practitioners use an *athame* to cast and dissolve the circle. With a blade (or a hand, used with intention), it becomes the "cutting" of a circle. You are cutting yourself out of the mundane world, and into a space that is amplified, protected, and sanctified.

Casting and opening a circle, as with any magickal act, must be done with intention as well as the actual function of movement. As you cast—and then open—the circle, visualize these things occurring. As you cast, envision the circle becoming a protective sphere. As you open, envision the sphere of sacred space dissolving into nothing.

You may choose to invoke Maiden with the first circle, Mother with the second, and Crone with the third. Or you can just "cast the circle, three times round . . ." You may do this as you voice an incantation (which you can write yourself, or find on web sites or in any number of books), or you can do the casting and opening in silence. Whichever route you take, employ the energy of visualization in the casting and opening. You can lend your energy to the casting and opening without even saying a word.

Calling (aka Invoking) the Quarters and Spiritual Entities

The calling of the quarters is a widespread Wiccan and Neopagan practice. It is also employed in the Ceremonial, Faerie, and many other traditions. Calling the quarters is asking the elements (or "guardians of the watchtowers") to be present in your working. Calling the quarters is performed as an aspect of the banishing, but if you choose to not perform the banishing, calling the quarters may be done in concert with circle casting.

You may call the four quarters (air, fire, water, and earth), or five (the four already listed, plus center, or the four already listed, plus the ancestors), or seven (the five already listed, plus above and below). You can also invoke Goddess, and God, if you desire.

With all callings, it is traditional to close with a statement such as, "So it is," or "So mote it be," or "Fire (or Earth, or She, or He) is here."

Working in this more intuitive manner, callings might go something like this:

For East
Spirits of air, I call upon you to bring clarity, inspiration, and ease of communication to this circle. I call the spirits of dawn, new ideas, and freedom of thought. Please be present here, and bring your blessings to this circle. So it is.

For South
Spirits of fire, I call upon you to bring passion, warmth, and transformation. I call upon fire to warm and transform this sacred space. Bring your heat, desire, and light. Burn bright in this circle. So it is.

And so on, through the other quarters and whatever energies/entities you choose to call.

The quarters are called in a clockwise progression, starting in many traditions with east/air, or with north/earth in some others. Starting from east, the progression would be east, south, west, north. Then, if you choose, you may call center, or the ancestors.

Then Goddess, then God. Or, you may call east, south, west, north, Goddess, God, and then the ancestors. Again, intuition is key. Do what feels right to you.

Releasing the Quarters and Spiritual Entities

At the end of the ritual, the entities and quarters that have been called will be released. Releasing goes in the opposite order as calling, starting with the last entity or quarter called and working back to the first. Releasing can be very simple, such as, "Spirits of earth, thank you for your presence, and your blessings on this circle."

Or, you can get as flowery as you'd like. In the tradition I grew up in, we would end the releasing with the statement "Go if you must, stay if you will." You can use whatever wording feels right.

Here are some concepts to work with when releasing:

- Expressing gratitude to the entities who attend.
- Granting them permission to move on if they must.
- Recognizing that they are ever present, and that it is our attention that leaves them.

The Most Obnoxiously Option-Oriented Ritual Outline You Have Ever Seen!

If you choose to take all of the steps offered so far, here's how the ritual will look:

1. Perform the banishing.
2. Cast the circle by circumambulating three times clockwise.
3. Call the quarters.
   a. Call air.
   b. Call fire.
   c. Call water.
   d. Call earth.
   e. Call center.
   f. Call Goddess.
   g. Call God.

4. Next, move on to the ritual outline for the week.

   a. Setting space (breathing, lighting of source candle).

   b. Consecration of altar (placing devotional items).

   c. Consecration of writing and art.

   d. Honoring with treats, water, and wine (communion).

   e. Ending of ritual.

5. Opening the circle.

   At the end of the circle, the practitioner "undoes" what she did at the beginning. Everything must be undone in the opposite order of how it was done—last to first. It's like you are walking back out into the world, and you want to retrace your steps. Starting with the last invocation, release each deity, guardian, or entity that you called. The releasing will move around the circle counterclockwise.

6. Releasing the quarters.

   a. Release God energy.

   b. Release Goddess energy.

   c. Release center.

   d. Release earth.

   e. Release water.

   f. Release fire.

   g. Release air.

7. Open the circle by circumambulating counterclockwise three times.

8. Perform the banishing counterclockwise.

Remember, you can use as many or as few of these elements as you'd like. If you choose to use just the outlines as they are presented in the sections devoted to each week's ritual, the following is the basic outline, though there will be some variations from week to week:

- Setting space (incense, breathing, lighting of candles).
- Consecration of writing, art, and altar.
- Bead consecration.

- Honoring with treats, water, and wine (communion).
- Ending of ritual.

Your Body Is a Temple

★ Suggestion: Consider consecrating your temple artifact (see "Magickal Act: Visiting the Temple" in chapter 1).

What You Will Need

- A bead. This week's bead should represent the body as temple, or the concept of sacred space.
- A platter of luscious morsels to eat. I recommend dates, figs, and other rich, sweet, dried fruits, as well as chocolate, cherries, and honey.
- Wine, if desired. See "Wines" in appendix I.
- Incense. See "Incenses" and incense recipes in appendix I.

How-To

- Build the altar with the items listed here and on the main altar list on page 140, or integrate any items not already present into your self-love altar (see "Magickal

Act: Creating an Altar to You! Invoking Self-Love" in chapter 1 for more info).
Your altar should be pleasing to the senses, and functional. For comfort and ease
in ritual space, place everything you need near where you will be seated.

- Make sure the charcoal is lit. It takes a few minutes for the charcoal to be ready
for the incense.

Outline

- Banishing (optional).
- Circle casting (optional).
- Calling of quarters and spirit entities (optional).
- Setting space.

Sprinkle a pinch of incense on the charcoal.

Focus on breathing deeply into your belly. As you breathe you may want to walk
around the space once, thinking of the qualities that this blend of resins will bring to the
space: love, purification, safety, healing, and connection with spirit. Then sit before your
altar. Breathe consciously for a few minutes, letting the scent of the incense permeate
your body, inside and out, and allowing your cells to absorb the positive qualities of the
incense. Perform this step until you feel present in your body, and in ritual space.

Record the following script in advance, or read it in ritual space:

Breathe deeply, allowing your breath to expand your chest, and then even more
deeply, letting your breath expand your belly, your lower abdomen. As you breathe,
allow the smoke of this special blend of incense to enter your body and infuse each cell
with blessing. Let this magickal and sacred blend of scents fill you with love, purification, safety, healing, and connection with spirit. As you breathe, allow your body to become the sacred temple where you worship.

Once you are fully present in your body, open your eyes, and come present in the
space. Take a moment to feel the energy you have already created by centering here in
this sacred space. Say:

I am in sacred space.

As you light the mother candle, say:

Lighting this flame, I invoke the sacredness of the body. I invoke the awareness that my body is a sacred temple that I consecrate to the purpose of my own growth, experience, and empowerment. I invoke not only self-acceptance but self-devotion.

From the source candle, light your personal candle. As you light this candle, say:

As I light my flame, I drop deeper into that space that allows for healing. I know my body as a sacred, wonderful temple. A space sacred and powerful. A space where I know the truth of my own being. I drop deeper into that space inside where I have true self-devotion, where I know that each act of self-love, self-adoration, and self-definition is a sacred act. The place where I alone define the boundaries of my temple; this sacred temple that is me.

As you place your lighted candle on your altar, say:

With this light I create a sacred circle that allows honor and devotion to grow, and my light shining becomes a beacon in the darkness that allows each seeker to find her own way home.

Consecration of Writing, Art, and Altar

Once your candle is placed on the altar, it is time to consecrate the items you created during the week. This may be one piece of writing and one piece of art you have created during the week, or it may be all of them. It depends only on how much time you want to devote to being in ritual space.

Lay whatever items you want to consecrate in front of the altar. You may compose your own words of consecration, or you can use the ones I offer here. Say:

I consecrate these works to the unfolding of self-awareness. May this act serve me, and may it serve all beings through the revelation of awareness. May my increasing awareness and presence serve to bring awareness of presence to all beings everywhere throughout space and time. So it is.

Take time to witness, honor, and cherish each item you are consecrating. Read your writing out loud if it feels comfortable (voicing words may add to their power). You may also want to pass the items through the smoke from the incense, or do some other act of purification and consecration.

If you feel inclined to add to your altar, this is the time to do it. What item from this week's exploration would like to live on your altar for the duration of your initiation cycle?

Bead Consecration

After you have consecrated your artifacts, consecrate this week's bead. Say:

> *I consecrate this bead in the journey of body-love. May it serve as a reminder to me that my body is a sacred space.*

Place the bead in your bead pouch.

Honoring with Treats, Water, and Wine

Bless the food, water, and wine. Say:

> *This food is not just a symbol of, but the true substance of, nurturance, and of the cycles of life. May the sacrifice of this that I am about to ingest feed my body, my spirit, and my soul. May I always experience, receive, and honor my hungers. May all true hungers be fulfilled.*
>
> *Water is life. Life, and regeneration, and healing. Let this water remind me of my origins; of the womb, and of the blessed sea, the birthplace of life and that which forms the flow.*
>
> *This wine is the blood of willing sacrifice. It represents the cycles of life, death, and birth. It offers succor, and a doorway to new perception. May this wine bless me with the awareness of choice, and with divine vision and ecstasy.*

Take time to honor your body with treats, water, and wine. As you eat and drink, sit in awareness of the magick of transmutation: how the food, water, and wine affect your senses, and how these edible items become part of the very fabric of your cells. Allow gratitude, honor, and acceptance of and for the elements you are bringing into your body.

Ending of Ritual

Sit before the altar again, and breathe, and then say:

> *Mine is the temple. As I walk through the world, I know that my body is a sacred vessel. It is consecrated to me, and to my unfolding and empowerment. As I learn to love*

and honor my body as the beautiful temple, wondrous tool, and amazing vehicle for transformation that it is, I become closer to the divine gift of creation.

Now, as I breathe again, inhaling the sacred scents, I prepare to walk forward into the world. I carry sacred space everywhere I go, and all I need is to remember: My body is sacred. My breath is sacred. My bones and blood and sweat and tears are sacred. My laughter is sacred, my voice is sacred, and my skin is sacred. I claim this mantra: this temple is mine.

Turn your focus inward, close your eyes, breathe, and relax. Allow yourself to slowly come back to the world you inhabit, the room you are sitting in, and your daily life. As you open your eyes, give yourself a hug, remembering that even as you reenter the world, your body remains a sacred temple of creation and empowerment.

- Releasing of quarters and entities (optional).
- Opening of circle (optional).
- Banishing (optional).

RITUAL TWO

I Love Me!

★ Suggestion: Consider consecrating the t-shirt you made this week, and an additional item to add to your altar (see "Magickal Act: D.I.Y. Fashion Statement" in chapter 2).

What You Will Need

- A bead. This week's bead should in some way represent body pride.
- Treats, as desired.
- Wine, if desired. See "Wines" in appendix I.
- Incense. See "Incenses" and incense recipes in appendix I.

How-To

- Build the altar with the items listed here and on the main altar list on page 140, or integrate any items not already present into your existing altar. For comfort and ease in ritual space, place everything you need near where you will be seated.
- Make sure the charcoal is lit.

Outline

- Banishing (optional).
- Circle casting (optional).
- Calling of quarters and spirit entities (optional).
- Setting space.

Sprinkle a pinch of incense on the charcoal.

Focus on breathing deeply into your belly. As you breathe you may want to walk around the space once, thinking of the qualities that this blend of resins will bring to the space: love, purification, safety, healing, and connection with spirit. Then sit before your altar. Breathe consciously for a few minutes, letting the scent of the incense permeate your body, inside and out, and allowing your cells to absorb the positive qualities of the incense. Perform this step until you feel present in your body, and in ritual space.

Record the following script in advance, or read it in ritual space:

Breathe deeply, allowing your breath to expand your chest, and then even more deeply, letting your breath expand your belly, your lower abdomen. As you breathe, allow the smoke of this special blend of incense to enter your body and infuse each cell with blessing. Let this magickal and sacred blend of scents fill you with love, purification, safety, healing, and connection with spirit. As you breathe, allow your body to become the sacred temple where you worship.

Once you are fully present in your body, open your eyes, and come present in the space. Take a moment to feel the energy you have already created by centering here in this sacred space. Say:

I am in sacred space.

As you light the mother candle, say:

Lighting this flame, I invoke body pride. I invoke the courage and power to be present in my body, to love my body, and to worship my body. I invoke the power of self-definition. I invoke the clarity and fullness of nurturance. I invoke a spirit of resistance and of celebration. I invoke power, and I invoke love. I invoke not only self-acceptance but self-devotion.

From the source candle, light your personal candle. As you light this candle, say:

> *As I light my flame, I drop deeper into that space that allows for healing. I know my body as a sacred, wonderful temple. A space sacred and powerful. A space where I know the truth of my own being. I drop deeper into that space inside where I have true self-devotion, where I know that each act of self-love, self-adoration, and self-definition is a sacred act. The place where I alone define the boundaries of my temple; this sacred temple that is me.*

As you place your lighted candle on your altar, say:

> *With this light I create a sacred circle that allows honor and devotion to grow, and my light shining becomes a beacon in the darkness that allows each seeker to find her own way home.*

Consecration of Writing, Art, and Altar

Once your candle is placed on the altar, it is time to consecrate the items you created during the week. This may be one piece of writing and one piece of art you have created during the week, or it may be all of them. It depends only on how much time you want to devote to being in ritual space.

Lay whatever items you want to consecrate in front of the altar. You may compose your own words of consecration, or you can use the ones I offer here. Say:

> *I consecrate these works to the unfolding of self-awareness. May this act serve me, and may it serve all beings through the revelation of awareness. May my increasing awareness and presence serve to bring awareness of presence to all beings everywhere throughout space and time. So it is.*

Take time to witness, honor, and cherish each item you are consecrating. Read your writing out loud if it feels comfortable (voicing words may add to their power). You may also want to pass the items through the smoke from the incense, or do some other act of purification and consecration.

If you feel inclined to add to your altar, this is the time to do it. What item from this week's exploration would like to live on your altar for the duration of your initiation cycle?

Bead Consecration

After you have consecrated your artifacts, consecrate this week's bead. Say:

> *I consecrate this bead in the journey of body-love. May it serve as a reminder to me that my body is a sacred space.*

Place the bead in your bead pouch.

Honoring with Treats, Water, and Wine

Bless the food, water, and wine. Say:

> *This food is not just a symbol of, but the true substance of, nurturance, and of the cycles of life. May the sacrifice of this that I am about to ingest feed my body, my spirit, and my soul. May I always experience, receive, and honor my hungers. May all true hungers be fulfilled.*

> *Water is life. Life, and regeneration, and healing. Let this water remind me of my origins; of the womb, and of the blessed sea, the birthplace of life and that which forms the flow.*

> *This wine is the blood of willing sacrifice. It represents the cycles of life, death, and birth. It offers succor, and a doorway to new perception. May this wine bless me with the awareness of choice, and with divine vision and ecstasy.*

Take time to honor your body with treats, water, and wine. As you eat and drink, sit in awareness of the magick of transmutation: how the food, water, and wine affect your senses, and how these edible items become part of the very fabric of your cells. Allow gratitude, honor, and acceptance of and for the elements you are bringing into your body.

Ending of Ritual

Sit before the altar again, and breathe, and then say:

> *Mine is the temple. As I walk through the world, I know that my body is a sacred vessel. It is consecrated to me, and to my unfolding and empowerment. As I learn to love and honor my body as the beautiful temple, wondrous tool, and amazing vehicle for transformation that it is, I become closer to the divine gift of creation.*

Now, as I breathe again, inhaling the sacred scents, I prepare to walk forward into the world. I carry sacred space everywhere I go, and all I need is to remember: My body is sacred. My breath is sacred. My bones and blood and sweat and tears are sacred. My laughter is sacred, my voice is sacred, and my skin is sacred. I claim this mantra: this temple is mine.

Turn your focus inward, close your eyes, breathe, and relax. Allow yourself to slowly come back to the world you inhabit, the room you are sitting in, and your daily life. As you open your eyes, give yourself a hug, remembering that even as you reenter the world, your body remains a sacred temple of creation and empowerment.

- Releasing of quarters and entities (optional).
- Opening of circle (optional).
- Banishing (optional).

RITUAL THREE

Pussy Power!

★ Suggestion: Consider consecrating your drawing-it pieces (see "Magickal Act: Drawing It" in chapter 3).

What You Will Need

- A bead. This week's bead should represent the wonderful vulva!
- A platter with a vulva cookie or candy.
- Wine, if desired. Try a light, floral, fruity dessert wine, like a white or rose Muscat.
- Incense. See "Incenses" and incense recipes in appendix I.

How-To

- Build the altar with the items listed here and on the main altar list on page 140, or integrate any items not already present into your existing altar. For comfort and ease in ritual space, place everything you need near where you will be seated.
- Make sure the charcoal is lit.

Outline

- Banishing (optional).
- Circle casting (optional).
- Calling of quarters and spirit entities (optional).
- Setting space.

Sprinkle a pinch of incense on the charcoal.

Focus on breathing deeply into your belly. As you breathe you may want to walk around the space once, thinking of the qualities that this blend of resins will bring to the space: love, purification, safety, healing, and connection with spirit. Then sit before your altar. Breathe consciously for a few minutes, letting the scent of the incense permeate your body, inside and out, and allowing your cells to absorb the positive qualities of the incense. Perform this step until you feel present in your body, and in ritual space.

Record the following script in advance, or read it in ritual space:

Breathe deeply, allowing your breath to expand your chest, and then even more deeply, letting your breath expand your belly, your lower abdomen. As you breathe, allow the smoke of this special blend of incense to enter your body and infuse each cell with blessing. Let this magickal and sacred blend of scents fill you with love, purification, safety, healing, and connection with spirit. As you breathe, allow your body to become the sacred temple where you worship.

Once you are fully present in your body, open your eyes, and come present in the space. Take a moment to feel the energy you have already created by centering here in this sacred space. Say:

I am in sacred space.

As you light the mother candle, say:

Lighting this flame, I invoke Pussy Pride! I invoke a sense of wonder, awe, adoration, and love for our amazing anatomy! I invoke the courage and power to be present in my body, to love my body, and to worship my body. I invoke not only self-acceptance but self-devotion.

From the source candle, light your personal candle. As you light this candle, say:

As I light my flame, I drop deeper into that space that allows for healing. I know my body as a sacred, wonderful temple. A space sacred and powerful. A space where I know the truth of my own being. I drop deeper into that space inside where I have true self-devotion, where I know that each act of self-love, self-adoration, and self-defini-tion is a sacred act. The place where I alone define the boundaries of my temple; this sacred temple that is me.

As you place your lighted candle on your altar, say:

With this light I create a sacred circle that allows honor and devotion to grow, and my light shining becomes a beacon in the darkness that allows each seeker to find her own way home.

Consecration of Writing, Art, and Altar

Once your candle is placed on the altar, it is time to consecrate the items you created during the week. This may be one piece of writing and one piece of art you have created during the week, or it may be all of them. It depends only on how much time you want to devote to being in ritual space.

Lay whatever items you want to consecrate in front of the altar. You may compose your own words of consecration, or you can use the ones I offer here. Say:

I consecrate these works to the unfolding of self-awareness. May this act serve me, and may it serve all beings through the revelation of awareness. May my increasing awareness and presence serve to bring awareness of presence to all beings everywhere throughout space and time. So it is.

Take time to witness, honor, and cherish each item you are consecrating. Read your writing out loud if it feels comfortable (voicing words may add to their power). You may also want to pass the items through the smoke from the incense, or do some other act of purification and consecration.

If you feel inclined to add to your altar, this is the time to do it. What item from this week's exploration would like to live on your altar for the duration of your initiation cycle?

Bead Consecration

After you have consecrated your artifacts, consecrate this week's bead. Say:

I consecrate this bead in the journey of vulval awe. May it serve as a reminder to me that my cunt is a sacred space.

Place the bead in your bead pouch.

Honoring with Treats, Water, and Wine

Bless the food, water, and wine. Say:

This food is not just a symbol of, but the true substance of, nurturance, and of the cycles of life. May the sacrifice of this that I am about to ingest feed my body, my spirit, and my soul. May I always experience, receive, and honor my hungers. May all true hungers be fulfilled.

Water is life. Life, and regeneration, and healing. Let this water remind me of my origins; of the womb, and of the blessed sea, the birthplace of life and that which forms the flow.

This wine is the blood of willing sacrifice. It represents the cycles of life, death, and birth. It offers succor, and a doorway to new perception. May this wine bless me with the awareness of choice, and with divine vision and ecstasy.

Take time to honor your body with treats, water, and wine. As you eat and drink, sit in awareness of the magick of transmutation: how the food, water, and wine affect your senses, and how these edible items become part of the very fabric of your cells. Allow gratitude, honor, and acceptance of and for the elements you are bringing into your body.

Ending of Ritual

Sit before the altar again, and breathe, and then say:

Mine is the temple. As I walk through the world, I know that my body is a sacred vessel. It is consecrated to me, and to my unfolding and empowerment. As I learn to love and honor my body as the beautiful temple, wondrous tool, and amazing vehicle for transformation that it is, I become closer to the divine gift of creation.

Now, as I breathe again, inhaling the sacred scents, I prepare to walk forward into the world. I carry sacred space everywhere I go, and all I need is to remember: My body is sacred. My breath is sacred. My bones and blood and sweat and tears are sacred. My laughter is sacred, my voice is sacred, and my skin is sacred. I claim this mantra: this temple is mine.

Turn your focus inward, close your eyes, breathe, and relax. Allow yourself to slowly come back to the world you inhabit, the room you are sitting in, and your daily life. As you open your eyes, give yourself a hug, remembering that even as you reenter the world, your body remains a sacred temple of creation and empowerment.

- Releasing of quarters and entities (optional).
- Opening of circle (optional).
- Banishing (optional).

RITUAL FOUR

The Descent

★ Suggestions:

1. Consider consecrating your blood art (see "Spell Working: Blood Magick" in chapter 4).

2. Consider performing a temple visualization in ritual space (see "Spell Working: The Womb Room" in chapter 4).

What You Will Need

- A bead. This week's bead should represent your blood or your uterus.
- A platter with dark bread or cakes of light. See the Cakes of Light recipe in appendix I.
- A blood-red wine, if desired. See "Wines" in appendix I.
- Incense. See "Incenses" and incense recipes in appendix I.

How-To

- Build the altar with the items listed here and on the main altar list on page 140, or integrate any items not already present into your existing altar. For comfort and ease in ritual space, place everything you need near where you will be seated.
- Make sure the charcoal is lit.

Outline

- Banishing (optional).
- Circle casting (optional).
- Calling of quarters and spirit entities (optional).
- Setting space.

Sprinkle a pinch of incense on the charcoal.

Focus on breathing deeply into your belly. As you breathe you may want to walk around the space once, thinking of the qualities that this blend of resins will bring to the space: love, purification, safety, healing, and connection with spirit. Then sit before your altar. Breathe consciously for a few minutes, letting the scent of the incense permeate your body, inside and out, and allowing your cells to absorb the positive qualities of the incense. Perform this step until you feel present in your body, and in ritual space.

Record the following script in advance, or read it in ritual space:

Breathe deeply, allowing your breath to expand your chest, and then even more deeply, letting your breath expand your belly, your lower abdomen. As you breathe, allow the smoke of this special blend of incense to enter your body and infuse each cell with blessing. Let this magickal and sacred blend of scents fill you with love, purification, safety, healing, and connection with spirit. As you breathe, allow your body to become the sacred temple where you worship.

Once you are fully present in your body, open your eyes, and come present in the space. Take a moment to feel the energy you have already created by centering here in this sacred space. Say:

I am in sacred space.

As you light the mother candle, say:

Lighting this flame, I invoke the journey we women have taken to get to where we are now. I invoke the courage and power of my ancestors of both blood and spirit; all the women who suffered and loved anyway, and made the world a more accepting place by living their lives with integrity. I invoke the courage to love and to worship our cunts, our wombs, and our blood. I invoke love, and I invoke devotion to our cunts, our wombs, and our scared blood.

From the source candle, light your personal candle. As you light this candle, say:

As I light my flame, I drop deeper into that space that allows for healing. I know my body as a sacred, wonderful temple. A space sacred and powerful. A space where I know the truth of my own being. I drop deeper into that space inside where I have true self-devotion, where I know that each act of self-love, self-adoration, and self-definition is a sacred act. The place where I alone define the boundaries of my temple; this sacred temple that is me.

As you place your lighted candle on your altar, say:

With this light I create a sacred circle that allows honor and devotion to grow, and my light shining becomes a beacon in the darkness that allows each seeker to find her own way home.

Consecration of Writing, Art, and Altar

Once your candle is placed on the altar, it is time to consecrate the items you created during the week. This may be one piece of writing and one piece of art you have created during the week, or it may be all of them. It depends only on how much time you want to devote to being in ritual space.

Lay whatever items you want to consecrate in front of the altar. You may compose your own words of consecration, or you can use the ones I offer here. Say:

I consecrate these works to the unfolding of self-awareness. May this act serve me, and may it serve all beings through the revelation of awareness. May my increasing awareness and presence serve to bring awareness of presence to all beings everywhere throughout space and time. So it is.

Take time to witness, honor, and cherish each item you are consecrating. Read your writing out loud if it feels comfortable (voicing words may add to their power). You may also want to pass the items through the smoke from the incense, or do some other act of purification and consecration.

If you feel inclined to add to your altar, this is the time to do it. What item from this week's exploration would like to live on your altar for the duration of your initiation cycle?

Bead Consecration

After you have consecrated your artifacts, consecrate this week's bead. Say:

> *I consecrate this bead in the journey of healing, and to the power of the Gods and of women: the power to create life. May it serve as a reminder to me that my womb, my blood, and my sex are sacred.*

Place the bead in your bead pouch.

Honoring with Treats, Water, and Wine

Bless the food, water, and wine. Say:

> *This food is not just a symbol of, but the true substance of, nurturance, and of the cycles of life. May the sacrifice of this that I am about to ingest feed my body, my spirit, and my soul. May I always experience, receive, and honor my hungers. May all true hungers be fulfilled.*
>
> *Water is life. Life, and regeneration, and healing. Let this water remind me of my origins; of the womb, and of the blessed sea, the birthplace of life and that which forms the flow.*
>
> *This wine is the blood of willing sacrifice. It represents the cycles of life, death, and birth. It offers succor, and a doorway to new perception. May this wine bless me with the awareness of choice, and with divine vision and ecstasy.*

Take time to honor your body with treats, water, and wine. As you eat and drink, sit in awareness of the magick of transmutation: how the food, water, and wine affect your senses, and how these edible items become part of the very fabric of your cells. Allow gratitude, honor, and acceptance of and for the elements you are bringing into your body.

Ending of Ritual

Sit before the altar again, and breathe, and then say:

> *Mine is the temple. As I walk through the world, I know that my body is a sacred vessel. It is consecrated to me, and to my unfolding and empowerment. As I learn to love and honor my body as the beautiful temple, wondrous tool, and amazing vehicle for transformation that it is, I become closer to the divine gift of creation.*

> *Now, as I breathe again, inhaling the sacred scents, I prepare to walk forward into the world. I carry sacred space everywhere I go, and all I need is to remember: My body is sacred. My breath is sacred. My bones and blood and sweat and tears are sacred. My laughter is sacred, my voice is sacred, and my skin is sacred. I claim this mantra: this temple is mine.*

Turn your focus inward, close your eyes, breathe, and relax. Allow yourself to slowly come back to the world you inhabit, the room you are sitting in, and your daily life. As you open your eyes, give yourself a hug, remembering that even as you reenter the world, your body remains a sacred temple of creation and empowerment.

- Releasing of quarters and entities (optional).
- Opening of circle (optional).
- Banishing (optional).

RITUAL FIVE

Coming to Our Senses

★ Suggestions:

1. Consider consecrating your Sensation Station toy box this week, as well as an item to add to your altar (see "Magickal Act: Sensation Station Toy Box" in chapter 5).

2. Consider performing your sensual bath as part of your initiation ritual (see "Spell Working, Day 7: The Sensual Bath" in chapter 5).

3. Consider playing with your Sensation Station in ritual space.

What You Will Need

- A bead. This week's bead should in some way represent your senses.

- Wine, if desired. See "Wines" in appendix I.

- Incense. See "Incenses" and incense recipes in appendix I.

How-To

- Build the altar with the items listed here and on the main altar list on page 140, or integrate any items not already present into your existing altar. For comfort and ease in ritual space, place everything you need near where you will be seated.
- Make sure the charcoal is lit.

Outline

- Banishing (optional).
- Circle casting (optional).
- Calling of quarters and spirit entities (optional).
- Setting space.

Sprinkle a pinch of incense on the charcoal.

Focus on breathing deeply into your belly. As you breathe you may want to walk around the space once, thinking of the qualities that this blend of resins will bring to the space: love, purification, safety, healing, and connection with spirit. Then sit before your altar. Breathe consciously for a few minutes, letting the scent of the incense permeate your body, inside and out, and allowing your cells to absorb the positive qualities of the incense. Perform this step until you feel present in your body, and in ritual space.

Record the following script in advance, or read it in ritual space:

Breathe deeply, allowing your breath to expand your chest, and then even more deeply, letting your breath expand your belly, your lower abdomen. As you breathe, allow the smoke of this special blend of incense to enter your body and infuse each cell with blessing. Let this magickal and sacred blend of scents fill you with love, purification, safety, healing, and connection with spirit. As you breathe, allow your body to become the sacred temple where you worship.

Once you are fully present in your body, open your eyes, and come present in the space. Take a moment to feel the energy you have already created by centering here in this sacred space. Say:

I am in sacred space.

As you light the mother candle, say:

Lighting this candle, I invoke revelations of the senses. I invoke a sense of awe at the power and sacred perfection of my body, which works exactly in the ways that it works. I invoke awe at my ability to smell, taste, hear, feel, and see. I claim this awe, and offer blessings and thankfulness to my body for all it does, and for all it is.

From the source candle, light your personal candle. As you light this candle, say:

As I light my flame, I drop deeper into that space that allows for healing. I know my body as a sacred, wonderful temple. A space sacred and powerful. A space where I know the truth of my own being. I drop deeper into that space inside where I have true self-devotion, where I know that each act of self-love, self-adoration, and self-definition is a sacred act. The place where I alone define the boundaries of my temple; this sacred temple that is me.

As you place your lighted candle on your altar, say:

With this light I create a sacred circle that allows honor and devotion to grow, and my light shining becomes a beacon in the darkness that allows each seeker to find her own way home.

Consecration of Writing, Art, and Altar

Once your candle is placed on the altar, it is time to consecrate the items you created during the week. This may be one piece of writing and one piece of art you have created during the week, or it may be all of them. It depends only on how much time you want to devote to being in ritual space.

Lay whatever items you want to consecrate in front of the altar. You may compose your own words of consecration, or you can use the ones I offer here. Say:

I consecrate these works to the unfolding of self-awareness. May this act serve me, and may it serve all beings through the revelation of awareness. May my increasing awareness and presence serve to bring awareness of presence to all beings everywhere throughout space and time. So it is.

Take time to witness, honor, and cherish each item you are consecrating. Read your writing out loud if it feels comfortable (voicing words may add to their power). You may also want to pass the items through the smoke from the incense, or do some other act of purification and consecration.

If you feel inclined to add to your altar, this is the time to do it. What item from this week's exploration would like to live on your altar for the duration of your initiation cycle?

Bead Consecration

After you have consecrated your artifacts, consecrate this week's bead. Say:

> *I consecrate this bead in the journey of sensual awareness. May it serve as a reminder to me that my senses are a sacred gift.*

Place the bead in your bead pouch.

Honoring with Treats, Water, and Wine

Bless the food, water, and wine. Say:

> *This food is not just a symbol of, but the true substance of, nurturance, and of the cycles of life. May the sacrifice of this that I am about to ingest feed my body, my spirit, and my soul. May I always experience, receive, and honor my hungers. May all true hungers be fulfilled.*
>
> *Water is life. Life, and regeneration, and healing. Let this water remind me of my origins; of the womb, and of the blessed sea, the birthplace of life and that which forms the flow.*
>
> *This wine is the blood of willing sacrifice. It represents the cycles of life, death, and birth. It offers succor, and a doorway to new perception. May this wine bless me with the awareness of choice, and with divine vision and ecstasy.*

Take time to honor your body with treats, water, and wine. As you eat and drink, sit in awareness of the magick of transmutation: how the food, water, and wine affect your senses, and how these edible items become part of the very fabric of your cells. Allow gratitude, honor, and acceptance of and for the elements you are bringing into your body.

Ending of Ritual

Sit before the altar again, and breathe, and then say:

> *Mine is the temple. As I walk through the world, I know that my body is a sacred vessel. It is consecrated to me, and to my unfolding and empowerment. As I learn to love*

and honor my body as the beautiful temple, wondrous tool, and amazing vehicle for transformation that it is, I become closer to the divine gift of creation.

Now, as I breathe again, inhaling the sacred scents, I prepare to walk forward into the world. I carry sacred space everywhere I go, and all I need is to remember: My body is sacred. My breath is sacred. My bones and blood and sweat and tears are sacred. My laughter is sacred, my voice is sacred, and my skin is sacred. I claim this mantra: this temple is mine.

Turn your focus inward, close your eyes, breathe, and relax. Allow yourself to slowly come back to the world you inhabit, the room you are sitting in, and your daily life. As you open your eyes, give yourself a hug, remembering that even as you reenter the world, your body remains a sacred temple of creation and empowerment.

- Releasing of quarters and entities (optional).
- Opening of circle (optional).
- Banishing (optional).

RITUAL SIX

Witch Power Rising (Dedication)

★ Suggestions:

1. Consider consecrating your creation artifact or your mentor icon this week (see "Spell Working: Creating Creation" and "Magickal Act: Creating a Mentor Icon" in chapter 6).

2. Consider performing a temple visualization in ritual space (see "Spell Working: Breath of Life" in chapter 6).

What You Will Need

- A bead. This week's bead should in some way represent one or more of your mentors, or your creation myth.

- Wine, if desired. See "Wines" in appendix I.

- A platter of star-shaped cookies.

- Your empowerment mantra. See "Spell Working: Creating an Empowerment Mantra" in chapter 6.
- Incense. See "Incenses" and incense recipes in appendix I.

How-To

- Build the altar with the items listed here and on the main altar list on page 140, or integrate any items not already present into your existing altar. For comfort and ease in ritual space, place everything you need near where you will be seated.
- Make sure the charcoal is lit.

Outline

- Banishing (optional).
- Circle casting (optional).
- Calling of quarters and spirit entities (optional).
- Setting space.

Sprinkle a pinch of incense on the charcoal.

Focus on breathing deeply into your belly. As you breathe you may want to walk around the space once, thinking of the qualities that this blend of resins will bring to the space: love, purification, safety, healing, and connection with spirit. Then sit before your altar. Breathe consciously for a few minutes, letting the scent of the incense permeate your body, inside and out, and allowing your cells to absorb the positive qualities of the incense. Perform this step until you feel present in your body, and in ritual space.

Record the following script in advance, or read it in ritual space:

Breathe deeply, allowing your breath to expand your chest, and then even more deeply, letting your breath expand your belly, your lower abdomen. As you breathe, allow the smoke of this special blend of incense to enter your body and infuse each cell with blessing. Let this magickal and sacred blend of scents fill you with love, purification, safety, healing, and connection with spirit. As you breathe, allow your body to become the sacred temple where you worship.

Once you are fully present in your body, open your eyes, and come present in the space. Take a moment to feel the energy you have already created by centering here in this sacred space. Say:

I am in sacred space.

As you light the mother candle, say:

> *Lighting this candle, I invoke the journey I have taken to get where I am now. I invoke the courage and power of my ancestors. I invoke lineage of spirit, and lineage of flesh. I invoke my strength as a leader, and I invoke my ability to find inspiration and support in my times of need. I invoke new stories of creation, new patterns to build my life upon, and new beginnings.*

From the source candle, light your personal candle. As you light this candle, say:

> *As I light my flame, I drop deeper into that space that allows for healing. I know my body as a sacred, wonderful temple. A space sacred and powerful. A space where I know the truth of my own being. I drop deeper into that space inside where I have true self-devotion, where I know that each act of self-love, self-adoration, and self-definition is a sacred act. The place where I alone define the boundaries of my temple; this sacred temple that is me.*

As you place your lighted candle on your altar, say:

> *With this light I create a sacred circle that allows honor and devotion to grow, and my light shining becomes a beacon in the darkness that allows each seeker to find her own way home.*

Consecration of Writing, Art, and Altar

Once your candle is placed on the altar, it is time to consecrate the items you created during the week. This may be one piece of writing and one piece of art you have created during the week, or it may be all of them. It depends only on how much time you want to devote to being in ritual space.

Lay whatever items you want to consecrate in front of the altar. You may compose your own words of consecration, or you can use the ones I offer here. Say:

> *I consecrate these works to the unfolding of self-awareness. May this act serve me, and may it serve all beings through the revelation of awareness. May my increasing awareness and presence serve to bring awareness of presence to all beings everywhere throughout space and time. So it is.*

Take time to witness, honor, and cherish each item you are consecrating. Read your writing out loud if it feels comfortable (voicing words may add to their power). You may also want to pass the items through the smoke from the incense, or do some other act of purification and consecration.

If you feel inclined to add to your altar, this is the time to do it. What item from this week's exploration would like to live on your altar for the duration of your initiation cycle?

Empowerment Mantra

Now, read aloud your empowerment mantra.

Bead Consecration

After you have consecrated your artifacts, consecrate this week's bead. Say:

> *I consecrate this bead in the journey of choice, regeneration, and lineage. May it serve as a reminder to me that my past and my future are sacred.*

Place the bead in your bead pouch.

Honoring with Treats, Water, and Wine

Bless the food, water, and wine. Say:

> *This food is not just a symbol of, but the true substance of, nurturance, and of the cycles of life. May the sacrifice of this that I am about to ingest feed my body, my spirit, and my soul. May I always experience, receive, and honor my hungers. May all true hungers be fulfilled.*

> *Water is life. Life, and regeneration, and healing. Let this water remind me of my origins; of the womb, and of the blessed sea, the birthplace of life and that which forms the flow.*

> *This wine is the blood of willing sacrifice. It represents the cycles of life, death, and birth. It offers succor, and a doorway to new perception. May this wine bless me with the awareness of choice, and with divine vision and ecstasy.*

Take time to honor your body with treats, water, and wine. As you eat and drink, sit in awareness of the magick of transmutation: how the food, water, and wine affect your senses, and how these edible items become part of the very fabric of your cells. Allow gratitude, honor, and acceptance of and for the elements you are bringing into your body.

Ending of Ritual

Sit before the altar again, and breathe, and then say:

> *Mine is the temple. As I walk through the world, I know that my body is a sacred vessel. It is consecrated to me, and to my unfolding and empowerment. As I learn to love and honor my body as the beautiful temple, wondrous tool, and amazing vehicle for transformation that it is, I become closer to the divine gift of creation.*
>
> *Now, as I breathe again, inhaling the sacred scents, I prepare to walk forward into the world. I carry sacred space everywhere I go, and all I need is to remember: My body is sacred. My breath is sacred. My bones and blood and sweat and tears are sacred. My laughter is sacred, my voice is sacred, and my skin is sacred. I claim this mantra: this temple is mine.*

Turn your focus inward, close your eyes, breathe, and relax. Allow yourself to slowly come back to the world you inhabit, the room you are sitting in, and your daily life. As you open your eyes, give yourself a hug, remembering that even as you reenter the world, your body remains a sacred temple of creation and empowerment.

- Releasing of quarters and entities (optional).
- Opening of circle (optional).
- Banishing (optional).

Goddess in the Mirror (Completion)

Have you chosen your witnesses? How many witnesses do you want to have at your seventh initiation? Your witnesses may be of any gender, and of any age. You can have just two, or as many as you'd like. Choose a number that feels right to you. You must have at least two.

In choosing, remember that these must be people you trust, people you love, and ideally people who will be in your life for a long, long time. In the future, these witnesses will have the responsibility of reminding you of your vows. During the ritual, they will play a part in your initiation. They will have the opportunity to see you honor the healing work you have done, and to offer their testimony to your unfolding. If you have a partner, this will be an amazing opportunity to create a new level of trust and depth in your relationship. Perhaps you have a mentor you'd like to have as witness, or maybe your best girlfriend or boyfriend.

Are you comfortable taking your vows in the nude? Will your witnesses be comfortable with your nudity? Nudity is not required, but it can be a powerful element of this ritual. In many cultures and since time began, nudity has been a common element in taking vows of initiation. There are a lot of symbolic reasons that nudity is a positive component of initiation. One is the idea of coming before the Divine with nothing to hide. Another is the act of "baring it all." Another element is that of worship. You have nothing to hide. This body of yours is an amazing and wondrous temple, dedicated to you and to the work you are doing.

Your witnesses will have an opportunity to honor you by taking on the facilitation and performance of part of this final ritual. Be prepared for some surprises, and place your trust in the process of initiation.

After the bead consecration section, there is a note in the ritual outline that says: "WITNESSES ONLY READ OUTLINE PAST THIS POINT!!!" Obviously, you shouldn't read past that point. You should, however, make sure to get this part to your witnesses well in advance of the ritual, and tell them to read it as soon as they can. After the part that they perform, you may either perform the food, water, and wine blessing, and the ending of ritual, or you may allow your witnesses do it. Let them know in advance which option you like better. You may also offer them personal candles to light in ritual space. It's up to you and your witnesses. This ritual will likely be longer than any of the others you have performed in the course of working *Sexy Witch*. Give it the time. I promise it'll be worth it. Plan for a whole afternoon and evening, and have a celebration after the ritual! It'll be like a début.

No really, do have a party after the ritual! Then you can invite as many of your peeps to honor your transition as you'd like, without having to share this very intimate ritual with all of them. You can be as overt or as covert as you wish. If you don't want to share all the wondrous details of your process with your buddies, just say you are having an "unbirthday" party, or that you just wanted to take some time to celebrate your wonderful self and your amazing circle of friends. If you want to open up the discussion about what's been putting that pretty grin on your face for the past few days, put out your altar and start answering questions once someone gets brave enough to ask them.

Now, on to your final Sexy Witch initiation!

Ritual Seven

★ Suggestions:

1. Allow one of your witnesses to prepare a ritual bath or at least a foot bath (see appendix 1 for recipes and instructions) for you before the initiation.

2. Treat this event as you would any momentous occasion. Do whatever makes you feel prepared to take your vows. Whether it's getting a pedicure or spending the morning in meditation, do what works to create a day that you will remember fondly for the rest of your life.

3. Make sure your witnesses can tolerate scents and smoke.

4. Allow one of your witnesses to prepare your treat platter.

5. Plan a more inclusive party for the evening, once your ritual is complete, to honor your new path.

What You Will Need

- Your witnesses!
- Comfy spaces for you and your witnesses to sit near the altar.
- Incense. See "Incenses" and incense recipes in appendix I.
- A bead. This week's bead should represent a doorway, a threshold, or a Witches' broom.
- Something to string your beads on (jeweler's wire, yarn, hemp rope). Make sure it is long enough to fashion a necklace or bracelet out of. You may want to purchase fastings/hooks, too, so you can remove and put on the talisman easily in the future.
- Wine, or champagne, if desired. See "Wines" in appendix I.
- A platter of cookies with a Witches' broom, a doorway, or a gateway on each of them. A platter of other treats as well. (Other treats are optional.)
- Your devotion oil. See appendix I for the recipe.
- Your empowerment contract. See "Magickal Act: Empowerment Contract" in chapter 7.
- Your vows of initiation. See "Spell Working: Vows of Initiation" in chapter 7.

- Your initiation talisman(s). See "Spell Working: Creating an Initiation Talisman" in chapter 7.

- Any works of art you created over the duration of your initiation cycle that you want to share with your witnesses.

- A pen.

Note: You must choose one direction for where your path is leading now (or where you want it to be leading), and one direction for the current/future home of your growth. (Tell your witnesses the directions you have chosen once you choose. They will need to know in advance of the ritual.)

In my personal cosmology, the west has a lot of correspondences that allow for female sexual empowerment, and many of the Goddesses I look to for inspiration in this arena are associated with the west. However, the south is also profoundly powerful and transformative. All the quarters have associations that make sense for either of the designations. What are your associations? For me, where the west represents nurturance, sensuality, and the womb, and often has a more gentle form of transformation to offer, the south is overtly sexual, creative, and powerful, and offers fundamental and complete transformation, as in fire burning wood to ash. The north represents grounding and solid nurturance, motherhood and stability. The east offers new beginnings and inspiration.

These are my associations. But this ritual is about *you,* not me. So, what are your associations? What direction are you heading toward? What element are you inviting to influence your life now? Air? Fire? Water? Earth? Where do you want the coming phase of your growth to take place? Rely on your intuition here, and find the directions that make the most sense to you. Choose your future path with intention.

How-To

- Build the altar with the items listed here and on the main altar list on page 140, or integrate any items not already present into your existing altar. For comfort and ease in ritual space, place everything you need near where you will be seated.

- Make sure the charcoal is lit.

- Give your devotion oil, empowerment contract, vows of initiation, and initiation talisman(s) to one of your witnesses before the ritual.

Outline

- Banishing (optional).
- Circle casting (optional).
- Calling of quarters and spirit entities (optional).
- Setting space.

Sprinkle a pinch of incense on the charcoal.

Focus on breathing deeply into your belly. As you breathe you may want to walk around the space once, thinking of the qualities that this blend of resins will bring to the space: love, purification, safety, healing, and connection with spirit. Then sit before your altar. Breathe consciously for a few minutes, letting the scent of the incense permeate your body, inside and out, and allowing your cells to absorb the positive qualities of the incense. Perform this step until you feel present in your body, and in ritual space.

Record the following script in advance, or read it in ritual space:

Breathe deeply, allowing your breath to expand your chest, and then even more deeply, letting your breath expand your belly, your lower abdomen. As you breathe, allow the smoke of this special blend of incense to enter your body and infuse each cell with blessing. Let this magickal and sacred blend of scents fill you with love, purification, safety, healing, and connection with spirit. As you breathe, allow your body to become the sacred temple where you worship.

Once you are fully present in your body, open your eyes, and come present in the space. Take a moment to feel the energy you have already created by centering here in this sacred space. Say:

I am in sacred space.

(If you wish, all participants may say together: *We are in sacred space.*)

As you light the mother candle, say:

Lighting this candle, I invoke gratitude for the journey I have taken in the past seven weeks. I invoke sweet anticipation for the journey that continues on the other side of this threshold. I invoke self-dedication, self-adoration, and self-respect. I invoke the vows of the initiate: To know, to will, to dare, and to be silent. I have revealed deep mysteries within me, and found new ways. I will continue to deepen as I walk the path before me.

From the source candle, light your personal candle. As you light this candle, say:

> *As I light my flame, I drop deeper into the ME that I am becoming, and I know my body as a sacred, wonderful temple. A space sacred and powerful. A space where I know the truth of my own being. I drop deeper into that space inside where I have true self-devotion, where I know that each act of self-definition, self-love, and self-adoration is a sacred act. The place where I alone define the boundaries of my temple; this sacred temple that is me. From this awareness, I create the new worlds I am building.*

(Witnesses may light personal candles as well. If so, instruct them by saying: *You may now light your own candles, and make a prayer of whatever sort feels right to you.*)

Consecration of Writing, Art, and Altar

Once your candle is placed on the altar, it is time to consecrate the items you created during the week. Lay whatever items you want to consecrate in front of the altar. You may compose your own words of consecration, or you can use the ones I offer here. Say:

> *I consecrate these works to the unfolding of self-awareness. May this act serve me, and may it serve all beings through the revelation of awareness. May my increasing awareness and presence serve to bring awareness of presence to all beings everywhere throughout space and time. So it is.*

Take time to witness, honor, and cherish each item you are consecrating. Read your writing out loud if it feels comfortable (voicing words may add to their power). You may also want to pass the items through the smoke from the incense, or do some other act of purification and consecration.

If you feel inclined to add to your altar, this is the time to do it. What item from this week's exploration would like to live on your altar for the duration of your initiation cycle?

Bead Consecration

After you have consecrated your artifacts, consecrate this week's bead. Say:

> *I consecrate this bead in the journey of body-love. May it serve as a reminder to me that my body is a sacred space.*

Now, take the stringing you have chosen, and string the beads. As you string them, you may speak aloud or just focus internally on what each bead represents. Once finished, hand this talisman of initiation to one of your witnesses.

WITNESSES ONLY READ OUTLINE PAST THIS POINT!!!

NOTE: WITNESSES, READ THIS WHOLE SECTION IN ADVANCE OF THE RITUAL DATE! It will be helpful to read the whole section titled "Ritual Seven: Goddess in the Mirror (Completion)," if you are willing, and if you are interested, you may also read chapter 7, "The Seventh Initiation: The Mirror and the Path."

As witness to this initiation rite, your most important and abiding job is to stand as witness for this initiation. As witness to the initiate's vows, it will be your responsibility in the future to support the initiate in striving to achieve and maintain her vows.

Your other job is become witness/Priest(ess) for the following section of this rite. You will allow the initiate the experience of entering her unknown future, and being born again into her own empowerment. The initiate has been instructed to expect surprises and to surrender to the process of her initiation.

The initiate will choose two directions—one for her gateway to her new future, and one for the home of her new path. In the gateway quarter, you will guide the initiate, blindfolded, to step over the broom. Stepping over the broom is a symbol of beginning on the path of the initiate, of crossing the threshold into a new phase of life.

During the Mirror Ceremony later in the ritual, all witnesses will have an opportunity to speak to their experience of the initiate's unfolding over the course of her initiation. It is not necessary for witnesses to write a testimony or statement in advance, but you may do so if you prefer having something prepared. Otherwise, each witness can just speak from his or her heart. Each should speak to their experience of the initiate's recent growth as she stands before the mirror, in addition to witnessing her vows of initiation.

What the Witness(es) Will Need

- A blindfold for the initiate. This doesn't need to be fancy, just functional. You can use a sleeping/relaxation mask (available for a few bucks at most drugstores and superstores, and at some beauty-supply boutiques), a strip of cloth, a bandana, or a silk scarf. Try the blindfold on yourself to make sure it will block sight.

- You will need to know the directions (north, east, south, and west) in the space where the ritual will be held.

- Ideally, a Witches' besom (broom), but the plain old kitchen variety of broom works, too. (The broom, when held parallel to the floor, becomes a symbol of the threshold. As practitioners step over the broom, they step through the doorway into their new lives. It also represents a "clean sweep," and new beginnings.) If you want to get really fancy, you can gift your loved one (the initiate) with a Witches' broom that's a real keeper. You may want to decorate a sweet little broom with herbs, dried flowers, and ribbon. This could become a treasured keepsake for the initiate that will remind her of this day for years to come.

- A full-length mirror that is freestanding or can be leaned against a wall. This mirror should be set up before the ritual, and covered with an opaque cloth so the initiate doesn't expect to confront it.

How-To

- Read through this outline in advance, and make a copy for each of you to have on hand during the section of the ritual you will be performing.

- Find out what directions the initiate has chosen for her path to take, and as her home. Place the broom in the path direction, and the mirror in the home direction, in advance of the ritual, according to the initiate's desired directions.

- The initiate will have given one of her witnesses some items: her vows, empowerment contract, initiation talisman, and devotion oil. These items should all be placed near the mirror. One of her talismans—a string of beads—will be created in the flow of the ritual. This should be placed with the other items listed here.

Preparation for Trust Walk and Mirror Ceremony

After the initiate performs her consecration of artifacts and altar, instruct her to sit in silence, close her eyes, and focus on the work she has done. One witness says:

> *Close your eyes, and allow yourself to remember all the wonderful, challenging, amazing, fun, revelatory work you have done in the past weeks. Feel who you are now, and how you have changed. Recall the moments of challenge, and the moments of insight. Let the new ways that you have found settle into your body, and make room for further growth. Allow yourself to look into the future, and notice how these changes will keep rippling through your life as you walk upon your path, more clear now than it has ever been, even as it is still shrouded in the mystery of the unknown.*

As one witness speaks, another witness blindfolds the initiate. The initiate has *not* been told this will happen, but has been told to expect some surprises and to trust in the process.

Trust Walk, Leap of Faith

Note: This section and the next are good ones for the initiate to perform naked. If she is comfortable with this, please ask her to disrobe while still blindfolded.

Two witnesses walk up to the initiate, and ask the direction she has chosen for her path to take. (Remember, the witnesses will need to know where the north, east, south, and west are in the space the ritual is being held in, and should already know what the initiate's answer will be. Place the broom and mirror in advance. Still ask the question in ritual space, and allow the initiate to answer.)

Walk the initiate to the direction, still blindfolded. At the appropriate "gate" (direction), both witnesses kneel down and hold the broom, symbolizing the threshold, and instruct the initiate to step, alone and blindfolded, into the unknown. Guide her if need be, but allow her step over the threshold unaided, if possible.

Goddess in the Mirror

Next, the witnesses guide the initiate to the mirror, and before removing her blindfold, they remove the mirror's cover. One witness removes the initiate's blindfold. Once the blindfold has been removed, instruct the initiate to behold herself in the mirror. One witness says:

Behold, the initiate. This woman has worked to claim her voice, has cried tears of purification and gratitude, has laughed, and has learned to love herself in all her imperfect perfection. She has chosen her path, and that path has lead her home to her own being.

As the initiate looks in the mirror, another witness (preferably the one *most* intimate with the initiate) anoints the initiate. Use the devotion oil for all the anointings if the initiate is unclothed. If she is clothed, use water on all the parts clothed, using the oil only on the unclothed parts.

Anointing

1. Wet finger and anoint the feet. Say:

   Blessed are your feet, which walk the Sacred Path.

2. Wet finger and anoint the knees. Say:

   Blessed are your knees, which touch the earth in humility and gratitude.

3. Wet finger and anoint the pubis, or the genitals if you are intimate enough with the initiate. Say:

   Blessed is your sex, which brings the gifts of pleasure and creation.

4. Wet finger and anoint the womb. Say:

   Blessed is your womb, the seat of life.

5. Wet finger and anoint the solar plexus (stomach region). Say:

   Blessed are your power and presence.

6. Wet finger and anoint the heart chakra (sternum). Say:

   Blessed is your heart, which loves with strength and beauty.

7. Wet finger and anoint the throat. Say:

   Blessed is your voice, which says what must be heard.

8. Wet finger and anoint the lips. Say:

Blessed are your lips, which speak the words of power.

9. Wet finger and anoint the third eye (center of forehead, just above the brow line). Say:

    Blessed be your vision, which sees the way things are, and the way things may become.

10. Wet finger and anoint the crown (top of the head). Say:

    Blessed be your crown, where you and all of creation are one.

11. Step back and say:

    Blessed are you, and blessed is your presence on the earth. Blessed is your body, your soul, and your spirit. Blessed is the world that you create, and blessed is your path in that world.

Vows

A witness hands the initiate her vows. Then, all witnesses flank the mirror. A witness says:

Do you have vows?

The initiate responds in the affirmative.

The witness says:

We are here to witness these vows, but these are vows you make to yourself. As you take these vows, look into the mirror and commit your vows to the person you are becoming.

The initiate reads her vows, looking at herself in the mirror.

Empowerment Contract

Once the initiate finishes reading her vows, the witness holding her empowerment contract hands the initiate her contract and a pen (which should be retrieved from the altar). The initiate signs her empowerment contract.

Talisman(s) of Initiation

Once the initiate finishes signing her contract, the witness holding her talisman(s) hands it/them to the initiate, and instructs her to put it/them on.

Honoring of Initiate

As the initiate continues facing the mirror, the witnesses honor her with blessings, compliments, and gratitude for her work, her growth, and her self-commitment. The initiate may look at the witnesses as they speak, but her attention should primarily be on watching herself be adored by those she loves and respects. Before beginning the honoring, a witness should say:

> *Allow us to honor you. As we speak, watch the image in the mirror. You are a woman worthy of worship, and we are here to worship you. We are here to honor your growth, your commitment to your growth, and your beautiful unfolding.*

Once the witnesses are done with the Honoring, a witness offers the initiate the chalice of wine, with this blessing:

> *To know, to will, to dare, to be silent.*

Another witness offers cake/cookie/scrumptious morsel, and says:

> *Blessed is the fruit of thy womb.*

Blessing of Treats, Water, and Wine

The witnesses should ask the initiate in advance of the ritual if she would like to bless the food, water, and wine. (If she doesn't, one of the witnesses will.) This section may be conducted in silence or near silence, aside from the blessing, or you may continue to honor the initiate as you eat and drink. The initiate may also be prompted to share some of her experiences after the blessing, while all participants eat and drink. A witness or the initiate says:

> *This food is not just a symbol of, but the true substance of, nurturance, and of the cycles of life. May the sacrifice of this that I am about to ingest feed my body, my spirit, and my soul. May I always experience, receive, and honor my hungers. May all true hungers be fulfilled.*

Water is life. Life, and regeneration, and healing. Let this water remind me of my origins; of the womb, and of the blessed sea, the birthplace of life and that which forms the flow.

This wine is the blood of willing sacrifice. It represents the cycles of life, death, and birth. It offers succor, and a doorway to new perception. May this wine bless me with the awareness of choice, and with divine vision and ecstasy.

Take time to honor your body with treats, water, and wine. As you eat and drink, sit in awareness of the magick of transmutation: how the food, water, and wine affect your senses, and how these edible items become part of the very fabric of your cells. Allow gratitude, honor, and acceptance of and for the elements you are bringing into your body.

Ending of Ritual

Again, this section may be performed by the initiate, or by one of the witnesses. Find out the initiate's preference in advance of the ritual. Say:

Mine is the temple. As I walk through the world, I know that my body is a sacred vessel. It is consecrated to me, and to my unfolding and empowerment. As I learn to love and honor my body as the beautiful temple, wondrous tool, and amazing vehicle for transformation that it is, I become closer to the divine gift of creation.

Now, as I breathe again, inhaling the sacred scents, I prepare to walk forward into the world. I carry sacred space everywhere I go, and all I need is to remember: My body is sacred. My breath is sacred. My bones and blood and sweat and tears are sacred. My laughter is sacred, my voice is sacred, and my skin is sacred. I claim this mantra: this temple is mine.

Turn your focus inward, close your eyes, breathe, and relax. Allow yourself to slowly come back to the world you inhabit, the room you are sitting in, and your daily life. As you open your eyes, give yourself a hug, remembering that even as you reenter the world, your body remains a sacred temple of creation and empowerment.

- Releasing of quarters and entities (optional).
- Opening of circle (optional).
- Banishing (optional).

RITUALS II

Rituals for Circles of Sexy Witches

Building Ritual, in Theory

If you have been working with your group of Witches for a while, you may already have an established way that you perform ritual. If you have a form of banishing, casting, invocation, or other ways of creating sacred space that work for you, I encourage you to integrate those aspects into the ritual outlines in this section.

Ritual, ceremony, and magick are about consciousness. Our relationship with magickal consciousness can be highly intuitive. However, there are also strengths to formal practice as well. It is my desire to give you as many options as possible in this section so that you can find, build, or create the ritual format that works the best for you. It's your magick—modify at Will!

I have purposefully left the basic ritual outlines very minimal. From a minimalist Mindful Magick or Conscious Intuitive Magick perspective, the rituals work as they are presented. If you want to add more structure, you may. I have included many elements of ritual performance that can be added to the basic ritual outlines. If working with a more traditional approach is most effective for you, stick with it.

Building Ritual, Sexy-Witch Style

In this section I offer the tools to create rituals that are tailor-fit to the needs of your group. I have included a description of Mindful/Conscious Intuitive Magick, a modified Lesser Banishing Ritual, some information on Wiccan circle casting, a few examples of ways to call the quarters, and then the more barebones, chapter-by-chapter ritual outlines.

There are opportunities built into the flow of each ritual to read from journal entries and to consecrate artifacts created while working the chapters. All participants may want to read the ritual section before gathering, as the ritual will flow more smoothly if everyone has an idea of what to expect.

Sharing Leadership

Depending on the needs and desires of your group, you may wish to rotate facilitation (the role of Priestess) for the weekly rituals. I suggest that you discuss as a group what would be the most comfortable way for you to proceed. If you are going to rotate, you may wish to host at different homes, or if one of you has a fabulous, spacious, comfortable home, perhaps you can use the same location, and just rotate the responsibility for facilitating and preparing for the rituals.

Some advantages of rotating facilitation include building leadership skills, sharing power and responsibility, and giving everyone the experience of shouldering the work. With effective sharing of responsibility, everyone will get a chance to both support and be supported. Everyone in the group who wants to have the experience of Priestessing will have it, and everyone will also have a chance to be guided; to totally give herself over to the experience of the ritual rather than having to focus on the flow so much.

One thing to keep in mind is that one of the responsibilities of any Priestess is to learn how to delegate. The Priestess has a lot to get together for rituals. As Priestess for the rite, it is not only all right but a really good idea to ask your circle mates to bring some items that are on the list for the ritual. There are also other ways in which all the circle mates can be involved with the circle as it is built. We will go into this in more detail later.

Sexy Witch Saturdays?

Try to allow enough time on your ritual days to really get into the material a bit. Sharing your experiences, talking about the work you have done, and sharing insights you have found and struggles you have overcome will reinforce the work. Of course, it doesn't need to be Saturday; it can be whatever day works best for your group.

You may want to plan a meal together before the ritual, and use that shared time to process through your experiences. Aside from reinforcing your personal grasp on the work you have done, this will reinforce the group dynamic and allow your group to become closer and stronger through shared experience. And, it may be the best day of your week—a whole chunk of time with your circle sisters, eating and chatting, and sharing your souls with each other. What could be more fun, enriching, and fulfilling?

Ideally, you will fit in time for whatever discussion of the chapter your group wants to do *before* the ritual. The idea is that each ritual will be an initiation, which is both an ending of one phase and a beginning of another. Give yourself and your circle mates the time to delve in and experience these transformations.

Doors of Perception

These weekly initiations, of which there will be seven—like the veils of Salome, or the gates that Inanna faced on her journey into the Underworld—are designed to be doorways between the chapters. You will move through the material in the chapters, find your depth, and then move ever deeper, toward the very core of your self. Each ritual will be a doorway that demarcates the transition from one chapter to the next, and also demarcates the spiraling journey in toward your center. It will be the pause between breaths, the transition point, the recognition and the act of transformation.

Tools: To Have, or Not to Have . . . That Is the Question

I have never felt a strong need for many magickal tools, though I have made some of my own, had some made, and been gifted with a few over the years. I have consecrated them and kept them on my altars. But I truly feel that anything that a wand can do in magickal space, a finger or hand can do as well. It's not the tool, it's how you use it!

I have my own superstitions about investing items with power, and feel most resourceful when my power is contained securely within my body. That is not to say that working with a wand doesn't make working certain magick easier for some Witches. If you have tools that make you feel strong, by all means, use them! Again, I am just reminding you of many possible options. It's your magick—own it!

Ritual Garb

I have more often than not been the Witch in street clothes. Or the Witch in a cocktail gown. Or the Witch in her birthday suit, if it's warm enough out. I almost never feel the need, and rarely have the desire, to dress in Renaissance-era garb for ritual, or wear a toga or a chitan, or a big, fancy cloak (unless it's performance ritual theatre, and costuming is required).

Yes, you wanna feel good. So, what does a Witch wear to perform ritual? Whatever she damn well pleases! You can wear your best dress or your nicest lingerie, or you can wear your pajamas if it's been that kind of week. The clothes *do not* make the Witch. Dress in whatever way makes you feel good. If that happens to be a ritual gown or cloak, more power to you. If it's not, more power to you as well. If there is certain dress that may assist you in any of the following rituals, it will be mentioned in that ritual's outline.

What to Bring to Circle

The following lists include items you will need for every ritual. The first list is for all participants, and the second list is for the Priestess. In the outline for each week's ritual, you will find an additional list that is specific to each ritual. Please make sure you have all items from this list *and* from the week's more specific list.

Also, where this Priestess' list says, "Priestess should bring . . .," it really means, "Priestess should make sure that someone is bringing . . ." Don't forget to offer the Priestess of the week a hand. You'll want help when it's your turn, too!

Participants' List

1. An individual candle. Tea lights or smaller votive candles are a good bet, and are available in most supermarkets. As the first one burns down, just replace it with another. You may dress these candles, if you'd like. (For dressing instructions, see appendix I.) Also, if your group decides to invite other witnesses to the seventh initiation, you may want to provide personal candles for your witnesses. (See the section "A Few Final Words Before Diving In" later in this chapter, and Ritual Seven in part 2, for more details about witnesses and their roles in your final initiation.)

2. Candle holder for tea light or smaller votive (be conscious in choosing your color). Each circle member will probably want to choose and purchase her own.

3. Each practitioner should bring her copy of *Sexy Witch* if she writes in the margins or needs to have the ritual outline at hand.

4. Each practitioner should bring her journal.

5. Each practitioner should bring any works of art or writings created while working the chapters that she wants to consecrate and share with her circle mates. One of these may become her weekly additional altarpiece for her personal self-love altar.

6. Each practitioner should bring a small pouch to put beads in.

Priestess' List

1. The altar—an altar space integrating all the ritual items. The altar should be pleasing to the senses, have a nice altar cloth (choose the color well), and have space for the artifacts that you and your circle mates will place on the it for sharing and consecration. The altar can be on the floor, or on a table.

2. A "source" or "mother" candle (this item should rotate with facilitation of the ritual). The source candle is a seven-day jar votive. This candle will be lit during every ritual, and extinguished afterward. Jar candles can be purchased in most supermarkets, in mercados mexicanos (Mexican markets), botanicas, and some carnecerias. Some of these jar votives will have the Catholic Saints, Jesus, or Mary on them, but you will also be able to find some without any decoration. Choose your color with intention. For group work, white may be the best, but if the group agrees, any color may be right. And, if your group has an affinity for *the* Mary (see appendix II), feel free to choose the Mary candle. You may dress this candle, if you'd like. (For dressing instructions, see appendix I.)

3. The Priestess should bring a basket, bowl, or other container with a bead for each participant (including herself). The weekly outlines will state what each week's bead should represent.

4. A censer for the incense.

5. Charcoal for the incense.

6. Incense (see appendix I).

7. A chalice for water.

8. A chalice for wine, if desired.

9. Wine, if desired (see appendix I).

10. Water.

11. Cookies, bread, or other edibles (see ritual outlines for details).

12. A box of tissue in case of tears.

13. The Priestess and other participants should bring any specific items mentioned in ritual outlines.

14. Don't forget things like matches or a lighter, a corkscrew (if needed), water, and a glass. Long matches (BBQ style) will be needed to light personal candles

from the source candle. (How-to: Each person lights a long match from the source candle, and then lights her personal candle from the match.)

15. Make sure there is enough comfy space for participants to sit in around the altar.

16. The Priestess should make sure that everyone can tolerate scents and smoke in an enclosed space. Incense can be intense, and can alter your senses in a good way, as long as it's not triggering an asthma attack or allergies.

All participants should always read the ritual outlines in advance of rituals so that everyone has all the necessary items on hand when it comes time to perform the ritual, and has an idea of the flow of the ritual. EXCEPTION: The outline for Ritual Seven should be read in full only by the Priestesses, of which there will be two instead of one for the final *Sexy Witch* initiation. Other practitioners should read only the section titled "What All Participants Will Need."

A Few Final Words Before Diving In

In working *Sexy Witch* with a posse, you will have choices to make as a group. One of those is about sharing leadership. Another may be regarding how much time you want to dedicate to your group work over the next seven weeks. Another will be how many aspects or layers of ritual you want to use in your group ritual format. You may, or may not, want to invite witnesses who are not part of the group for the seventh initiation.

In creating community in general, there can be conflict. This is also part of the work. I encourage you all to explore the extent to which you are able to make space in your life for the group-work aspect, and to create ritual outlines and shared duties accordingly.

In the ritual outlines, there are words to recite. Of course, as always, the words I have written down are optional. You can use mine, or you can make up your own if you'd like. You can make them rhyme, or not (I have not).

The words I have written are not based on a secret formula. The magick that will be done in these rituals of initiation is you and your group getting together and working ritual, and doing so with intention, focus, and growing skill. The magick is a circle of women, sharing sacred space, growth, and transformation.

There are certain benefits to using a standardized set of words, as ritual may flow more smoothly if everyone can expect basically the same outline from week to week. If you decide that you want to create your own words in place of mine, you may want to do so as a group, and adhere to a standard outline created by your group. On the other hand, some people really enjoy the free flow of improvised ritual. It's *your* magick. Make it work for you!

Mindful Magick

In my magick working, I often take a minimalist approach to ritual. It's what currently works for me. I call it Mindful Magick, Mindfulness Magick, or Conscious Intuitive Magick. I do a lot of focusing inward, breathing, centering, sensing, and being.

Some of the concepts that I'm working with in creating ritual space at this time include recognizing space as sacred, rather than creating a space that is sacred. I focus on my body as a sacred space, and center in that. I focus on the world around me as a sacred space, and honor that. I encourage you to work with these concepts as well.

Use the outlines I have provided, but follow your intuition. Do what feels right. It's your magick. Create it. Shape it. Ride it. Follow it.

A Witch's Banishing Ritual, Modified from the Ceremonial Lesser Banishing Ritual of the Pentagram

The Lesser Banishing is a simple and profoundly effective way to clear ritual space, cast the circle, and call on the guardians of the gates in one fell swoop. It is a beautiful piece of ritual when executed well, and can be modified to encompass your group's orientation.

This modification of the Lesser Banishing Ritual of the Pentagram was created by myself and assorted ritual partners over the years. Throughout the instructions I will give you options that will allow you to modify it even further yourself, and ideally to make it your own.

1. The Priestess chosen to lead the ritual enters the circle.
2. The other participants follow in a clockwise flow, creating a loose circle around the Priestess.
3. The Tree of Life, performed at the center of the circle.
   a. The Priestess points the index and middle fingers of her right hand, folding the other fingers.

b. Touching her forehead with the extended fingers, she says:

    I am I,

c. Pointing to the sky, she says:

    in harmony with the heavens,

d. Pointing to the ground, she says:

    with the earth,

e. Touching her right shoulder, she says:

    with the sun,

f. Circling to her left shoulder, she says:

    and with the moon,

g. Bringing her hands to the prayer position, she says:

    forever and ever.

h. Placing her left hand, palm down, on top of her right hand, palm up, she says:

    So it is.

i. All participants say:

    So it is.

4. The banishing.

   For the banishing, you can use whatever words make you feel that the guardian, entity, energy, or intention of a direction has been brought present. This can be done by assigning a Goddess to each quarter (e.g., Aurora in the east, Pele in the south, Oshun in the west, and Kali in the north); or by saying the name of the direction, or an idea that the direction represents (e.g., inspiration in the east, passion in the south, regeneration in the west, wisdom in the north); or you can use any of the words that have been used by any of the Ceremonial magickians. There are many, and you can easily find them by doing a web search on the Lesser Banishing Ritual of the Pentagram.

a. The Priestess walks to the eastern edge of the circle and draws a pentagram in the air with her finger or her wand. In drawing the pentagram, start at the left lower point, and draw upward to the apex on the pentagram. This is the basic earth-invoking pentagram, but can be used at all quarters.

b. Starting with her arms at her sides, the Priestess slowly raises them, focusing intently on the pentagram she has drawn in front of her, and the word she will use to invoke the direction.

c. Once her arms are pointing out from her shoulders, parallel to the ground, the Priestess brings her hands to the sides of her face, palms facing back.

d. Next, she steps forward with her right foot, and while forcefully thrusting the energy with her hands towards the direction she is facing, she says the word out loud.

e. She will then step forward with her left foot meeting the right, and bring the index and middle fingers of her right hand to her lips in the sign of "shh…" (This is the sign of the initiate. For more information on the significance of this sign, do your research.)

f. Next, the Priestess will go to the south, and do the same, using whatever word she has chosen for the south.

g. The same in the west.

h. And in the north.

i. And she completes the circle at the east.

5. The center.

a. Again the Priestess stands in the center of the circle, facing east. She stands with her arms outstretched at her sides, parallel to the ground.

b. All participants face east and stand the same way.

c. All say:

Before me the rushing wind, behind me the raging sea, to my right hand the leaping fire, and to my left hand the cool and trembling earth. For about me is the omnipresence of her body, and within me is the consciousness of the continuity of existence.

6. The Tree.

    a. The Priestess performs the Tree again, as in step 3.

7. The Priestess joins the circle. All participants face the center, and sit or stand.

Sort of Wiccan Circle Casting and Opening

Depending on your orientation, you may perform only this circle casting, and then move on to the rituals as I have written them for this book. Or, you may perform the circle casting and the calling of the quarters (see the next section), and then the ritual. Or, you may perform the banishing just described, then this circle casting, and the calling the quarters (and deities, if you'd like), and then the ritual.

You may also choose to do none of the above, and use just the simple format of the rituals written here. Remember, it's your magick! Perform it as you Will.

Many Witches use the *Rule of Three* as a basis for ritual and magick. The circle casting for most Witches relies on a three-time circumambulation. To cast a circle in the Wiccan, Dianic, Faerie, and many other traditions, you walk the perimeter of the circle three times clockwise to cast the circle, and three times counterclockwise to open it. Depending on the tradition, you will have different assignations for the three times around.

To cast a circle is to create a bubble, or sphere, of sacred space. Many practitioners use an *athame* to cast and dissolve the circle. With a blade (or a hand, used with intention), it becomes the "cutting" of a circle. You are cutting yourself out of the mundane world, and into a space that is amplified, protected, and sanctified.

Casting and opening a circle, as with any magickal act, must be done with intention as well as the actual function of movement. As you cast—and then open—the circle, visualize these

★ ——————————

The Basics: To cast the circle, walk clockwise, also known as sun-wise, or *deosil.* To open (remove, dissolve) the circle, walk counterclockwise, otherwise known as *widdershins.* In many traditions, clockwise is the direction of building, and counterclockwise is the direction of dissolution.

—————————— ★

things occurring. As you cast, envision the circle becoming a protective sphere. As you open, envision the sphere of sacred space dissolving into nothing.

The Basics: The calling of the quarters and deities or energy forms can be done in many different ways. Many traditions have their own script for callings. Another way to do it is just to focus on the representations that the entities hold for you, the practitioner. If you want some correspondences for the quarters, see "Correspondences: Quarters, Elements, Directions, and Other Entities" in appendix I.

You may choose to invoke Maiden with the first circle, Mother with the second, and Crone with the third. Or you can just "cast the circle, three times round . . ." You may do this as you voice an incantation (which you can write yourself, or find on web sites or in any number of books), or you can do the casting and opening in silence. Whichever route you take, employ the energy of visualization in the casting and opening. You can lend your energy to the casting and opening without even saying a word.

Calling (aka Invoking) the Quarters and Spiritual Entities

The calling of the quarters is a widespread Wiccan and Neopagan practice. It is also employed in the Ceremonial, Faerie, and many other traditions. Calling the quarters is asking the elements (or "guardians of the watchtowers") to be present in your working. Calling the quarters is performed as an aspect of the banishing, but if you choose to not perform the banishing, calling the quarters may be done in concert with circle casting.

A really nice aspect of calling the quarters is that you can employ more people in the function of creating sacred space. You may have four people call the four quarters (air, fire, water, and earth), or five (the four already listed, plus center), or seven (the five already listed, plus above and below). You can also invoke Goddess, and God, if you desire. You may also invoke the ancestors.

With all callings, it is traditional to close with a statement such as, "So it is," or "So mote it be," or "Fire (or Earth, or She, or He) is here." It is also traditional for the other participants to respond, with the same words, to the statement.

Working in this more intuitive manner, callings might go something like this:

For East

Priestess:

> *Spirits of air, I call upon you to bring clarity, inspiration, and ease of communication to this circle. I call the spirits of dawn, new ideas, and freedom of thought. Please be present here, and bring your blessings to this circle. So it is.*

Group response:

> *So it is.*

For South

Priestess:

> *Spirits of fire, I call upon you to bring passion, warmth, and transformation. I call upon fire to warm and transform this sacred space. Bring your heat, desire, and light. Burn bright in this circle. So it is.*

Group response:

> *So it is.*

And so on, through the other quarters and whatever energies/entities you choose to call.

The quarters are called in a clockwise progression, starting in many traditions with east/air, or with north/earth in some others. Starting from east, the progression would be east, south, west, north. Then, if you choose, you may call center, or the ancestors. Then Goddess, then God. Or, you may call east, south, west, north, Goddess, God, and then the ancestors. Again, intuition is key. Do what feels right to you and your group.

Releasing the Quarters and Spiritual Entities

At the end of the ritual, the entities and quarters that have been called will be released. Releasing goes in the opposite order as calling, starting with the last entity or quarter called and working back to the first. Releasing can be very simple, such as, "Spirits of earth, thank you for your presence, and your blessings on this circle."

Or, you can get as flowery as you'd like. In the tradition I grew up in, we would end the releasing with the statement "Go if you must, stay if you will." You can use whatever wording feels right.

Here are some concepts to work with when releasing:

- Expressing gratitude to the entities who attend.

- Granting them permission to move on if they must.

- Recognizing that they are ever present, and that it is our attention that leaves them.

The Most Obnoxiously Option-Oriented Ritual Outline You Have Ever Seen!

If you choose to take all of the steps offered so far, here's how the ritual will look:

1. The Priestess chosen to lead the ritual performs the banishing.

2. The Priestess casts the circle by circumambulating three times clockwise.

3. Call the quarters.

    a. One circle mate calls air.

    b. One calls fire.

    c. One calls water.

    d. One calls earth.

    e. One calls center.

    f. One calls Goddess.

    g. One calls God.

4. Next, the group moves on, with the Priestess leading, to the ritual outline for the week.

    a. Setting space (breathing, lighting of source candle).

    b. Consecration of altar (placing devotional items) and lighting of candles.

    c. Sharing of writing and art.

    d. Honoring with treats, water, and wine (communion).

    e. Ending of ritual.

5. Opening the circle.

    At the end of the circle, each participant "undoes" what she did at the beginning. Everything must be undone in the opposite order of how it was done—last to first. It's like you are walking back out into the world, and you want to retrace your steps. Starting with the last invocation, each participant releases each deity, guardian, or entity that she called. The releasing will move around the circle counterclockwise. If working with all seven quarters listed, that would look like this:

6. Releasing the quarters.

    a. Release God energy.

    b. Release Goddess energy.

    c. Release center.

    d. Release earth.

    e. Release water.

    f. Release fire.

    g. Release air.

7. The Priestess opens the circle by circumambulating counterclockwise three times.

8. The Priestess performs the banishing counterclockwise.

Remember, you can use as many or as few of these elements as you'd like. If you choose to use only the weekly outlines as they are presented, the following is the basic outline, though there will be some variations from week to week:

a. Setting space (breathing, lighting of source candle).

b. Sharing of writing and art.

c. Consecration of writing and art.

d. Bead consecration.

e. Honoring with treats, water, and wine (communion).

f. Ending of ritual.

Your Body Is a Temple

★ Suggestions:

1. Bring items to share and consecrate. This week, consider bringing your temple artifact (see "Magickal Act: Visiting the Temple" in chapter 1). One (or more) of the items you consecrate may also be added to your personal altar if you choose to expand it.

2. Your journal. Choose one piece (or more) of writing from this week that you will share with the group.

3. Consider wearing something that makes you feel beautiful, sexy, hot, really comfy, or all of these.

What the Facilitator/Priestess Will Need

- Beads for all the participants. This week's bead should represent the body as temple, or the concept of sacred space.

- A platter of luscious morsels to eat. I recommend dates, figs, and other rich, sweet, dried fruits, as well as chocolate, cherries, and honey.
- Sweet red wine (like Muscat). See "Wines" in appendix I.
- DON'T FORGET: Make sure everyone in your group can tolerate scents and smoke. Incense can be intense, and can alter your senses in a good way, as long as it's not triggering an asthma attack or allergies.

How-To

Before everyone gathers around the altar, the Priestess will:

- Create the altar with the items listed here and on the main altar list on page 205. The altar should be pleasing to the senses, and functional. The Priestess should place everything she will need near where she will be seated.
- Make sure the charcoal is lit. It takes a few minutes for the charcoal to be ready for the incense.
- Have everyone change into, or strip down to, their fun/sexy/comfy attire.
- Have everyone gather their items (personal candles/holders, journals, copy of *Sexy Witch*, bead pouch, works of art, comfort items) to bring to circle.
- Choose a person to bless the treats/water/wine, or the Priestess can do this.
- Describe the flow (outline) of the ritual so the participants will know what to prepare for (although ideally, everyone will have already read it).

Outline

- Banishing (optional).
- Circle casting (optional).
- Calling of quarters and spirit entities (optional).
- Setting space.

Once the attendees gather, the Priestess sprinkles a pinch of incense on the charcoal. She instructs everyone to focus on breathing, deeply into their bellies. The Priestess says:

Breathe deeply, allowing your breath to expand your chest, and then even more deeply, letting it expand your belly, your lower abdomen.

As everyone breathes together, the Priestess may want to walk around the space once, thinking of the qualities that this blend of resins will bring to the space: love, purification, safety, healing, and connection with spirit. Then she sits with the other participants in a circle. Breathe together as a group for a few minutes, letting the scent of the incense permeate your bodies, inside and out, allowing your cells to absorb the positive qualities of the incense. The Priestess says:

> *Allow the smoke of this special blend of incense to enter your body and infuse each cell with blessing. Let this magickal and sacred blend of scents fill you with love, purification, safety, healing, and connection with spirit. As you breathe, allow your body to become the sacred temple where you worship.*

Once everyone is fully present in their bodies, the Priestess instructs everyone to open their eyes, and come present in the space. As a group, you may want to take a moment and hold hands, feeling the shared energy you have already created by centering here in this sacred space. All participants may say together:

> *We are in sacred space.*

The Priestess lights the mother candle so that everyone will be able to light their individual candles from the source. As she lights the mother candle, the Priestess says:

> *Lighting this flame, I invoke the sacredness of the body. I invoke the awareness that our bodies are sacred temples that we consecrate to the purpose of our own growth, experience, and empowerment. I invoke not only self-acceptance but self-devotion.*

As each participant lights her personal flame, you will all drop deeper into that space where you know your body as a sacred, wonderful temple. A space sacred and powerful. A space where you know the truth of your own being. You will find that space inside where you have achieved true self-devotion, where you know that each act of self-love, self-adoration, and self-definition is a sacred act. The place where you alone define the boundaries of your temple: the sacred temple that is each of us.

Each participant may state a prayer, a wish, or an intention as she lights her candle.

Lighting of Personal Candles

Each person in the group now approaches the altar and lights her candle from the source candle. The Priestess says:

One by one, as you feel moved, approach the altar and light your candle, and place it at the perimeter of the altar cloth. With this light we create a sacred circle that allows honor and devotion to grow, and we become a beacon in the darkness that allows each seeker to find her own way home.

Sharing of Writing and Art

Once the candles are lighted, it is time to start sharing the items created during the week. Ideally, each participant (including the Priestess) will share one piece of artwork and one piece of writing (or more, if you have made that agreement as a group) in ritual space. The Priestess says:

Now is the time to share the works you created this week. Reading your writing out loud in ritual space and talking about your artifacts, with all of us as witnesses, adds to their power. Who would like to start?

You all may choose to conduct this sharing in a clockwise (deosil) flow, though only if it feels necessary to your group.

Consecration of Writing and Art

Once everyone has had a chance to share, it's time for the consecration. Each participant will lay whatever items she wants to consecrate out in front of herself, or around the altar. All together, say:

I consecrate these works to the unfolding of self-awareness. May this act serve me, and may it serve all beings through the revelation of awareness. May my increasing aware-ness and presence serve to bring awareness of presence to all beings everywhere throughout space and time. So it is.

Take time to witness, honor, and cherish each item being consecrated. The participants may want to pass the items through the smoke from the incense, or do some other act of purification and consecration.

In adding to your personal/home altar, you will use one or more of the items you have consecrated. What item(s) from this week's exploration would like to live on your altar for the duration of your initiation cycle?

Consecration of Beads

After each participant has shared with the group, she will take a bead from the basket and consecrate it. All together, say:

> *I consecrate this bead in the journey of self-love. May this bead serve as a reminder to me that my body is a sacred space.*

Each participant places her bead in her bead pouch.

Blessing the Treats, Water, and Wine

Bless the food, water, and wine. All together, say:

> *This food is not just a symbol of, but the true substance of, nurturance, and of the cycles of life. May the sacrifice of this that I am about to ingest feed my body, my spirit, and my soul. May I always experience, receive, and honor my hungers. May all true hungers be fulfilled.*
>
> *Water is life. Life, and regeneration, and healing. Let this water remind me of my origins; of the womb, and of the blessed sea, the birthplace of life and that which forms the flow.*
>
> *This wine is the blood of willing sacrifice. It represents the cycles of life, death, and birth. It offers succor, and a doorway to new perception. May this wine bless me with the awareness of choice, and with divine vision and ecstasy.*

As a group, take time to honor your bodies with treats, water, and wine. As you eat and drink, sit in awareness of the magick of transmutation: how the food, water, and wine affect your senses, and how these edible items become part of the very fabric of your cells. Allow gratitude, honor, and acceptance of and for the elements you are bringing into your bodies.

Honoring with Treats, Water, and Wine

Each person will take a turn feeding and honoring another. Pair up, and feed your partner, in a gentle and sensuous way. The one who is being honored must state exactly how she wants to be honored. With words? With touch? With which foods? Once one partner has fed and honored the other, switch roles. The honored one becomes the honoring one, and vice versa.

The water chalice is passed from person to person with the blessing "Water shared is life shared." The wine chalice is passed with the blessing "Wine offered is choice given and received." Food is passed with the blessing "May all true hungers be fulfilled."

Ending of Ritual

All participants sit in circle once again and breathe. The Priestess says:

> *Yours is the temple. As you walk through the world, know that your body is a sacred vessel. It is consecrated to you, and to your unfolding and empowerment. As we learn to love and honor our bodies as the beautiful temples, wondrous tools, and amazing vehicles for transformation that they are, we grow closer to the divine gift of creation.*

Now, as each of you breathe again, inhaling the sacred scents, you prepare to walk forward into the world. You carry sacred space everywhere you go, and all you need is to remember: your body is sacred. Your breath is sacred. Your bones and blood and sweat and tears are sacred. Your laughter is sacred, your voice is sacred, and your skin is sacred. All together, state aloud and claim this mantra:

> *This temple is mine.*

Turn your focus inward, close your eyes, breathe, and relax. Allow yourself to slowly come back to the world you inhabit, the room you are sitting in, and your daily life. As you open your eyes, give yourself a hug, remembering that even as you reenter the world, your body remains a sacred temple of creation and empowerment.

- Releasing of quarters and entities (optional).
- Opening of circle (optional).
- Banishing (optional).

RITUAL TWO

I Love Me!

★ Suggestion: This week, consider consecrating the t-shirt you made, and an additional item to add to your home altar (see "Magickal Act: D.I.Y. Fashion Statement" in chapter 2).

What the Facilitator/Priestess Will Need

- Beads for all the participants. This week's bead should represent body pride, or the concept of self-definition.
- A platter of treats to eat.
- Wine, if desired. See "Wines" in appendix I.
- DON'T FORGET: Make sure everyone in your group can tolerate scents and smoke. Incense can be intense, and can alter your senses in a good way, as long as it's not triggering an asthma attack or allergies.

How-To

Before everyone gathers around the altar, the Priestess will:

- Create the altar with the items listed here and on the main altar list on page 205. The altar should be pleasing to the senses, and functional. The Priestess should place everything she will need near where she will be seated.
- Make sure the charcoal is lit. It takes a few minutes for the charcoal to be ready for the incense.
- Have everyone change into, or strip down to, their fun/sexy/comfy attire.
- Have everyone gather their items (personal candles/holders, journals, copy of *Sexy Witch*, bead pouch, works of art, comfort items) to bring to circle.
- Choose a person to bless the treats/water/wine, or the Priestess can do this.
- Describe the flow (outline) of the ritual so the participants will know what to prepare for (although ideally, everyone will have already read it).

Outline

- Banishing (optional).
- Circle casting (optional).
- Calling of quarters and spirit entities (optional).
- Setting space.

Once the attendees gather, the Priestess sprinkles a pinch of incense on the charcoal. She instructs everyone to focus on breathing, deeply into their bellies. The Priestess says:

> Breathe deeply, allowing your breath to expand your chest, and then even more deeply, letting it expand your belly, your lower abdomen.

As everyone breathes together, the Priestess may want to walk around the space once, thinking of the qualities that this blend of resins will bring to the space: love, purification, safety, healing, and connection with spirit. Then she sits with the other participants in a circle. Breathe together as a group for a few minutes, letting the scent of the incense permeate your bodies, inside and out, allowing your cells to absorb the positive qualities of the incense. The Priestess says:

Allow the smoke of this special blend of incense to enter your body and infuse each cell with blessing. Let this magickal and sacred blend of scents fill you with love, purification, safety, healing, and connection with spirit. As you breathe, allow your body to become the sacred temple where you worship.

Once everyone is fully present in their bodies, the Priestess instructs everyone to open their eyes, and come present in the space. As a group, you may want to take a moment and hold hands, feeling the shared energy you have already created by centering here in this sacred space. All participants may say together:

We are in sacred space.

The Priestess lights the mother candle so that everyone will be able to light their individual candles from the source. As she lights the mother candle, the Priestess says:

Lighting this flame, I invoke body pride, and the power and willingness to self-define. I invoke the courage and power to be present in our bodies, to love our bodies, and to worship our bodies, in all their many shapes. I invoke the clarity and fullness of self-nurturance. I invoke a spirit of resistance and of celebration. I invoke power, and I invoke love. I invoke not only self-acceptance but self-devotion.

As each participant lights her personal flame, you will all drop deeper into that space where you know your body as a sacred, wonderful temple. A space sacred and powerful. A space where you know the truth of your own being. You will find that space inside where you have achieved true self-devotion, where you know that each act of self-love, self-adoration, and self-definition is a sacred act. The place where you alone define the boundaries of your temple: the sacred temple that is each of us.

Each participant may state a prayer, a wish, or an intention as she lights her candle.

Lighting of Personal Candles

Each person in the group now approaches the altar and lights her candle from the source candle. The Priestess says:

One by one, as you feel moved, approach the altar and light your candle, and place it at the perimeter of the altar cloth. With this light we create a sacred circle that allows honor and devotion to grow, and we become a beacon in the darkness that allows each seeker to find her own way home.

Sharing of Writing and Art

Once the candles are lighted, it is time to start sharing the items created during the week. Ideally, each participant (including the Priestess) will share one piece of artwork and one piece of writing (or more, if you have made that agreement as a group) in ritual space. The Priestess says:

> *Now is the time to share the works you created this week. Reading your writing out loud in ritual space and talking about your artifacts, with all of us as witnesses, adds to their power. Who would like to start?*

You all may choose to conduct this sharing in a clockwise (deosil) flow, though only if it feels necessary to your group.

Consecration of Writing and Art

Once everyone has had a chance to share, it's time for the consecration. Each participant will lay whatever items she wants to consecrate out in front of herself, or around the altar. All together, say:

> *I consecrate these works to the unfolding of self-awareness. May this act serve me, and may it serve all beings through the revelation of awareness. May my increasing awareness and presence serve to bring awareness of presence to all beings everywhere throughout space and time. So it is.*

Take time to witness, honor, and cherish each item being consecrated. The participants may want to pass the items through the smoke from the incense, or do some other act of purification and consecration.

In adding to your personal/home altar, you will use one or more of the items you have consecrated. What item(s) from this week's exploration would like to live on your altar for the duration of your initiation cycle?

Consecration of Beads

After each participant has shared with the group, she will take a bead from the basket and consecrate it. All together, say:

> *I consecrate this bead in the journey of self-definition. May this bead serve as a reminder to me that my self-image is a sacred mirror.*

Each participant places her bead in her bead pouch.

Blessing the Treats, Water, and Wine

Bless the food, water, and wine. All together, say:

> *This food is not just a symbol of, but the true substance of, nurturance, and of the cycles of life. May the sacrifice of this that I am about to ingest feed my body, my spirit, and my soul. May I always experience, receive, and honor my hungers. May all true hungers be fulfilled.*
>
> *Water is life. Life, and regeneration, and healing. Let this water remind me of my origins; of the womb, and of the blessed sea, the birthplace of life and that which forms the flow.*
>
> *This wine is the blood of willing sacrifice. It represents the cycles of life, death, and birth. It offers succor, and a doorway to new perception. May this wine bless me with the awareness of choice, and with divine vision and ecstasy.*

The water chalice is passed from person to person with the blessing "Water shared is life shared." The wine chalice is passed with the blessing "Wine offered is choice given and received." Food is passed with the blessing "May all true hungers be fulfilled."

As a group, take time to honor your bodies with treats, water, and wine. As you eat and drink, sit in awareness of the magick of transmutation: how the food, water, and wine affect your senses, and how these edible items become part of the very fabric of your cells. Allow gratitude, honor, and acceptance of and for the elements you are bringing into your bodies.

Ending of Ritual

All participants sit in circle once again and breathe. The Priestess says:

> *Yours is the temple. As you walk through the world, know that your body is a sacred vessel. It is consecrated to you, and to your unfolding and empowerment. As we learn to love and honor our bodies as the beautiful temples, wondrous tools, and amazing vehicles for transformation that they are, we grow closer to the divine gift of creation.*

Now, as each of you breathe again, inhaling the sacred scents, you prepare to walk forward into the world. You carry sacred space everywhere you go, and all you need is to remember: your body is sacred. Your breath is sacred. Your bones and blood and sweat

and tears are sacred. Your laughter is sacred, your voice is sacred, and your skin is sacred. All together, state aloud and claim this mantra:

This temple is mine.

Turn your focus inward, close your eyes, breathe, and relax. Allow yourself to slowly come back to the world you inhabit, the room you are sitting in, and your daily life. As you open your eyes, give yourself a hug, remembering that even as you reenter the world, your body remains a sacred temple of creation and empowerment.

- Releasing of quarters and entities (optional).
- Opening of circle (optional).
- Banishing (optional).

RITUAL THREE

Pussy Power!

★ Suggestion: This week, Consider consecrating your drawing-it sketches (see "Magickal Act: Drawing It" in chapter 3).

What the Facilitator/Priestess Will Need

- Beads for all the participants. This week's bead should represent the vivacious vulva!
- A platter of treats to eat, preferably yoni-shaped cookies.
- Wine, if desired. Perhaps a fruity, floral dessert wine. See "Wines" in appendix I.
- DON'T FORGET: Make sure everyone in your group can tolerate scents and smoke. Incense can be intense, and can alter your senses in a good way, as long as it's not triggering an asthma attack or allergies.

How-To

Before everyone gathers around the altar, the Priestess will:

- Create the altar with the items listed here and on the main altar list on page 205. The altar should be pleasing to the senses, and functional. The Priestess should place everything she will need near where she will be seated.
- Make sure the charcoal is lit. It takes a few minutes for the charcoal to be ready for the incense.
- Have everyone change into, or strip down to, their fun/sexy/comfy attire.
- Have everyone gather their items (personal candles/holders, journals, copy of *Sexy Witch*, bead pouch, works of art, comfort items) to bring to circle.
- Choose a person to bless the treats/water/wine, or the Priestess can do this.
- Describe the flow (outline) of the ritual so the participants will know what to prepare for (although ideally, everyone will have already read it).

Outline

- Banishing (optional).
- Circle casting (optional).
- Calling of quarters and spirit entities (optional).
- Setting space.

Once the attendees gather, the Priestess sprinkles a pinch of incense on the charcoal. She instructs everyone to focus on breathing, deeply into their bellies. The Priestess says:

Breathe deeply, allowing your breath to expand your chest, and then even more deeply, letting it expand your belly, your lower abdomen.

As everyone breathes together, the Priestess may want to walk around the space once, thinking of the qualities that this blend of resins will bring to the space: love, purification, safety, healing, and connection with spirit. Then she sits with the other participants in a circle. Breathe together as a group for a few minutes, letting the scent of the incense permeate your bodies, inside and out, allowing your cells to absorb the positive qualities of the incense. The Priestess says:

Allow the smoke of this special blend of incense to enter your body and infuse each cell with blessing. Let this magickal and sacred blend of scents fill you with love, purifica-

tion, safety, healing, and connection with spirit. As you breathe, allow your body to
become the sacred temple where you worship.

Once everyone is fully present in their bodies, the Priestess instructs everyone to open
their eyes, and come present in the space. As a group, you may want to take a moment
and hold hands, feeling the shared energy you have already created by centering here in
this sacred space. All participants may say together:

We are in sacred space.

The Priestess lights the mother candle so that everyone will be able to light their individual candles from the source. As she lights the mother candle, the Priestess says:

*Lighting this flame, I invoke Pussy Pride! I invoke a sense of wonder, awe, adoration,
and love for our amazing anatomy! I invoke the courage and power to be present in
our very canals and sweet folds, to love our bodies, to pleasure ourselves, and to worship the amazing power of pleasure and satisfaction.*

As each participant lights her personal flame, you will all drop deeper into that space
where you know your body as a sacred, wonderful temple. A space sacred and powerful.
A space where you know the truth of your own being. You will find that space inside
where you have achieved true self-devotion, where you know that each act of self-love,
self-adoration, and self-definition is a sacred act. The place where you alone define the
boundaries of your temple: the sacred temple that is each of us.

Each participant may state a prayer, a wish, or an intention as she lights her candle.

Lighting of Personal Candles

Each person in the group now approaches the altar and lights her candle from the
source candle. The Priestess says:

*One by one, as you feel moved, approach the altar and light your candle, and place it
at the perimeter of the altar cloth. With this light we create a sacred circle that allows
honor and devotion to grow, and we become a beacon in the darkness that allows each
seeker to find her own way home.*

Sharing of Writing and Art

Once the candles are lighted, it is time to start sharing the items created during the week. Ideally, each participant (including the Priestess) will share one piece of artwork and one piece of writing (or more, if you have made that agreement as a group) in ritual space. The Priestess says:

> *Now is the time to share the works you created this week. Reading your writing out loud in ritual space and talking about your artifacts, with all of us as witnesses, adds to their power. Who would like to start?*

You all may choose to conduct this sharing in a clockwise (deosil) flow, though only if it feels necessary to your group.

Consecration of Writing and Art

Once everyone has had a chance to share, it's time for the consecration. Each participant will lay whatever items she wants to consecrate out in front of herself, or around the altar. All together, say:

> *I consecrate these works to the unfolding of self-awareness. May this act serve me, and may it serve all beings through the revelation of awareness. May my increasing awareness and presence serve to bring awareness of presence to all beings everywhere throughout space and time. So it is.*

Take time to witness, honor, and cherish each item being consecrated. The participants may want to pass the items through the smoke from the incense, or do some other act of purification and consecration.

In adding to your personal/home altar, you will use one or more of the items you have consecrated. What item(s) from this week's exploration would like to live on your altar for the duration of your initiation cycle?

Consecration of Beads

After each participant has shared with the group, she will take a bead from the basket and consecrate it. All together, say:

> *I consecrate this bead in the journey of love, passion, power, and pleasure. May this bead serve as a reminder to me that my cunt is a sacred space.*

Each participant places her bead in her bead pouch.

Blessing the Treats, Water, and Wine

Bless the food, water, and wine. All together, say:

> *This food is not just a symbol of, but the true substance of, nurturance, and of the cycles of life. May the sacrifice of this that I am about to ingest feed my body, my spirit, and my soul. May I always experience, receive, and honor my hungers. May all true hungers be fulfilled.*

> *Water is life. Life, and regeneration, and healing. Let this water remind me of my origins; of the womb, and of the blessed sea, the birthplace of life and that which forms the flow.*

> *This wine is the blood of willing sacrifice. It represents the cycles of life, death, and birth. It offers succor, and a doorway to new perception. May this wine bless me with the awareness of choice, and with divine vision and ecstasy.*

The water chalice is passed from person to person with the blessing "Water shared is life shared." The wine chalice is passed with the blessing "Wine offered is choice given and received." Food is passed with the blessing "May all true hungers be fulfilled."

As a group, take time to honor your bodies with treats, water, and wine. As you eat and drink, sit in awareness of the magick of transmutation: how the food, water, and wine affect your senses, and how these edible items become part of the very fabric of your cells. Allow gratitude, honor, and acceptance of and for the elements you are bringing into your bodies.

Ending of Ritual

All participants sit in circle once again and breathe. The Priestess says:

> *Yours is the temple. As you walk through the world, know that your body is a sacred vessel. It is consecrated to you, and to your unfolding and empowerment. As we learn to love and honor our bodies as the beautiful temples, wondrous tools, and amazing vehicles for transformation that they are, we grow closer to the divine gift of creation.*

Now, as each of you breathe again, inhaling the sacred scents, you prepare to walk forward into the world. You carry sacred space everywhere you go, and all you need is to remember: your body is sacred. Your breath is sacred. Your bones and blood and sweat

and tears are sacred. Your laughter is sacred, your voice is sacred, and your skin is sacred. All together, state aloud and claim this mantra:

This temple is mine.

Turn your focus inward, close your eyes, breathe, and relax. Allow yourself to slowly come back to the world you inhabit, the room you are sitting in, and your daily life. As you open your eyes, give yourself a hug, remembering that even as you reenter the world, your body remains a sacred temple of creation and empowerment.

- Releasing of quarters and entities (optional).
- Opening of circle (optional).
- Banishing (optional).

RITUAL FOUR

The Descent

★ Suggestions:

1. This week, consider consecrating your blood art, or your reusable menstrual products (see "Spell Working: Blood Magick" in chapter 4). Okay, maybe that seems kinda gross at first, but think about it: maybe making your cloth pads a ritual tool will make it easier to remember why you use them instead of the throwaway products you can so *conveniently* pick up at the grocery store . . .

2. Up for group discussion: Perhaps you will want to conduct the temple visualization from chapter 4 during this ritual, in honor of healing our wombs (see "Spell Working: The Womb Room"). If so, the Priestess may read the visualization from the end of chapter 4.

What the Facilitator/Priestess Will Need

- Beads for all the participants. This week's bead should represent blood, or the uterus.

- A platter with dark bread or cakes of light. See the Cakes of Light recipe in appendix I.
- A blood-red wine, if desired. Maybe a Merlot, Chianti, or Shiraz. See "Wines" in appendix I.
- DON'T FORGET: Make sure everyone in your group can tolerate scents and smoke. Incense can be intense, and can alter your senses in a good way, as long as it's not triggering an asthma attack or allergies.

How-To

Before everyone gathers around the altar, the Priestess will:

- Create the altar with the items listed here and on the main altar list on page 205. The altar should be pleasing to the senses, and functional. The Priestess should place everything she will need near where she will be seated.
- Make sure the charcoal is lit. It takes a few minutes for the charcoal to be ready for the incense.
- Have everyone change into, or strip down to, their fun/sexy/comfy attire.
- Have everyone gather their items (personal candles/holders, journals, copy of *Sexy Witch*, bead pouch, works of art, comfort items) to bring to circle.
- Choose a person to bless the treats/water/wine, or the Priestess can do this.
- Describe the flow (outline) of the ritual so the participants will know what to prepare for (although ideally, everyone will have already read it).

Outline

- Banishing (optional).
- Circle casting (optional).
- Calling of quarters and spirit entities (optional).
- Setting space.

Once the attendees gather, the Priestess sprinkles a pinch of incense on the charcoal. She instructs everyone to focus on breathing, deeply into their bellies. The Priestess says:

Breathe deeply, allowing your breath to expand your chest, and then even more deeply, letting it expand your belly, your lower abdomen.

As everyone breathes together, the Priestess may want to walk around the space once, thinking of the qualities that this blend of resins will bring to the space: love, purification, safety, healing, and connection with spirit. Then she sits with the other participants in a circle. Breathe together as a group for a few minutes, letting the scent of the incense permeate your bodies, inside and out, allowing your cells to absorb the positive qualities of the incense. The Priestess says:

Allow the smoke of this special blend of incense to enter your body and infuse each cell with blessing. Let this magickal and sacred blend of scents fill you with love, purification, safety, healing, and connection with spirit. As you breathe, allow your body to become the sacred temple where you worship.

Once everyone is fully present in their bodies, the Priestess instructs everyone to open their eyes, and come present in the space. As a group, you may want to take a moment and hold hands, feeling the shared energy you have already created by centering here in this sacred space. All participants may say together:

We are in sacred space.

The Priestess lights the mother candle so that everyone will be able to light their individual candles from the source. As she lights the mother candle, the Priestess says:

Lighting this flame, I invoke the journey we women have taken to get to where we are now. I invoke the courage and power of our ancestors of both blood and spirit; all the women who suffered and loved anyway, and made the world a more accepting place by living their lives with integrity. I invoke the courage to love and to worship our cunts, our wombs, and our blood. I invoke love, and I invoke devotion to our cunts, our wombs, and our scared blood.

As each participant lights her personal flame, you will all drop deeper into that space where you know your body as a sacred, wonderful temple. A space sacred and powerful. A space where you know the truth of your own being. You will find that space inside where you have achieved true self-devotion, where you know that each act of self-love, self-adoration, and self-definition is a sacred act. The place where you alone define the boundaries of your temple: the sacred temple that is each of us.

Each participant may state a prayer, a wish, or an intention as she lights her candle.

Lighting of Personal Candles

Each person in the group now approaches the altar and lights her candle from the source candle. The Priestess says:

> *One by one, as you feel moved, approach the altar and light your candle, and place it at the perimeter of the altar cloth. With this light we create a sacred circle that allows honor and devotion to grow, and we become a beacon in the darkness that allows each seeker to find her own way home.*

Temple Visualization (Optional)

If you decide to perform the temple visualization from chapter 4 as part of this ritual, it should be inserted here.

Sharing of Writing and Art

Once the candles are lighted, it is time to start sharing the items created during the week. Ideally, each participant (including the Priestess) will share one piece of artwork and one piece of writing (or more, if you have made that agreement as a group) in ritual space. The Priestess says:

> *Now is the time to share the works you created this week. Reading your writing out loud in ritual space and talking about your artifacts, with all of us as witnesses, adds to their power. Who would like to start?*

You all may choose to conduct this sharing in a clockwise (deosil) flow, though only if it feels necessary to your group.

Consecration of Writing and Art

Once everyone has had a chance to share, it's time for the consecration. Each participant will lay whatever items she wants to consecrate out in front of herself, or around the altar. All together, say:

> *I consecrate these works to the unfolding of self-awareness. May this act serve me, and may it serve all beings through the revelation of awareness. May my increasing awareness and presence serve to bring awareness of presence to all beings everywhere throughout space and time. So it is.*

Take time to witness, honor, and cherish each item being consecrated. The participants may want to pass the items through the smoke from the incense, or do some other act of purification and consecration.

In adding to your personal/home altar, you will use one or more of the items you have consecrated. What item(s) from this week's exploration would like to live on your altar for the duration of your initiation cycle?

Consecration of Beads

After each participant has shared with the group, she will take a bead from the basket and consecrate it. All together, say:

> *I consecrate this bead in the journey of healing, and to the power of the Gods and of women: the power to create life. May it serve as a reminder to me that my womb, my blood, and my sex are sacred.*

Each participant places her bead in her bead pouch.

Blessing the Treats, Water, and Wine

Bless the food, water, and wine. All together, say:

> *This food is not just a symbol of, but the true substance of, nurturance, and of the cycles of life. May the sacrifice of this that I am about to ingest feed my body, my spirit, and my soul. May I always experience, receive, and honor my hungers. May all true hungers be fulfilled.*

> *Water is life. Life, and regeneration, and healing. Let this water remind me of my origins; of the womb, and of the blessed sea, the birthplace of life and that which forms the flow.*

> *This wine is the blood of willing sacrifice. It represents the cycles of life, death, and birth. It offers succor, and a doorway to new perception. May this wine bless me with the awareness of choice, and with divine vision and ecstasy.*

The water chalice is passed from person to person with the blessing "Water shared is life shared." The wine chalice is passed with the blessing "Wine offered is choice given and received." Food is passed with the blessing "May all true hungers be fulfilled."

As a group, take time to honor your bodies with treats, water, and wine. As you eat and drink, sit in awareness of the magick of transmutation: how the food, water, and wine affect your senses, and how these edible items become part of the very fabric of your cells. Allow gratitude, honor, and acceptance of and for the elements you are bringing into your bodies.

Ending of Ritual

All participants sit in circle once again and breathe. The Priestess says:

> *Yours is the temple. As you walk through the world, know that your body is a sacred vessel. It is consecrated to you, and to your unfolding and empowerment. As we learn to love and honor our bodies as the beautiful temples, wondrous tools, and amazing vehicles for transformation that they are, we grow closer to the divine gift of creation.*

Now, as each of you breathe again, inhaling the sacred scents, you prepare to walk forward into the world. You carry sacred space everywhere you go, and all you need is to remember: your body is sacred. Your breath is sacred. Your bones and blood and sweat and tears are sacred. Your laughter is sacred, your voice is sacred, and your skin is sacred. All together, state aloud and claim this mantra:

> *This temple is mine.*

Turn your focus inward, close your eyes, breathe, and relax. Allow yourself to slowly come back to the world you inhabit, the room you are sitting in, and your daily life. As you open your eyes, give yourself a hug, remembering that even as you reenter the world, your body remains a sacred temple of creation and empowerment.

- Releasing of quarters and entities (optional).
- Opening of circle (optional).
- Banishing (optional).

RITUAL FIVE

Coming to Our Senses

★ Suggestions:

1. Consider consecrating your Sensation Station toy box this week, as well as an item to add to your altar (see "Magickal Act: Sensation Station Toy Box" in chapter 5).

2. Bring your Sensation Station toy box for use in ritual.

What Facilitator/Priestess Will Need

- Beads for all the participants. This week's bead should represent the senses.

- A platter of treats that are sumptuous and enjoyable, as well as some tastes that may seem unusual. For example, honey can be served on toothpicks, tiny key lime pies can be served with the fingers, or whipped cream can be scooped onto pitted cherries. Some different flavors to work with: Greek olives, smoked salmon, caviar.

- A blood-red wine, if desired. Maybe a Merlot, Chianti, or Shiraz. See "Wines" in appendix I.

- DON'T FORGET: Make sure everyone in your group can tolerate scents and smoke. Incense can be intense, and can alter your senses in a good way, as long as it's not triggering an asthma attack or allergies.

How-To

Before everyone gathers around the altar, the Priestess will:

- Create the altar with the items listed here and on the main altar list on page 205. The altar should be pleasing to the senses, and functional. The Priestess should place everything she will need near where she will be seated.

- Make sure the charcoal is lit. It takes a few minutes for the charcoal to be ready for the incense.

- Have everyone change into, or strip down to, their fun/sexy/comfy attire.

- Have everyone gather their items (personal candles/holders, journals, copy of *Sexy Witch,* bead pouch, works of art, comfort items) to bring to circle.

- Choose a person to bless the treats/water/wine, or the Priestess can do this.

- Describe the flow (outline) of the ritual so the participants will know what to prepare for (although ideally, everyone will have already read it).

Outline

- Banishing (optional).

- Circle casting (optional).

- Calling of quarters and spirit entities (optional).

- Setting space.

Once the attendees gather, the Priestess sprinkles a pinch of incense on the charcoal. She instructs everyone to focus on breathing, deeply into their bellies. The Priestess says:

Breathe deeply, allowing your breath to expand your chest, and then even more deeply, letting it expand your belly, your lower abdomen.

As everyone breathes together, the Priestess may want to walk around the space once, thinking of the qualities that this blend of resins will bring to the space: love, purification, safety, healing, and connection with spirit. Then she sits with the other participants in a circle. Breathe together as a group for a few minutes, letting the scent of the incense permeate your bodies, inside and out, allowing your cells to absorb the positive qualities of the incense. The Priestess says:

> *Allow the smoke of this special blend of incense to enter your body and infuse each cell with blessing. Let this magickal and sacred blend of scents fill you with love, purification, safety, healing, and connection with spirit. As you breathe, allow your body to become the sacred temple where you worship.*

Once everyone is fully present in their bodies, the Priestess instructs everyone to open their eyes, and come present in the space. As a group, you may want to take a moment and hold hands, feeling the shared energy you have already created by centering here in this sacred space. All participants may say together:

> *We are in sacred space.*

The Priestess lights the mother candle so that everyone will be able to light their individual candles from the source. As she lights the mother candle, the Priestess says:

> *Lighting this flame, I invoke revelations of the senses. I invoke a sense of awe at the power and sacred perfection of our bodies, which work exactly in the ways that they work. I invoke awe at our ability to smell, taste, hear, feel, and see. Claim this awe, and offer blessings and thankfulness to your body for all it does, and for all it is.*

As each participant lights her personal flame, you will all drop deeper into that space where you know your body as a sacred, wonderful temple. A space sacred and powerful. A space where you know the truth of your own being. You will find that space inside where you have achieved true self-devotion, where you know that each act of self-love, self-adoration, and self-definition is a sacred act. The place where you alone define the boundaries of your temple: the sacred temple that is each of us.

As you drop deeper into that space that allows for healing, you know again that each act that creates self-awareness and self-knowledge is a sacred act. With this awareness, we alone define the New World we are creating.

Each participant may state a prayer, a wish, or an intention as she lights her candle.

Lighting of Personal Candles

Each person in the group now approaches the altar and lights her candle from the source candle. The Priestess says:

> *One by one, as you feel moved, approach the altar and light your candle, and place it at the perimeter of the altar cloth. With this light we create a sacred circle that allows honor and devotion to grow, and we become a beacon in the darkness that allows each seeker to find her own way home.*

Sharing of Writing and Art

Once the candles are lighted, it is time to start sharing the items created during the week. Ideally, each participant (including the Priestess) will share one piece of artwork and one piece of writing (or more, if you have made that agreement as a group) in ritual space. The Priestess says:

> *Now is the time to share the works you created this week. Reading your writing out loud in ritual space and talking about your artifacts, with all of us as witnesses, adds to their power. Who would like to start?*

You all may choose to conduct this sharing in a clockwise (deosil) flow, though only if it feels necessary to your group.

Consecration of Writing and Art

Once everyone has had a chance to share, it's time for the consecration. Each participant will lay whatever items she wants to consecrate out in front of herself, or around the altar. All together, say:

> *I consecrate these works to the unfolding of self-awareness. May this act serve me, and may it serve all beings through the revelation of awareness. May my increasing awareness and presence serve to bring awareness of presence to all beings everywhere throughout space and time. So it is.*

Take time to witness, honor, and cherish each item being consecrated. The participants may want to pass the items through the smoke from the incense, or do some other act of purification and consecration.

In adding to your personal/home altar, you will use one or more of the items you have consecrated. What item(s) from this week's exploration would like to live on your altar for the duration of your initiation cycle?

Coming to Our Senses

Have all the participants pair up, and choose one of each pair to be the guide first, and one to be the explorer. The explorer allows the guide to take her on a journey through her senses.

- Negotiation of boundaries and desires: The guide asks the explorer to state any boundaries she wants to make clear (like no touch in certain areas of the body), as well as desires she would like to have fulfilled (requesting touch in certain areas, or asking to have her hair brushed or played with).
- The guide blindfolds the explorer.
- The guide treats the explorer to scents (essential oils, slices of orange, chocolate, etc.), touch sensations (massage, hair brushing, touching with soft clothes and faux fur, etc.), tastes (delicacies from the platter of treats, offered in no particular order), sound (shaker instruments played softly by the ears, drums, etc.), and ending with the removal of the blindfold with a mirror in place so the first thing the explorer sees is herself.
- Then, the explorer and the guide switch roles.

Consecration of Beads

After each participant has had the opportunity to be both explorer and guide, she will take a bead from the basket and consecrate it. All together, say:

I consecrate this bead in the journey of sensual awareness. May it serve as a reminder to me that my senses are a sacred gift.

Each participant places her bead in her bead pouch.

Blessing the Treats, Water, and Wine

Bless the food, water, and wine. All together, say:

This food is not just a symbol of, but the true substance of, nurturance, and of the cycles of life. May the sacrifice of this that I am about to ingest feed my body, my spirit, and my soul. May I always experience, receive, and honor my hungers. May all true hungers be fulfilled.

Water is life. Life, and regeneration, and healing. Let this water remind me of my origins; of the womb, and of the blessed sea, the birthplace of life and that which forms the flow.

This wine is the blood of willing sacrifice. It represents the cycles of life, death, and birth. It offers succor, and a doorway to new perception. May this wine bless me with the awareness of choice, and with divine vision and ecstasy.

The water chalice is passed from person to person with the blessing "Water shared is life shared." The wine chalice is passed with the blessing "Wine offered is choice given and received." Food is passed with the blessing "May all true hungers be fulfilled."

As a group, take time to honor your bodies with treats, water, and wine. As you eat and drink, sit in awareness of the magick of transmutation: how the food, water, and wine affect your senses, and how these edible items become part of the very fabric of your cells. Allow gratitude, honor, and acceptance of and for the elements you are bringing into your bodies.

Ending of Ritual

All participants sit in circle once again and breathe. The Priestess says:

Yours is the temple. As you walk through the world, know that your body is a sacred vessel. It is consecrated to you, and to your unfolding and empowerment. As we learn to love and honor our bodies as the beautiful temples, wondrous tools, and amazing vehicles for transformation that they are, we grow closer to the divine gift of creation.

Now, as each of you breathe again, inhaling the sacred scents, you prepare to walk forward into the world. You carry sacred space everywhere you go, and all you need is to remember: your body is sacred. Your breath is sacred. Your bones and blood and sweat and tears are sacred. Your laughter is sacred, your voice is sacred, and your skin is sacred. All together, state aloud and claim this mantra:

This temple is mine.

Turn your focus inward, close your eyes, breathe, and relax. Allow yourself to slowly come back to the world you inhabit, the room you are sitting in, and your daily life. As you open your eyes, give yourself a hug, remembering that even as you reenter the world, your body remains a sacred temple of creation and empowerment.

- Releasing of quarters and entities (optional).
- Opening of circle (optional).
- Banishing (optional).

RITUAL SIX

Witch Power Rising (Dedication)

★ Suggestions:

1. Consider consecrating your creation artifact this week, as well as your mentor icon (see "Spell Working: Creating Creation" and "Magickal Act: Creating a Mentor Icon" in chapter 6).

2. Don't forget to bring your empowerment mantra! (See "Spell Working: Creating an Empowerment Mantra" in chapter 6.)

3. Up for group discussion: Consider performing a temple visualization in ritual space (see "Spell Working: Breath of Life" in chapter 6).

What the Facilitator/Priestess Will Need

• Beads for all the participants. This week's bead should represent the concept of mentors, or the concept of creating creation.

- A platter of treats. I recommend star-shaped cookies.
- Wine, if desired. See "Wines" in appendix I.
- DON'T FORGET: Make sure everyone in your group can tolerate scents and smoke. Incense can be intense, and can alter your senses in a good way, as long as it's not triggering an asthma attack or allergies.

How-To

Before everyone gathers around the altar, the Priestess will:

- Create the altar with the items listed here and on the main altar list on page 205. The altar should be pleasing to the senses, and functional. The Priestess should place everything she will need near where she will be seated.
- Make sure the charcoal is lit. It takes a few minutes for the charcoal to be ready for the incense.
- Have everyone change into, or strip down to, their fun/sexy/comfy attire.
- Have everyone gather their items (personal candles/holders, journals, copy of *Sexy Witch,* bead pouch, works of art, comfort items) to bring to circle.
- Choose a person to bless the treats/water/wine, or the Priestess can do this.
- Describe the flow (outline) of the ritual so the participants will know what to prepare for (although ideally, everyone will have already read it).

Outline

- Banishing (optional).
- Circle casting (optional).
- Calling of quarters and spirit entities (optional).
- Setting space.

Once the attendees gather, the Priestess sprinkles a pinch of incense on the charcoal. She instructs everyone to focus on breathing, deeply into their bellies. The Priestess says:

Breathe deeply, allowing your breath to expand your chest, and then even more deeply, letting it expand your belly, your lower abdomen.

As everyone breathes together, the Priestess may want to walk around the space once, thinking of the qualities that this blend of resins will bring to the space: love, purification, safety, healing, and connection with spirit. Then she sits with the other participants in a circle. Breathe together as a group for a few minutes, letting the scent of the incense permeate your bodies, inside and out, allowing your cells to absorb the positive qualities of the incense. The Priestess says:

> *Allow the smoke of this special blend of incense to enter your body and infuse each cell with blessing. Let this magickal and sacred blend of scents fill you with love, purification, safety, healing, and connection with spirit. As you breathe, allow your body to become the sacred temple where you worship.*

Once everyone is fully present in their bodies, the Priestess instructs everyone to open their eyes, and come present in the space. As a group, you may want to take a moment and hold hands, feeling the shared energy you have already created by centering here in this sacred space. All participants may say together:

> *We are in sacred space.*

The Priestess lights the mother candle so that everyone will be able to light their individual candles from the source. As she lights the mother candle, the Priestess says:

> *Lighting this flame, I invoke the journey we have each taken to get to where we are now. I invoke the courage and power of our ancestors. I invoke the lineage of spirit, and the lineage of flesh. I invoke our strength as leaders, and I invoke our ability to seek, find, and accept inspiration and support in our times of need. I invoke new stories of creation, new patterns to build our lives upon, and the revolutionary and evolutionary power of new beginnings.*

As each participant lights her personal flame, you will all drop deeper into that space where you know your body as a sacred, wonderful temple. A space sacred and powerful. A space where you know the truth of your own being. You will find that space inside where you have achieved true self-devotion, where you know that each act of self-love, self-adoration, and self-definition is a sacred act. The place where you alone define the boundaries of your temple: the sacred temple that is each of us.

As you drop deeper into that space that allows for healing, you know again that each act that creates self-awareness and self-knowledge is a sacred act. With this awareness, we alone define the New World we are creating.

Each participant may state a prayer, a wish, or an intention as she lights her candle.

Lighting of Personal Candles

Each person in the group now approaches the altar and lights her candle from the source candle. The Priestess says:

> *One by one, as you feel moved, approach the altar and light your candle, and place it at the perimeter of the altar cloth. With this light we create a sacred circle that allows honor and devotion to grow, and we become a beacon in the darkness that allows each seeker to find her own way home.*

Breath of Life Visualization (Optional)

If you have agreed to perform the breath of life visualization in ritual space, insert it here.

Sharing of Writing and Art

Once the candles are lighted, it is time to start sharing the items created during the week. Ideally, each participant (including the Priestess) will share one piece of artwork and one piece of writing (or more, if you have made that agreement as a group) in ritual space. The Priestess says:

> *Now is the time to share the works you created this week. Reading your writing out loud in ritual space and talking about your artifacts, with all of us as witnesses, adds to their power. Who would like to start?*

You all may choose to conduct this sharing in a clockwise (deosil) flow, though only if it feels necessary to your group.

Consecration of Writing and Art

Once everyone has had a chance to share, it's time for the consecration. Each participant will lay whatever items she wants to consecrate out in front of herself, or around the altar. All together, say:

> *I consecrate these works to the unfolding of self-awareness. May this act serve me, and may it serve all beings through the revelation of awareness. May my increasing aware-*

ness and presence serve to bring awareness of presence to all beings everywhere throughout space and time. So it is.

Take time to witness, honor, and cherish each item being consecrated. The participants may want to pass the items through the smoke from the incense, or do some other act of purification and consecration.

In adding to your personal/home altar, you will use one or more of the items you have consecrated. What item(s) from this week's exploration would like to live on your altar for the duration of your initiation cycle?

Empowerment Mantra

Now, read aloud your empowerment mantra.

Consecration of Beads

After each participant has shared with the group, she will take a bead from the basket and consecrate it. All together, say:

> *I consecrate this bead in the journey of choice, regeneration, and lineage. May it serve as a reminder to me that my past and my future are sacred.*

Each participant places her bead in her bead pouch.

Blessing the Treats, Water, and Wine

Bless the food, water, and wine. All together, say:

> *This food is not just a symbol of, but the true substance of, nurturance, and of the cycles of life. May the sacrifice of this that I am about to ingest feed my body, my spirit, and my soul. May I always experience, receive, and honor my hungers. May all true hungers be fulfilled.*

> *Water is life. Life, and regeneration, and healing. Let this water remind me of my origins; of the womb, and of the blessed sea, the birthplace of life and that which forms the flow.*

> *This wine is the blood of willing sacrifice. It represents the cycles of life, death, and birth. It offers succor, and a doorway to new perception. May this wine bless me with the awareness of choice, and with divine vision and ecstasy.*

The water chalice is passed from person to person with the blessing "Water shared is life shared." The wine chalice is passed with the blessing "Wine offered is choice given and received." Food is passed with the blessing "May all true hungers be fulfilled."

As a group, take time to honor your bodies with treats, water, and wine. As you eat and drink, sit in awareness of the magick of transmutation: how the food, water, and wine affect your senses, and how these edible items become part of the very fabric of your cells. Allow gratitude, honor, and acceptance of and for the elements you are bringing into your bodies.

Ending of Ritual

All participants sit in circle once again and breathe. The Priestess says:

> *Yours is the temple. As you walk through the world, know that your body is a sacred vessel. It is consecrated to you, and to your unfolding and empowerment. As we learn to love and honor our bodies as the beautiful temples, wondrous tools, and amazing vehicles for transformation that they are, we grow closer to the divine gift of creation.*

Now, as each of you breathe again, inhaling the sacred scents, you prepare to walk forward into the world. You carry sacred space everywhere you go, and all you need is to remember: your body is sacred. Your breath is sacred. Your bones and blood and sweat and tears are sacred. Your laughter is sacred, your voice is sacred, and your skin is sacred. All together, state aloud and claim this mantra:

> *This temple is mine.*

Turn your focus inward, close your eyes, breathe, and relax. Allow yourself to slowly come back to the world you inhabit, the room you are sitting in, and your daily life. As you open your eyes, give yourself a hug, remembering that even as you reenter the world, your body remains a sacred temple of creation and empowerment.

- Releasing of quarters and entities (optional).
- Opening of circle (optional).
- Banishing (optional).

Goddess in the Mirror
(Completion)

Note: This ritual requires *two* Priestesses. Only the Priestesses should read this entire outline. The element of surprise is important. The other participants should read only the "What All Participants Will Need" section. Also, be prepared for some surprises, and place your trust in the process of initiation. This ritual will likely be longer than any of the others you have performed in the course of working *Sexy Witch*. Give it the time. I promise it'll be worth it.

Here are some things to discuss as a group before planning this initiation:

- Are people in the group comfortable with the idea of taking their vows "skyclad" (otherwise known as nekkid)?
- Will witnesses, other than the core group, be invited?

- What do you think of planning a more inclusive party for the evening, once your ritual is complete, to honor your new path?

My Comments on Nudity in Ritual

The nudity question may seem out of the blue, but what more empowering experience is there than to be naked in front of our sisters in magick? After all, much of the work that has been done in these chapters is about claiming our bodies as sacred space, and there is a profound sense of liberation possible when sharing nudity with others. You get to see the real thing: other women's actual bodies. Not airbrushed, false representations of the "perfect body," but actual, innate, perfectly imperfect, dimpled, asymmetrical, natural beauty. And you get to sit in your own skin, proud and accepting, nervous and bold, with nothing to hide.

In many cultures and since time began, nudity has been a common element in taking vows of initiation. There are a lot of symbolic reasons that nudity is a positive component of initiation. A concept to work with is the idea of coming before the Divine as a newborn does, naked as a babe being born to her new life. Another concept to work with is the idea of exposing all that you are in your willingness to make a clean start.

Obviously, nudity is not required for the ritual, but it is an opportunity to create a whole new relationship with your body. The opportunity to do so will be made clear in the course of the ritual. In my experience, it has been an amazing breakthrough point for women to bare their bodies in the company of others, and especially to do so in ritual space. It may be so for you and your crew to get courageous enough to bare your bodies in front of each other. Remember, this body of yours is an amazing and wondrous temple, dedicated to you and to the work you are doing.

To be or not to be nude is your choice to make as a group. I strongly encourage going for it, but it's your ritual. Perform it as you wish. Be comfortable in your choice, but remember that risk taking may lead to watershed moments and astounding, instantaneous growth. Risk taking is also a nearly universal component of initiation.

The Question of Witnesses

Your group must decide collectively if you want to invite additional witnesses for this final initiation. After working with an exclusive group for this long, it may feel strange to introduce new people into the mix, but it may be important for some of the people in your lives to witness this moment on your path of initiation.

One reason to invite witnesses is to allow people who are close to you, and ideally who will be in your life for a long time, to witness your transition. Another reason is to have people in your daily life who will understand the vows you have made, and will support you in holding to those vows.

If you decide as a group to invite witnesses to attend, remember that these must be people you trust, people you love, and ideally people who will be in your life for a long, long time. In the future, these witnesses will have the responsibility of reminding you of your vows. During the ritual, they will play a part in your initiation. They will have the opportunity to see you honor the healing work you have done, and to offer their testimony to your unfolding.

If you have a partner, this will be an amazing opportunity to create a new level of trust and depth in your relationship. Perhaps you have a mentor you'd like to have as witness, or maybe your best girlfriend or boyfriend.

If you have decided to have nudity be an element of this ritual, will these witnesses be comfortable with your nudity and the nudity of the others in your group? Will you all be comfortable with the witnesses *witnessing* your nudity? As I have already stated, nudity is not required, but it can be a powerful element of this ritual.

Planning A Sexy Witch Soirée

Plan for a whole afternoon and evening, and have a celebration after the ritual! It'll be like a début. No really, do have a party after the ritual! Then you can invite as many of your peeps to honor your transition as you'd like, without having to share this very intimate ritual with all of them.

Your group can be as overt or as covert as you'd like about your cause for celebration. If you don't want to share all the wondrous details of your process with your buddies, just say you are having an mutual "unbirthday" party, or that you just wanted to take some time to celebrate your wonderful selves and your amazing circle of friends. If you want to open up the discussion about what's been putting that pretty grin on your face for the past few days, put out your altar and start answering questions once someone gets brave enough to ask them.

This is the end of an amazing process, and the beginning of the rest of your lives. Cherish this time at this threshold.

Where to from Here?

Each of you must now choose one direction for where your path is leading (or where you want it to be leading), and one direction for the current/future home of your growth.

In my personal cosmology, the west has a lot of correspondences that allow for female sexual empowerment, and many of the Goddesses I look to for inspiration in this arena are associated with the west. However, the south is also profoundly powerful and transformative. All the quarters have associations that make sense for either of the designations. What are your associations? For me, where the west represents nurturance, sensuality, and the womb, and often has a more gentle form of transformation to offer, the south is overtly sexual, creative, and powerful, and offers fundamental and complete transformation, as in fire burning wood to ash. The north represents grounding and solid nurturance, motherhood and stability. The east offers new beginnings and inspiration.

These are my associations. But this ritual is about *you,* not me. So, what are your associations? What direction are you heading toward? What element are you inviting to influence your life now? Air? Fire? Water? Earth? Where do you want the coming phase of your growth to take place? Rely on your intuition here, and find the directions that make the most sense to you. Choose your future path with intention.

Once you have made your choices, tell the Priestesses of this final rite the directions you have chosen. They will need to know in advance of the ritual.

Now, on to your final Sexy Witch initiation!

Ritual Seven

★ Suggestions:

  • Treat this event as you would any momentous occasion. Do whatever makes you feel prepared to take your vows. Whether it's getting a pedicure or spending the morning in meditation, do what works to create a day that you will remember fondly for the rest of your life.

What All Participants Will Need

- Your devotion oil. See appendix I for the recipe.
- Your empowerment contract. See "Magickal Act: Empowerment Contract" in chapter 7.
- Your vows of initiation. See "Spell Working: Vows of Initiation" in chapter 7.
- Your initiation talisman(s). See "Spell Working: Creating an Initiation Talisman" in chapter 7.
- Give your devotion oil, empowerment contract, vows of initiation, and initiation talisman to one of the Priestesses before the ritual. Make sure it is wrapped up in a tidy bundle, and recognizably yours so you don't take someone else's vows!
- Your bead pouch.
- A pen.
- Your copy of *Sexy Witch*.
- Your journal. Choose one piece of writing from this week that you will share with the group.
- Your witness(es), if your group has decided to invite others to attend.
- Up for group discussion: Consider performing a Foot Bath Ceremony in ritual space. See appendix I.

ONLY THE PRIESTESSES FOR THIS RITUAL READ PAST THIS POINT!!!

What the Facilitators/Priestesses Will Need

- Beads for all the participants. This week's bead should represent a doorway, a threshold, or a Witches' broom.
- Something for everyone to string their beads on (jeweler's wire, yarn, hemp rope). Make sure it is long enough to fashion a necklace or bracelet out of. You may want to purchase fastenings/hooks, too, so these talismans can be easily removed in the future.
- A platter of treats.

- Wine, or champagne, if desired. See "Wines" in appendix I.

Additional Items for This Ritual

- A full-length mirror that is freestanding or can be stood up against a wall.
- A cloth to use as a shroud (cover) for the mirror.
- Blindfolds for all the practitioners.
- Ideally, a Witches' besom (broom), but the plain old kitchen variety of broom works, too. (The broom, when held parallel to the floor, becomes a symbol of the threshold. As practitioners step over the broom, they step through the doorway into their new lives. It also represents a "clean sweep," and new beginnings.) Note: In my mirror-working rituals, I have always placed the mirror in the west. For me the west has a lot of correspondences that allow for female sexual empowerment, and many of the Goddesses I look to for inspiration in this arena are associated with the west. However, there are reasons that the south would work as well, or any of the quarters. Where the west represents nurturance, sensuality, and the womb, and often has a more gentle form of transformation to offer, the south is overtly sexual, creative, and powerful, and offers fundamental and complete transformation, as in fire burning wood to ash. Again, rely on your intuition here, and place the mirror accordingly. You may want to pose this question to the group, without mentioning the mirror.

How-To

For simplicity's sake, choose one of the two of you to be Priestess 1 (P1) and the other to be Priestess 2 (P2). In the following outline you will understand the need for this. Together, do the following:

- DON'T FORGET: Make sure everyone in your group can tolerate scents and smoke. Incense can be intense, and can alter your senses in a good way, as long as it's not triggering an asthma attack or allergies.
- Create the altar with the items listed here and on the main altar list on page 205. The altar should be pleasing to the senses, and functional. For this ritual, the altar should not be placed in the center of the circle. There will be more movement than usual. Place the altar on a table, to the side of the mirror.

- Make sure the charcoal is lit. It takes a few minutes for the charcoal to be ready for the incense.
- Have everyone gather items (personal candles/holders, journals, copy of *Sexy Witch*, bead pouch, works of art, comfort items) to bring to circle.
- Choose a person to bless the treats/water/wine, or one of the Priestesses can do this.

Place the mirror before the initiates gather. They should not see the mirror before it is revealed in the course of the ritual. Wherever the mirror is set, it should be covered with a shroud, so participants will not see what it is until faced with it.

Also, participants will step over the broom (a symbol of the threshold) at whichever quarter they choose. Stepping over the broom is a symbol of beginning on the path of the initiate, of crossing the threshold into a new phase of life. Be sure that everyone has chosen their directions.

Outline

- Banishing (optional).
- Circle casting (optional).
- Calling of quarters and spirit entities (optional).
- Setting space.

Note: Priestess 1 and Priestess 2 should read through the outline, and decide which Priestess will perform which parts of the ritual. You may note "P1" or "P2" in the margin accordingly, or on a copy of the outline.

Once the attendees gather, P1 or P2 sprinkles a pinch of incense on the charcoal. She instructs everyone to focus on breathing, deeply into their bellies. She says:

> *Breathe deeply, allowing your breath to expand your chest, and then even more deeply, letting it expand your belly, your lower abdomen.*

As everyone breathes together, the Priestess may want to walk around the space once, thinking of the qualities that this blend of resins will bring to the space: love, purification, safety, healing, and connection with spirit. Then she sits with the other participants in a circle. Breathe together as a group for a few minutes, letting the scent of the incense permeate your bodies, inside and out, allowing your cells to absorb the positive qualities of the incense. The Priestess says:

> *Allow the smoke of this special blend of incense to enter your body and infuse each cell with blessing. Let this magickal and sacred blend of scents fill you with love, purification, safety, healing, and connection with spirit. As you breathe, allow your body to become the sacred temple where you worship.*

Once everyone is fully present in their bodies, the Priestess instructs everyone to open their eyes, and come present in the space. As a group, you may want to take a moment and hold hands, feeling the shared energy you have already created by centering here in this sacred space. All participants may say together:

> *We are in sacred space.*

The Priestess lights the mother candle so that everyone will be able to light their individual candles from the source. As she lights the mother candle, the Priestess says:

> *Lighting this flame, I invoke gratitude for the journey we have taken together in the past seven weeks. I invoke sweet anticipation for the journey that continues on the other side of this threshold. I invoke self-dedication, self-adoration, and self-respect. I invoke the vows of the initiate: To know, to will, to dare, and to be silent. We have shared deep mysteries, and found new ways. We will continue to deepen. We have revealed deep mysteries within ourselves, and found new ways. Each of us will continue to deepen as we walk the paths before us.*

As each participant lights her personal flame, you will all drop deeper into that space where you know your body as a sacred, wonderful temple. A space sacred and powerful. A space where you know the truth of your own being. You will find that space inside where you have achieved true self-devotion, where you know that each act of self-love, self-adoration, and self-definition is a sacred act. The place where you alone define the boundaries of your temple: the sacred temple that is each of us.

As you drop deeper into that space that allows for healing, you know again that each act that creates self-awareness and self-knowledge is a sacred act. With this awareness, we alone define the New World we are creating.

Each participant may state a prayer, a wish, or an intention as she lights her candle.

Lighting of Personal Candles

Each person in the group now approaches the altar and lights her candle from the source candle. P1 or P2 says:

> *One by one, as you feel moved, approach the altar and light your candle, and place it at the perimeter of the altar cloth. With this light we create a sacred circle that allows honor and devotion to grow, and we become a beacon in the darkness that allows each seeker to find her own way home.*

Sharing of Writing and Art

Once the candles are lighted, it is time to start sharing the items created during the week. Ideally, each participant (including the Priestesses) will share one piece of artwork and one piece of writing (or more, if you have made that agreement as a group) in ritual space. P1 or P2 says:

> *Now is the time to share the works you created this week. Reading your writing out loud in ritual space and talking about your artifacts, with all of us as witnesses, adds to their power. Who would like to start?*

You all may choose to conduct this sharing in a clockwise (deosil) flow, though only if it feels necessary to your group.

Consecration of Writing and Art

Once everyone has had a chance to share, it's time for the consecration. Each participant will lay whatever items she wants to consecrate out in front of herself, or around the altar. All together, say:

> *I consecrate these works to the unfolding of self-awareness. May this act serve me, and may it serve all beings through the revelation of awareness. May my increasing awareness and presence serve to bring awareness of presence to all beings everywhere throughout space and time. So it is.*

Take time to witness, honor, and cherish each item being consecrated. The participants may want to pass the items through the smoke from the incense, or do some other act of purification and consecration.

In adding to your personal/home altar, you will use one or more of the items you have consecrated. What item(s) from this week's exploration would like to live on your altar for the duration of your initiation cycle?

Bead Consecration

After each initiate is done with the consecration of artifacts, she will take a bead from the basket and consecrate it. All together, say:

> *I consecrate this bead in the journey of initiation. May it serve as a reminder to me that my path is my own, and is constantly unfolding in accordance with Love and Will.*

Now, P1 or P2 says:

> *Take a length of string, and in this sacred space, string the beads that serve as reminders of the steps you have taken on this path of initiation. As you string them, you may speak aloud or just focus internally on what each bead represents. Once finished, hand this talisman of initiation to one of the Priestesses.*

Preparation for Mirror Ceremony

P1 or P2 instructs the initiates to sit in silence, close their eyes, and focus on the work they have done. P1 says:

> *Close your eyes, and allow yourself to remember all the wonderful, challenging, amazing, fun, revelatory work you have done in the past weeks. Feel who you are now, and how you have changed. Recall the moments of challenge, and the moments of insight. Let the new ways that you have found settle into your body, and make room for further growth. Allow yourself to look into the future, and notice how these changes will keep rippling through your life as you walk upon your path, more clear now than it has ever been, even as it is still shrouded in the mystery of the unknown.*

As P1 speaks, P2 blindfolds the initiates. The initiates have *not* been told this will happen, but have been told to expect some surprises and to trust in the process.

P1 keeps speaking until all the participants are blindfolded.

They're Blindfolded, Now Get Them Naked!

No, really . . . if your group has decided to employ nudity, this is the time to encourage it. Ask everyone to remove their clothes, with blindfolds in place. Yeah, it may be a bit challenging, but who said initiation was supposed to be easy? Besides, after all the intense work you have all done over the past weeks, this is a piece of cake!

Trust Walk, Leap of Faith

P1 and P2 approach each initiate in turn. They ask the direction each initiate has chosen for her path to take, and walk the initiate to the direction, still blindfolded. At the appropriate "gate" (direction), both Priestesses kneel down and hold the broom, symbolizing the threshold, and instruct the initiate to step, alone and blindfolded, into the unknown. They guide her if need be, but allow her to step over the threshold unaided if possible.

Goddess in the Mirror

The Priestesses uncover the mirror, and assemble the initiates, still blindfolded and naked, in a semicircle, facing the mirror. The Priestesses then find the initiates' bundles of artifacts of initiation, and place them at the feet of the initiates.

If witnesses are present, the Priestesses may integrate them into the circle beside their loved one, or create a second semicircle standing behind the initiates. P1 stands to one side of the mirror, and P2 to the other. P2 says:

You may now remove your blindfolds, and behold the path before you.

Once the blindfold has been removed, P1 instructs each initiate, in turn, to behold herself in the mirror. P1 says:

Behold, the initiate. This woman has worked to claim her voice, has cried tears of purification and gratitude, has laughed, and has learned to love herself in all her imperfect perfection. She has chosen her path, and that path has lead her home to her own being.

P2 says:

One by one, please pick up your bundle of artifacts of initiation, and approach the mirror. As each of your circle sisters stands in witness of her own reflection, honor her with your attention.

As each initiate in turn approaches and looks in the mirror, the Priestess *most* intimate with the particular initiate anoints her. If figuring that out seems too complicated, you can take turns between the two of you, or you can choose one of you to do all the anointings. Use the devotion oil for all the anointings if the initiate is unclothed. If she is clothed, use water on all the parts clothed, using the oil only on the unclothed parts.

Anointing

1. Wet finger and anoint the feet. Say:

   Blessed are your feet, which walk the Sacred Path.

2. Wet finger and anoint the knees. Say:

   Blessed are your knees, which touch the earth in humility and gratitude.

3. Wet finger and anoint the pubis, or the genitals if you are intimate enough with the initiate. Say:

   Blessed is your sex, which brings the gifts of pleasure and creation.

4. Wet finger and anoint the womb. Say:

   Blessed is your womb, the seat of life.

5. Wet finger and anoint the solar plexus (stomach region). Say:

   Blessed are your power and presence.

6. Wet finger and anoint the heart chakra (sternum). Say:

   Blessed is your heart, which loves with strength and beauty.

7. Wet finger and anoint the throat. Say:

   Blessed is your voice, which says what must be heard.

8. Wet finger and anoint the lips. Say:

   Blessed are your lips, which speak the words of power.

9. Wet finger and anoint the third eye (center of forehead, just above the brow line). Say:

   Blessed be your vision, which sees the way things are, and the way things may become.

10. Wet finger and anoint the crown (top of the head). Say:

    Blessed be your crown, where you and all of creation are one.

11. Step back and say:

    Blessed are you, and blessed is your presence on the earth. Blessed is your body, your soul, and your spirit. Blessed is the world that you create, and blessed is your path in that world.

Vows

To each initiate facing the mirror, P1 says:

Do you have vows?

Each initiate responds in the affirmative.

P1 says:

We are here to witness these vows, but these are vows you make to yourself. As you take these vows, look into the mirror and commit your vows to the person you are becoming.

Each initiate reads her vows, looking at herself in the mirror.

Empowerment Contract

Once each initiate finishes reading her vows, P2 hands her a pen, and says:

Now, find your empowerment contract, and sign it before the witnesses assembled here.

Each initiate signs her empowerment contract.

Talisman(s) of Initiation

Once each initiate finishes signing her contract, P1 says:

Find your talismans of initiation, and put them on. You wear these talismans as a re-minder of the path you have taken to get to this moment, and as a commitment to walking the path that stretches forth from here.

Honoring of Initiates

One by one, as each initiate continues facing the mirror, the circle of her ritual sisters and her witness(es), if present, honor her with blessings, compliments, and gratitude for her work, her growth, and her self-commitment. The initiate may look at the witnesses as they speak, but her attention should be primarily on watching herself be adored by those she loves and respects. Before beginning the honoring, P2 says to the initiate:

Allow us to honor you. As we speak, watch the image in the mirror. You are a woman worthy of worship, and we are here to worship you. We are here to honor your growth, your commitment to your growth, and your beautiful unfolding.

Once the honoring of this initiate is complete, P1 offers the initiate the chalice of wine or water, and says:

To know, to will, to dare, to be silent.

P2 offers the initiate cake/cookie/a scrumptious morsel, and says:

Blessed is the fruit of thy womb.

Once she has taken the wine and food, the initiate goes back to semicircle, and allows the next initiate to approach. This can be performed in a clockwise flow, or as you please.

Once all initiates have been honored, P1 performs the Goddess in the Mirror for P2, then P2 for P1, allowing P1 and P2 to be anointed, take vows, sign contracts, don their talismans, be honored by the circle, and receive the wine and cakes of initiation.

Blessing the Treats, Water, and Wine

After the blessing, you may choose to have more informal sharing time in circle here. Eat, drink, and be merry! This may be your last circle together, so enjoy it. You may con-tinue to honor one another as you eat and drink, or talk about the amazing things you have learned about one another. Keep it positive, as you are still in sacred circle, and are actively creating the future you will each walk into from this moment on. Then P1 or P2 says:

> *This food is not just a symbol of, but the true substance of, nurturance, and of the cycles of life. May the sacrifice of this that I am about to ingest feed my body, my spirit, and my soul. May I always experience, receive, and honor my hungers. May all true hungers be fulfilled.*
>
> *Water is life. Life, and regeneration, and healing. Let this water remind me of my origins; of the womb, and of the blessed sea, the birthplace of life and that which forms the flow.*
>
> *This wine is the blood of willing sacrifice. It represents the cycles of life, death, and birth. It offers succor, and a doorway to new perception. May this wine bless me with the awareness of choice, and with divine vision and ecstasy.*

The water chalice is passed from person to person with the blessing "Water shared is life shared." The wine chalice is passed with the blessing "Wine offered is choice given and received." Food is passed with the blessing "May all true hungers be fulfilled."

As a group, take time to honor your bodies with treats, water, and wine. As you eat and drink, sit in awareness of the magick of transmutation: how the food, water, and wine affect your senses, and how these edible items become part of the very fabric of your cells. Allow gratitude, honor, and acceptance of and for the elements you are bringing into your bodies.

Ending of Ritual

All participants sit in circle once again and breathe. P1 or P2 says:

> *Yours is the temple. As you walk through the world, know that your body is a sacred vessel. It is consecrated to you, and to your unfolding and empowerment. As we learn to love and honor our bodies as the beautiful temples, wondrous tools, and amazing vehicles for transformation that they are, we grow closer to the divine gift of creation.*

Now, as each of you breathe again, inhaling the sacred scents, you prepare to walk forward into the world. You carry sacred space everywhere you go, and all you need is to remember: your body is sacred. Your breath is sacred. Your bones and blood and sweat

and tears are sacred. Your laughter is sacred, your voice is sacred, and your skin is sacred. All together, state aloud and claim this mantra:

This temple is mine.

As a group, turn your focus inward, close your eyes, breathe, and relax. Allow yourself to slowly come back to the world you inhabit, the room you are sitting in, and your daily life. As you open your eyes, give yourself a hug, remembering that even as you reenter the world, your body remains a sacred temple of creation and empowerment.

- Releasing of quarters and entities (optional).
- Opening of circle (optional).
- Banishing (optional).

Recipes, Correspondences, and Other Details You Might Need to Know

Just for the heck of it, read through this appendix. There may be something here that makes it easier to understand other parts of this book!

Magickal Tools: An Overview

In the Wiccan tradition, there are four basic tools; one for each direction, element, or quarter.

East

Blade, athame, knife, sword.

South

Wand.

West

Chalice, cup, goblet.

North

A disc or dish with a pentagram (five-pointed star) painted on it, or inscribed or carved into the surface.

Many people work with their own correspondences. Some use incense to represent the east, or a candle for the south. As I stated in Part Two: The Rituals, I believe that ritual work and all kinds of magick working may be performed just as effectively without tools. But if tools work for you, work it, grrl! (See also "Tools: To Have, or Not to Have . . . That Is the Question" in Rituals I and II.)

Candle Dressing

Use a carrier oil, and add a few drops of essential oil. Choose an essential oil that will support the magick you are working. Always use pure oils, especially if you are going to be burning the oil, as with a candle.

Apply the oil to the candle, thinking of the magick you will be working as you burn it. You may create a mantra to chant while you do the dressing, or you may just think thoughts related to the desired outcome or the emotional state of the working.

Many people dress taper candles from the center to the top, then the center to the bottom. Do it that way if you wish, but what matters the most is that what you are doing feels right to you, and works for you.

Chakras: Energy in the Body

Chakra is a Sanskrit word that means "wheel," and is a name that is used to refer to energy centers in our bodies. One may visualize these energy spots as spinning wheels of energy or colored light. There are many chakras, and they are located in slightly different spots according to the different systems. Most Western practitioners focus primarily on the seven chakras that are located in the trunk of the body.

If you are interested in working with these energy spots, I suggest that you study up on them a bit, and then investigate where they are in your body. There are millions of books out there on chakras, chakra systems, chakra work, and more. Many of these books say slightly different things, and no body is totally the same as any other. A general guideline that might hold more often than not: the seven chakras that I cover here are in the core of the body near the spine, and have openings at the front and back of the body. Here are those seven:

First Chakra

Sanskrit Name: Muladhara; Often Referred to as: Root chakra; Represents: Survival; Color: Red; Location: Perineum.

Second Chakra

Sanskrit Name: Svadhisthana; Often Referred to as: Sex chakra; Represents: Sexuality; Color: Orange; Location: Genitals.

Third Chakra

Sanskrit Name: Manipura; Often Referred to as: Power chakra; Represents: Power; Color: Yellow; Location: Somewhere between the solar plexus and the navel.

Fourth Chakra

Sanskrit Name: Anahata; Often Referred to as: Heart chakra; Represents: Love; Color: Green; Location: Sternum.

Fifth Chakra

Sanskrit Name: Vishuddha; Often Referred to as: Throat chakra; Represents: Voice; Color: Blue; Location: Throat.

Sixth Chakra

Sanskrit Name: Ajna; Often Referred to as: Third Eye chakra; Represents: Vision; Color: Lavender; Location: Above, and in triangulation to, the eyes.

Seventh Chakra

Sanskrit Name: Sahasrara; Often Referred to as: Crown chakra; Represents: Ascension; Color: Crystalline; Location: At or just above the top of the head.

Other chakras can be found throughout the body. For further reading suggestions, please see appendix III, and look for "Chakras" under the heading for chapter 1.

Color Correspondences: A Primer

Black

Depth, entering the mystery.

Red

Sex, blood magick.

Orange

Security, wealth.

Yellow

Power, inspiration.

Green

Regeneration, growth, verdancy.

Blue

Loyalty, truth.

Purple

Vision.

White

Purity, innocence.

Mantra Building, Sigil-Style

The idea behind this form of mantra building is to create a mantra that can affect your subconscious mind without having to confront the resistance of your conscious thoughts. Sometimes it's best to skirt the full-frontal assault. Creating a mantra that holds the intention of an affirmation, but doesn't have the ability to attract your own self-debilitating shields, can be very effective.

1. Write your mantra, like: *I love myself.*

2. Cross out all letters that repeat. Include each letter that appears only once, even if it appears multiple times. In other words, drop repeats of any letter. This will leave you with: *ILOVEMYSF.*

3. Take these letters and rearrange them into an unrecognizable word, or set of words, like: *SYF VO ELEM.* Work with it until the sound and feel of the word or phrase work for you.

4. Chant this mantra in place of your original phrase.

Incenses

Making your own incense to burn over charcoal is easy. It's also cleaner and purer than stick incense or other processed blends, and it's loaded with your personal intention because you have created, ground, and mixed it.

I provide three incense blends here, but you may, of course, create your own blends. Magickal herbal and aromatherapy correspondence charts abound on the web. A correspondence chart, your own intuition, some supplies, and some time and patience with which to experiment are all you need to become an incense-making mad woman.

If you choose to opt for my blends, I recommend using the first blend for Rituals One through Four, switching to the second blend for Ritual Five: Coming to Our Senses, and staying with that through Ritual Seven. The third blend may be used for any guided visualization or meditation.

To store your incense blends, you can get small, glass jam jars at crafting shops or even in some grocery stores. On the label, you may include ingredients and measurements, the properties of the ingredients, your intentions, and the date.

When creating an incense blend, feel your way through it. Always work with sensing the measurements, and lend your energy to the process of creation. Visualize the energy you are charging the blend with as you grind and mix. Make sure you are using your intention to create a magickal charge that supports the properties of the mix.

My blend recipes are guidelines. Experiment to make them work for you. There is no universal magickal formula. Always test your creations (including the ones based on my recipes, obviously) before using them in ritual space. And, a word of warning: Powdered incense burns quickly, and produces a lot of smoke. Use it sparingly but often. A little dab'll do ya!

Blend One: Devotion

Rose (love, healing, protection), copal (love and purification), and frankincense (protection, exorcism, spirit).

- Dried rose petals.
- Copal resin, either powdered or unprocessed.
- Frankincense resin, either powdered or unprocessed.
- Mortar and pestle.
- Storage bottle.

Mix equal parts copal and frankincense, and a third as much dried rose petals. Put in mortar, and grind until uniform. As you grind the materials, focus on the properties of the substances you are mixing. Use intention to create the magick of the incense.

Blend Two: Purely Empowered

Copal (love and purification), ylang ylang (peace, happiness, mood elevation), allspice (willpower, healing, courage), and benzoin (success, knowledge, stabilization).

- Copal resin, either tears or powdered.
- Benzoin resin, either tears or powdered.
- Allspice, ground or crushed.
- Ylang ylang oil, pure or in an organic base.
- Mortar and pestle.
- Mixing bowl.
- Storage bottle.

Mix equal parts copal and benzoin in the mortar, and add one-third part allspice. Mix with pestle until of a uniform, coarsely powdered consistency. Pour powdered mixture into mixing bowl, and add a few drops of ylang ylang oil. Mix. The blend will become crumbly and gummy as the powder absorbs the oil. It will remain this way. This mixture burns a bit more slowly than straight powder, but you should still use it sparingly.

Blend Three: Inner Vision

All ingredients listed here have meditative and clairvoyant properties. This incense is not going to make your house smell all nice and pretty, but it will help you get into an altered state of consciousness that will make visualization and meditation easier and more effective.

The last two items listed, tobacco and henbane, are toxic in large quantities, so use sparingly. For the tobacco, try to get unprocessed, raw tobacco leaves. The henbane you may be able to find at a botanica or a magickal supply store, or you can order it on the web. If you do not want to use the toxic components, you may just leave them out, or you may replace them with any of the following: thyme, poppy flowers, juniper, eyebright, or sage. The mixture may not be as strong, but it will still work fine.

- Wormwood *(Artemisia absinthium)*. Wormwood leaves can be purchased at magickal supply stores or on-line.
- Mugwort *(Artemisia vulgaris)*. Mugwort leaves can be purchased at magickal supply stores or on-line. Caution: contact with mugwort may cause dermatitis.
- Bay laurel leaves. Whole leaves can be purchased in the spices section of the grocery.
- Cedar. Dried cedar can be wildcrafted and dried or purchased at magickal supply stores.
- Yarrow. Yarrow flowers can be purchased at magickal supply stores or health food stores. Caution: contact with yarrow may cause dermatitis.
- Cinnamon. Powdered cinnamon can be purchased in the spices section of the grocery.
- Nutmeg. Powdered nutmeg can be purchased in the spices section of the grocery.
- Tobacco (toxic!). Use whole, dried, unprocessed leaves, if possible. They can be purchased at magickal supply stores or on-line.
- Henbane (toxic!). Henbane leaves can be purchased at magickal supply stores or on-line.
- Mortar and pestle.
- Mixing bowl.
- Storage bottle.

Mix equal parts wormwood and mugwort with the mortar and pestle. Add one whole dried bay leaf, crumbled. Add a generous pinch of cedar, and a generous pinch of yarrow. Grind and mix with pestle until the mixture is of uniform consistency. Once uniform and fairly powdery, add a pinch of cinnamon and a small pinch of nutmeg. Mix, and pour this mixture into the mixing bowl. Next, take a small portion of the tobacco leaf and a small bit of henbane, and put in the mortar. Mix with the pestle until the mixture is uniform. Add to the mixing bowl pinch by pinch, according to feel.

Wines

If you have a favorite ritual wine, use it. Otherwise, I recommend that you try different wines for different rituals. Think about what fits for you. If you want a sweet, fruity wine (perhaps for Ritual One: Your Body Is a Temple, and Ritual Five: Coming to Our Senses), try a Muscat (sweet, fruity), Port (sweet to crisp, rich) or Sherry (sweet, fruity, sometimes floral). If you want a deep red wine (perhaps for Ritual Four: The Descent), try a Shiraz (spicy, smooth), Cabernet (woody, deep), or Chianti (rich, complex). For Ritual Seven: Goddess in the Mirror (Completion), I suggest champagne or sparkling wine, to invoke the spirit of celebration!

Cookies, Cakes, Bread, and Other Edibles

Ritual cakes are generally small, cookie-like cakes, made by hand for the purpose of the ritual being performed. If you have the time and energy, I recommend creating your ritual cakes from scratch, and decorating them with appropriate symbols for the week's ritual. This may be done by the Priestess pro tem, or as a group project, if you are working with a group.

If you do not have the time or energy to commit to making your own cakes, you may buy something simple, yet sufficient, at the store. We used store-bought ginger snaps in a ritual group with which I worked dark moon ritual for a thirteen-moon cycle. The ginger snaps looked like dark moons, and they were yummy, too! So, you can find ready-to-purchase items that work.

Again, I want to say, though, that there's something to making your devotional offerings with your own hands. If you can do this at least once (perhaps for the first ritual, to see if it's a good fit), I really recommend it. It's possible (and often totally intuitive) to work a lot of magick into the cakes as you make them. Think of the movie *Like Water for Chocolate*. If you haven't seen that movie, see it! It's all about kitchen alchemy.

As you decorate the cakes, you can make this part of your ritual dedication. If you choose this route, here are symbols to work with for each week's ritual:

Ritual One: Temple.

Ritual Two: Breasts.

Ritual Three: Yoni.

Ritual Four: Uterus.

Ritual Five: Spiral.

Ritual Six: Stars.

Ritual Seven: Gateway, threshold, or Witches' broom.

You can find recipes for making magickal or ritual cakes on the internet, or you can create your own recipe, using any cookie recipe that you like as a starting point. If you are a natural-born "Kitchen Witch," start from scratch and see what you can do! Some good choices as starting points for intuitive Kitchen-Witchery include corn meal mixed with wheat flour, honey as sweetener, and wine for flavor and charge.

You may make savory cakes or sweet ones, depending on your desires and the work at hand. Either way, you may use seasonings, herbs, and other items that will amp up the work being done in a given ritual. For instance, in the cakes for Ritual Two: I Love Me!, you may want to include some rose water for love and healing.

Some of the rituals call for additional foods. That is covered in the ritual outlines in part 2.

Cakes of Light

Cakes of light are a Thelemic obsession. If you are adventurous, committed to Thelemic magick, or just curious, give it a go.

"For perfume, mix meal & honey & thick leavings of red wine: then oil of Abramelin and olive oil, and afterward soften & smooth down with rich fresh blood."

—*Liber Al vel Legis* (*The Book of the Law* by Aleister Crowley), III:23

If you want to know more, check here:
http://www.billheidrick.com/tlc1991/tlc0191.htm#hyatm. It offers the best advice I have yet found on the topic of how to actually make cakes of light.

Disposing of Ritual Offerings

To dispose of leftover ritual foods and drink (just what's in the chalice, not what's in the bottle; that may be used for future ritual . . . or polished off in ritual space if there are enough of you to drink it!), you may leave extra offerings out for the spirits/faeries/critters, you may cast them into a forested area, or you may use them to fertilize your favorite plants or your garden.

Correspondences: Quarters, Elements, Directions, and Other Entities

East = Air

Inspiration, communication, breath, clarity, vision.

South = Fire

Passion, transformation, heat, sexuality, desire.

West = Water

Emotion, birth, death, spirits, surrender, moist, flowing.

North = Earth

Wisdom, solidity, grace, depth, grounding, ancestors, stability.

Center = Core

Consciousness, focus, focal point, axis, inside.

Above = Sky or Heavens

Above/Sky/the Heavens is often seen as the Father aspect of the Mother/Father duality in many traditions. Sky, Father, God, Zeus, Jehovah, Judgment, guidance.

Below = Planet Earth

Below/Planet Earth is often seen as the Mother aspect of the Mother/Father duality.

Essential Oil Correspondence Chart

This is a mini-list. There are tons of essential oils out there. Again, these are my personal correspondences for these oils. You may have a totally different relationship with the oils listed than I do. Trust yourself. Purchase a few oils, and write down the images and emotions that come to mind when you smell them. Truly, I would rather that you didn't even *read* this chart . . . just gather your own associations, and use your oils accordingly. However, if you need some help, here's a starting point for you.

- Amber: Grounding, sensual awareness.

- Jasmine: Sex, money, prophesy, power, secrets, night.

- Lavender: Peace, calming, relaxation, healing.

- Rose: Love, whether romantic, sexual, soulful, or all of these! Peace, beauty, dedicated to Aphrodite. (Rose oil is expensive when you get the good stuff, but it goes a long way.)

- Rosemary: Focus, healing, purification, protection.

- Sandalwood: Earth, clarity, sensual awareness, strength.

- Tangerine: Power, strength, energy, excitement.

- Ylang ylang: Peace, calming, sensuality, mood revitalizer, depression fighter.

Foot Bath

Ahhh, one of the nicest things you and a friend can do for one another. So easy, too!

What You Will Need

- A friend to trade roles with.

- A basin. A plastic dish washing tub is fine. The only requirement: your feet need to fit.

- Hot water.

- Nice, clean foot towels.

- Foot lotion or other soothing, thick, creamy oil.

Optional items:

- Epsom or other bath salts.

- Oils. Bath oils, olive oil, jojoba, etc.

- Essential oils. A few drops will do.

- Foot-scrubbing products.
- Loofa sponge.
- Pumice stone.
- Calendula or lavender flowers, rose petals.

If you wanna get really fancy, and add in a pedicure:

- Cuticle cream.
- Nail file.
- Nail polish.

How-To

- Set the tub in front of a chair. Your friend should be sitting in the chair.
- Fill the tub with nice, warm water.
- Add other items.
- Wash and rub your friend's feet, while telling her all the things you love about her, and especially making a magickal act of honoring her feet, and the path she walks upon.
- Massage your friend's feet, toes, calves. Use scrubby stuff, if you want.
- Dry feet.
- Massage feet and calves with foot lotion.
- Optional: follow with pedicure.
- And *switch!*

Sensual Bath Salts

- Two cups Epsom salt, Dead Sea salts, or other mineral salts.
- Mixing bowl.
- Storage container, if you are not going to use right away. The two-cup measurement is good for one use. You may increase the amounts in this recipe if you want more than one use.
- Mortar and pestle for grinding flowers and herbs (optional).

To this base you may add any essential oil blend that you like to bathe with (sandalwood, rose, ylang ylang, lavender). You may also add dried flowers (lavender, rose petals, calendula) and herbs (basil, mugwort, rosemary, mint). Mix in the bowl, making sure that all materials are fairly evenly distributed. You may grind the flowers and herbs if you don't like having full leaves, petals, or flower heads in your bath.

If you prefer not to have the herbal solids floating in your bath, you may instead make an herbal mix and put it in a fine mesh bag. Add this bag of herbs to the bath water.

Optional Sensual Bath Additions

Clay
You may use a clay beauty mask mix, or you may use raw or dried clay or mineral mud. This additive is great for purifying and softening the skin.

Whole Milk
Milk is perfect for soothing, clarifying, and softening the skin. Use about one quart, warmed.

Calendula Flowers, or Calendula Milk
Calendula softens and conditions the skin. To make calendula milk, just add one-half to one cup dried calendula flowers to the warming milk. Allow it to steep until the milk is a warm, golden color.

Honey
Honey is mildly astringent, antibacterial, moisturizing, and purifying. Use two to four tablespoons. Heat first to liquefy, then add to warm bath water.

Oil
If you have dry skin, adding oil to your bath water is a great way to reduce the drying effects of water. You may use almond, jojoba, or olive oil. Jojoba is luxurious but pricey. Almond is light, versatile, and affordable. Olive is heavier. A little bit goes a long way.

You may also infuse oils with different herbs or flowers. You can find the directions for this on web sites and in many herbal books.

You may also use almond or jojoba oil to stretch your pure essential oils. To do so, partially fill a one-ounce bottle with oil, then add a few drops of whatever essential oil you want to stretch. You can figure out your ratios by feel. Keep a chart and track your progress if you like, so that you won't have to figure the ratio out again each time you create a blend. The diluted oil won't be as intense as the pure oils, but with some essential oils this is a really good thing! Never use lemon oil, for example, directly on your skin or in your bath unless it has been diluted.

Devotion Oil

You will use this oil in Ritual Seven, and in your daily practice for chapter 7. Who knows, it may even become your "signature scent." You may wear it whenever and wherever you like, and it will have the power to remind you of the Goddess you are! Choose the oils based on scent, attribution (you can decide what oils best invoke the qualities you want to devote yourself to), intuition, or feeling. Here's what you will need:

- A one-ounce glass bottle with a cap. You can get this sort of bottle at many health food stores, or you can order them on-line.
- A small funnel. The opening must fit in the neck of the one-ounce bottle.
- Up to three of your favorite essential oils.
- Almond, jojoba, or grape seed oils as a carrier oil.

Fill the bottle about two-thirds full with the carrier oil. To create the right mix, start by adding only a few drops of each of the essential oils to the carrier oil. Add to your own liking, until you have created a personalized scent that is all yours!

The Vow of the Bodhisattva

The Vow of the Bodhisattva is a Buddhist vow that comes from two branches of Buddhism: Mahayana and Vajrayana. This is a vow to remain embodied, to forgo Nirvana, or enlightenment, until all beings have reached enlightenment. It is a vow of love and compassion for all beings, based in the belief that our continuing to return to the earthly plane and to practice the Way of the Buddha, life after life, will assist all in reaching Buddhahood.

Here is another adaptation of the vow that is truer to the original form, but is still interfaith.

> *Beings are without number. I vow to be one.*
>
> *Suffering is inexhaustible. I vow to extinguish it.*
>
> *Paths to enlightenment are innumerable. I vow to walk them.*
>
> *Enlightenment is not a goal. I vow to achieve it.*

For more information on the Bodhisattva Vow (including links to more traditional versions of it), Buddhism, and the Tibetan Bodhisattva and Goddess Tara, please see appendix III.

A Compendium of S/heroes

Okay, so maybe *s/heroes* sounds a little dorky, or, even worse, revisionist. What word would you prefer that I use? Heroine? I just can't. I have a couple of reasons why. One is that I don't want to be reminded of a drug—heroin—every time I think of or talk about the women I admire. The other is the "–ine" part. It just makes female heroes sound more dainty, flowery, and weak. I'm not down!

Technically, *hero* is a word that may be used for male or female heroes, but it's not generally used that way. Hero is almost always used to describe a man. English is a living language! It's evolved massively lately. I say let's use some of the current fluidity to create new terms for women. So, s/heroes it is, for now. You'll get used to it! Maybe in a decade or so, we can all use the word heroes and know that it applies to both men and women.

Each category in this compendium has three subcategories: "Archetypes," "Historical Figures," and "Current Pop-Culture Icons." I hope you will enjoy researching the names I have listed, and the occasional mini-bio I have provided. I hope also that you will be inspired by this work to seek out more information on the lives of any s/heroes who really reach out to you, whatever the context. Maybe this will inspire you to take time to interview your mother, or look up your third-grade teacher. There are s/heroes everywhere!

The internet is an amazing resource on this front. Many of these amazing women and archetypes have fan sites, bios, and even shrines to them built on the fertile frontier of cyberspace. Many also have biographies or autobiographies that are easy to find in your local bookstore, or even at your library.

One caveat: this is a very partial listing of the female heroes out there. I have left many out, and this list is weighted toward the women I have learned something from in my research and in my life. If I left your favorite out, don't get mad, get even! Send me a note, and perhaps I will be able to add her to my list for future projects. You could even use the opportunity to create your own tribute website in honor of the women who have influenced your life.

Above all, enjoy this compendium (as limited as it is), and search out more info about the rich and fascinating history of women who changed, and are still changing, the rules.

Virgins and Maidens

While the terms *maiden* and *virgin* imply chastity, to me that element is not the defining aspect of maidenhood. In the way I am using these terms, it's more about a subset of that concept: a girl or women belonging to herself.

Throughout the ages there have been women who chose not to marry, and made this choice for many reasons. Unfortunately, many of their stories are lost to the sands of time. We do know, though, that often a woman who loved women would be considered a virgin. She couldn't very well correct those who assumed, could she?

Artemis and Diana are "virgin" archetypes who consorted only with their equally "virginal" nymphs in the wild hills of Greece and Rome. The Virgin Queen may or may not have ever bedded any of her suitors. Dr. Elizabeth Blackwell never married, and was arrested repeatedly for dressing in men's attire.

Archetypes

Artemis

This Greek Goddess is a virgin, Goddess of the hunt, a midwife, and a protector of women and children. She is armed with a bow and a quiver of arrows. Artemis lives free of the bonds of cultural convention, running free in the hills with her hounds, the animals of the forest, and her virginal Nymphs.

—http://messagenet.com/myths/bios/artemis.html.

Diana

Diana is the Roman name for the Goddess Artemis. Later she also became Queen of the Witches, with a whole subset of Goddess worship bearing her name. Dianic Witchcraft is woman-oriented Goddess worship. Dianic covens are often for women only.

—http://www.thewhitegoddess.co.uk/goddess/diana.html.

Kore

In the Ancient Greek, *Kore* means "young girl," or "daughter." Kore is one of the deities honored in the great Eleusinian Mysteries. Kore is the innocent, young daughter of Demeter, the Grain Mother, and Zeus, the patriarch of the Olympian Gods. Kore represents eternal springtime, and the hope that is born again with each sprouting shoot.

—http://www.spiralgoddess.com/Demeter.html.

Hestia/Vesta

Hestia is the Greek Goddess of the hearth. She is sister to Zeus, and the daughter of Rhea and Cronos. She was known as Vesta to the Romans, and her Priestesses were known as Vestal Virgins.

—http://www.paralumun.com/romevesta.htm.

The Valkyrie

Odin's shield-maidens were fierce warriors and protectors.

—http://www.dolls-n-daggers.com/Valkyrie.html.

Historical Figures

Joan of Arc, 1412–1431

http://www.newadvent.org/cathen/08409c.htm.

Queen Elizabeth I

"You may have many a wiser prince sitting in this seat, but you never have had, or shall have, any who loves you better."

—From Elizabeth's "Golden Speech of 1601," http://www3.newberry.org/elizabeth/forthemedia/elizhistory.html.

The Virgin Queen remained unmarried through her life, though she had many suitors. She was responsible for England's final conversion to the Protestant faith, and single-handedly ruled England for over forty-four years.

—http://englishhistory.net/tudor/monarchs/eliz1.html.

Elizabeth Blackwell, M.D., 1821–1910

http://campus.hws.edu/his/blackwell/biography.html.

Susan B. Anthony

http://www.susanbanthonyhouse.org/biography.htm.

Emily Dickinson

http://www.online-literature.com/dickinson.

Mary Cassatt

http://www.ibiblio.org/wm/paint/auth/cassatt.

Current Pop-Culture Icons

Mary-Kate and Ashley Olsen

The last virgins in America. In using the term *virgin* here, I am not speaking to whether these young women have taken lovers or not. I am pointing rather to the fact that their mutual image is based in the identity of innocence and self-containment.

—http://www.marykateandashley.com.

Mothers, Healers, and Wives

When I first started this section, it was Mothers only. I added Healers and Wives with the dawning realization that there are other aspects to this stage of life (duh!). Also, I found that there were few mothers in the historical category. By broadening this category to include women who may not be mothers but are known to have contributed in some traditionally "motherly" way to culture, I found that I could honor their stories as well.

Archetypes

Gaia

The primary mother in the Greek Pantheon, Gaia is one of the elder Greek Goddesses. From her, many of the other Gods and Goddesses were born. Gaia is the earth herself, and all the creatures who live on her are born of her womb.

—http://www.kheper.net/topics/Gaia/goddess.htm.

Demeter

Another of the deities given homage and memory in the Eleusinian Rites, Demeter is the Grain Mother, mother of growing things. Her daughter is Kore, the eternal springtime. In the Homeric Hymns, Demeter is credited with gifting humankind with agriculture.

—http://www.pantheon.org/articles/d/demeter.html.

Ceres

While having her own origins, Ceres came to possess many of the attributes of Demeter as the Hellenic culture was assimilated by the Romans. Ceres also became the Goddess of the Plebeians in Roman culture, with the office of protecting the plebes from the patricians. She governed the fair distribution of grain, and marriage and divorce law.

—http://www.astrostar.com/articles/Ceres.htm.

Isis

The principal Goddess of Ancient Egypt, Isis is the daughter of Geb and Nut, the earth her father and the heavens her mother. Isis was many things: Goddess of Love, Magick Maker, Goddess of Fertility and Healing, and Queen of the Underworld. She is wife to Osiris, and mother to Horus. Isis is often represented as a winged Goddess, and she always carries an ankh, the Egyptian symbol of life, death, and rebirth. She is the mother of the God Who Dies and Is Reborn, a cycle that has many manifestations in religions the globe over.

—http://www.touregypt.net/isis.htm.

Mary, Mother of God

A younger Goddess but one of the most widely worshipped today, by far, Mary is a wonderful and compassionate Mother Goddess.

—http://www.newadvent.org/cathen/15464b.htm.

Brighid, Bride, Breed

Healer, Goddess, and Catholic saint, Bride has stood the test of time. There are shrines dedicated to her in Ireland to this day.

—http://www.seaofstorms.com/mecca/goddess.html.

Hera

The iconic mother and wife to Zeus, Hera stands for the hearth, the family, and propriety. Among other things, she is a jealous wife with a philandering husband. Not the happiest of tales, but it makes for some good Greek myths.

—http://www.promotega.org/asu30020/hera.html.

Historical Figures

Florence Nightingale, 1820–1910

Nightingale was a woman with a calling. The reforms she worked for and the writings she authored still influence the practice of medicine today.

—http://www.florence-nightingale.co.uk/flo2.htm.

Sacagawea

http://www.pbs.org/weta/thewest/people/s_z/sacagawea.htm.

Martha Washington

Our first First Lady.

—http://www.whitehouse.gov/history/firstladies/mw1.html.

Eleanor Roosevelt

The first First Lady to go in with a plan.

—http://www.whitehouse.gov/history/firstladies/ar32.html.

Jackie O.

The First Lady with the most amazing sense of style, a beautiful husband, and beautiful children. O, Jackie!

—http://www.whitehouse.gov/history/firstladies/jk35.html.

Princess Diana

A princess story come to life, Princess Di lived the dream and did magick with it. As Diana grew into herself and out of the Royal House, she used her almost accidental influence in positive ways.

—http://www.royal.gov.uk/output/page151.asp.

June Carter Cash

A truly iconic, inimitable mother and wife.

—http://maninblack.net/June.html.

Current Pop-Culture Icons

Coretta Scott King

A mother who never sacrificed ideals for family, nor family for ideals. A true warrior of love.

—http://www.africana.com/research/encarta/csking.asp.

Rosie O'Donnell

This is what a mom looks like.

—http://www.eonline.com/On/Holly/Shows/Odonnell/bio.html.

Angelina Jolie

Yep, this is what a mom looks like, too!

—http://www.celebrity-fansites.com/stars/angelina_jolie/bio.html.

Pamela Anderson

And this!

—http://www.pamwatch.com/bio.html.

Kim Gordon

This mother is a Sonic Youth who toured for years while raising her kid. She's the reason we're still punk rock.

—http://en.wikipedia.org/wiki/Kim_Gordon.

J. K. Rowling

http://gaga.essortment.com/jkrowlingbiogr_reak.htm.

Lovers and Sacred Whores

Here we are at the *whore* word. I promised you an explanation of this one, and it is my pleasure to offer that to you here. You may have heard of the concept of the sacred whore, or the temple prostitute. If the mystical and magickal aspects of giving on the sexual level appeal to you, I encourage you to do some research on this subject.

At this juncture, I offer you an etymological basis for understanding these words. They are such loaded terms, and both have beautiful subtextual meaning. The term *prostitute* comes from the Latin *pro* and *stituere*. *Pro* means "before," and *stituere* means "to stand." The word *prostitute* literally means "to stand before." *Whore* comes from the Indo-European root *Ka,* which means "to like or desire," from which *carus,* the Latin for *dear,* leads us to *caress, cherish,* and *charity.* Whore also shares its root with the word *queen.*

Archetypes

Ishtar

http://sangha.net/messengers/ishtar.htm.

Babalon

http://www.sexmagick.com/aisha/mywork/procession.htm.

Aphrodite

The ever popular Hellenic Goddess of Love, mother to Cupid, and lover of Dionysus, this lady knows how to party!

—http://messagenet.com/myths/bios/aphrodite.html.

Mary Magdalene

The second Mary, this Mary is also prayed to. Not by most Catholics, though. Rumored by some to be a prostitute, and by others to be the wife of Christ, and by still others to be a prostitute *and* the wife of Christ, Magdalene is a woman shrouded in mystery. We do know that she washed Christ's feet, though, and that's pretty sexy.

—http://www.magdalene.org.

Historical Figures

Veronica Franco , 1546–1591

Have you seen the movie *Dangerous Beauty?* See it!

—http://www.jazzbabies.com/home/franco.htm.

Mae West

"Marriage is a great institution, but I'm not ready for an institution."

—http://www.quotationspage.com/quote/405.html, http://www.bookrags.com/bio graphy/mae-west/.

Marilyn Monroe

"That's the trouble, a sex symbol becomes a thing. But if I'm going to be a symbol of something, I'd rather have it sex than some other things we've got symbols of."

—http://www.ariga.com/frosties/monroemarilyn.shtml, http://www.marilynmonroe. com/about/bio.html.

Josephine Baker, 1906–1975

All the rage in Paris in the '20s, Baker was an amazing woman who was not afraid to flaunt what she had: gorgeous dark skin, beautiful lips, amazing breasts, and a dance style to die for. Josephine was a lover, though she knew how to fight, too.

—http://www.harlemlive.org/shethang/profiles/josephinebaker/jbaker.html.

Current Pop-Culture Icons

Annie Sprinkle

Have you seen her movie *Sluts and Goddesses?* See it!!!

—http://www.sexuality.org/l/art/sprinbio.htm.

Nina Hartley

More than twenty years in porn, and still going strong. Oh, and she's smart, politically aware, spiritually conscious, sweet, and HOT HOT HOT!

—http://www.adultfilmfan.com/ninahartley.php.

Susie Bright

The original "sexpert." I believe she coined the term!

—http://susiebright.blogs.com/about.html.

Crones and Hags

In researching the etymology of the word *crone,* I found that its root meaning is "carrion" (from the Vulgar Latin *coronia).* However, the root of *crony* is a newer word, and is assumed to be based on the Greek *kronos,* meaning time. I say we keep using the term crone, and assume that meaning!

Hag is a word with a rich and varied past, and has carried the meaning of everything from Witch, to wise old woman with magickal powers, to hedge-rider.

Archetypes

Hecate

The Hellenic Crone aspect. She travels with a pack of hounds, stands at the crossroads, and is a midwife, leading beings into and out of their earthly incarnations.

—http://www.goddessgift.com/goddess-myths/goddess_hecate.htm.

Cailleach

This Gaelic Winter Goddess brings the cold, storms, and snow. She is also credited with being the cause of weather, and is fond of animals.

—http://www.joellessacredgrove.com/Celtic/deitiesc.html.

Historical Figures

Mother Jones

Mother Jones was afforded, along with a choice few others during different time periods, the title of "the most dangerous woman in America." This white-haired, angelic-faced woman of a certain age was a self-proclaimed "hell raiser" who fought long and hard for workers' rights. She battled steadfastly for the eight-hour work day, organized strikers and strikers' wives, and spearheaded the Children's Crusade against child labor. She had her own children, but lost them all to yellow fever. Out of her loss she built a legacy, and all the workers of America became the children of Mother Jones.

—http://womenshistory.about.com/library/weekly/aa010430.htm.

Katharine Hepburn

http://womenshistory.about.com/cs/quotes/a/qu_k_hepburn.htm.

Current Pop-Culture Icons

The Queen Mother

http://womenshistory.about.com/library/bio/blbio_elizabeth_mum.htm.

Angelica Huston

http://www.imdb.com/name/nm0001378.

Dark Queens

The Dark Queens are a certain type of woman. Secretive perhaps, mysterious, hidden. She lives in the shadows, or often in the chthonic realm—the Underground—and is no stranger to sacrifice. Many of the Dark Queens find some form of meaning, or even resurrection and eternal life, through their own sacrifices.

Archetypes

Caryatid

http://www.absoluteastronomy.com/encyclopedia/c/ca/caryatid.htm.

Red Queen

Ereshkigal

http://www.gotojassminesitenow.com/goddesses/ereshkigal.html.

Persephone

http://www.goddessgift.com/goddess-myths/goddess_persephone.htm.

Virgin of Guadalupe

http://www.mexonline.com/virginofguadalupe.htm.

Historical Figures

Frida Kahlo

http://cgfa.sunsite.dk/kahlo/kahlo_bio.htm.

Marlene Dietrich

http://www.marlene.com.

Bettie Page

http://www.bettiepage.com.

Martha Graham

http://womenshistory.about.com/library/bio/blbio_martha_graham.htm.

Mata Hari

http://www.bookrags.com/biography/mata-hari.

Isadora Duncan

http://www.sfmuseum.org/bio/isadora.html.

Billie Holiday

"You can be up to your boobies in white satin, with gardenias in your hair and no sugar cane for miles, but you can still be working on a plantation."

　　—http://afroamhistory.about.com/od/billieholiday/a/lhorne.htm, http://www.cmgww.com/music/holiday/bio.html.

Edna St. Vincent Millay

http://www.poets.org/poet.php/prmPID/160.

Current Pop-Culture Icons

Sinead O'Connor

http://www.iband.com/music/o_bios/Sinead_O_Connor.html.

Dita Von Teese

http://suicidegirls.com/words/Dita+von+Teese+by+Laura+Nixon, www.dita.net/bio.php.

Siouxsie Sioux

http://siberia82.tripod.com/siouxbio.html.

P. J. Harvey

http://www.mp3.com/pj-harvey/artists/21900/summary.html.

Rule Breakers, World Shapers

This category needs little introduction. This is the hall of fame for those women and archetypes who busted out of the other boxes, perhaps even while fulfilling them. These s/heroes lived lives where they put everything on the line, and often had a blast doing it, even against the odds and in the midst of danger.

Natalie Angier

http://www.secularhumanism.org/library/fi/angier_24_5.htm.

Starhawk

http://www.starhawk.org.

Susan Sarandon

http://www.nndb.com/people/762/000024690.

Emily Dickinson

http://www.cswnet.com/~erin/emily.htm.

Goddesses

Kali

http://www.goddess.ws/kali.html.

Pele

http://www.thewhitemoon.com/gallery/Pele2.html.

Nemesis

http://waltm.net/nemesis.htm.

Tara

http://www.goddessgift.com/goddess-myths/goddess_tara_white.htm.

Historical Figures

Hypatia, 355?–415 CE

"Reserve your right to think, for even to think wrongly is better than not to think at all."

—http://space.about.com/od/astronomerbiographies/a/hypatiabio.htm.

Hypatia was a natural philosopher and taught mathematics and natural sciences in Alexandria, Egypt. Little more is known about Hypatia except that she was daughter of Theon, who taught at the School of the Alexandrine Library. Hypatia made tools for her scientific experiments, and wrote treatises in the areas of geography, algebra, and astronomy. She is rumored to have been Pagan, and to have had a hand in politics. She died a violent death at the hands of a mob of Christian monks, or possibly was lynched as part of a political intrigue.

—http://pages.prodigy.net/fljustice/hypatia.htm.

Sojourner Truth, 1797–1883

"I feel that if I have to answer for the deeds done in my body just as much as a man, I have a right to have just as much as a man. There is a great stir about colored men getting their rights, but not a word about the colored women; and if colored men get their rights, and not colored women theirs, you see the colored men will be masters over the women, and it will be just as bad as it was before."

—Excerpted from a speech by Sojourner Truth in New York, 1867, http://afroamhistory.about.com/library/blsojourner_truth_1867speech.htm.

Sojourner Truth was a woman of faith. Raised in slavery, Sojourner had a hard life, but always relied on her faith to carry her through. After emancipation, she spent years walking the east coast states and preaching. She was also took part in many utopian communities. Truth spoke for the rights of women, and of all the disenfranchised. She campaigned until her death for equality for all.

—http://search.eb.com/women/articles/Truth_Sojourner.html.

Emma Goldman, 1869–1940

" . . . I had seen enough of the horrors of married life in my own home. Father's harsh treatment of mother, the constant wrangles and bitter scenes that ended in mother's fainting spells . . . Together with my own marital experiences they had convinced me that binding people for life was wrong . . .

"If ever I love a man again, I will give myself to him without being bound by the rabbi or the law . . . and when that love dies, I will leave without permission."

—Emma Goldman, *Living My Life.*

Red Emma is the most famous female anarchist in history, and a foremost figure in the American Anarchist movement. Goldman believed in the freedom to love without bonds, never had children, and lived her life on her own terms. Emma was arrested numerous times for her activities on many issues, including providing impoverished women with information about birth control. (This was a good bit before Margaret Sanger came along.) She spent her life fighting for workers' rights, women's rights, and the rights of the poor, and organized against the draft during WWI.

—http://www.jewwatch.com/jew-mindcontrol-anarchism-emmagoldman.html.

Victoria Claflin Woodhull, 1838–1927

"While others of my sex devoted themselves to a crusade against the laws that shackle the women of the country, I asserted my individual independence . . . While others sought to show that there was no valid reason why a woman should be treated . . . as being inferior to man, I boldly entered the arena of politics and business and exercised the rights I already possessed. I therefore claim the right to speak for the unenfranchised women of the country and . . . I now announce myself as a candidate for the Presidency."

—Victoria Claflin Woodhull, from Barbara Goldsmith's *Other Powers,* pp. 212.

Woodhull was the first female stockbroker, and she ran for the Presidency in 1872, nearly fifty years before American women had won the right to vote. Victoria's vice presidential running mate, Fredrick Douglass, was a former slave. Victoria's platform was short skirts and free love . . . or, the right of women to wear hems above the ankle, and the right to divorce. She was hailed as "Mrs. Satan" by the press of her day. Talk about a woman ahead of her times!

—http://us.history.wisc.edu/hist102/bios/17.html.

Harriet Tubman

http://www.civilwarhome.com/tubmanbio.htm.

Simone de Beauvoir

http://www.philosophypages.com/ph/beav.htm.

Janis Joplin

http://www.officialjanis.com/bio.html.

Rosa Parks

http://www.achievement.org/autodoc/page/par0pro-1.

Evita Peron

http://womenshistory.about.com/od/peroneva.

Martha Graham

"Great dancers are not great because of their technique, they are great because of their passion."

—http://www.brainyquote.com/quotes/quotes/m/marthagrah133358.html.

Indira Gandhi

http://www.multied.com/bio/people/gandhi.html.

Denise Levertov

http://www.bookrags.com/biography/denise-levertov.

Current Pop-Culture Icons

Madonna/Esther

She grabbed her crotch, simulated masturbation on stage, had a child on her own, founded a multimillion-dollar empire, and has never stopped looking damn good while doing, and having, it all.

—http://www.angelfire.com/co3/bigbother/madonna.htm.

Karen Finley

Finley is a fearless artist who has talked about subjects such as rape, AIDS, death, and sex. Primarily known for her performance art, she has also worked with environmental art, and a number of other mediums. As likely her largest claim to fame, Finley was the main respondent in the Supreme Court case of "the NEA Four." It was an ongoing battle that revolved around the funding of her work, and the work of three other artists, by the National Endowment for the Arts. Finley is a feminist whose work deals with sexuality, among other topics.

—http://www.artfacts.net/index.php/pageType/artistInfo/artist/29173.

bell hooks

http://www.bookrags.com/biography/bell-hooks.

Patti Smith

http://www.aristarec.com/psmith/smithbio.html.

Katherine Dunham

"I used to want the words 'She tried' on my tombstone. Now I want 'She did it.'"

—http://www.brainyquote.com/quotes/quotes/k/katherined166859.html, http://www.bookrags.com/biography/katherine-dunham.

Diane di Prima

http://www.ksu.edu/english/janette/installations/MaryV/biography.htm.

Ani DiFranco

Known as "the Little Folk Singer Who Could," Ani is a self-made woman, and she does it her way. With a number of self-produced albums under her belt, she has chosen to remain independent. In the process she ended up founding her own label, Righteous Babe Records, which gives voice to other indie artists who would have a hard time being heard without Ani's support.

—http://www.askmen.com/women/singer_200/216_ani_difranco.html.

Mystic

http://evilmonito.com/007/mystic/mystic.htm.

Nadine Strossen

Long-time president of the ACLU and author of *Defending Pornography: Free Speech, Sex and the Fight for Women's Rights.*

—http://ome.ksu.edu/lectures/dorothy/bio/strossen.html.

Gloria Steinem

http://www.nwhp.org/tlp/biographies/steinem/steinem_bio.html.

Chief Wilma Mankiller

The first female Chief of the Cherokee Nation, Mankiller brought a sense of pride back to her people, and while she faced plenty of adversity along the way, she did it all without losing her sense of humor, honor, and humility.

—http://www.bookrags.com/biography/wilma-mankiller.

The '91ers

The American women's soccer team, widely known as "the '91ers" after their first big win at the World Cup in 1991, took gold in the '04 Olympics. It was a bittersweet and emotional moment, as Mia Hamm, Joy Fawcett, and Julie Foudy, three of the five original team members (Hamm, Foudy, Fawcett, Kristine Lilly, and Brandi Chastain) had announced plans for retirement preceding the Olympic Games. At the time of the Olympics win, not one of the five was under thirty-two years of age. In the thirteen years that these women took the soccer world by storm, they changed the rules for all the female athletes that come after them.

—http://www.unitedsoccerathletes.com.

APPENDIX III

Informational Resources

This is a chapter-by-chapter listing of on-topic websites, books, and other resources. There is also an additional section for resources that are not on-topic to any specific chapter, but seem in-line with the vibe of *Sexy Witch*.

Chapter One: Your Body Is a Temple

Altar of Self-Love

Vulva Pillows

The Velvet Vulva™, http://www.artgoddess.com/vulva-page.html.
Kinda pricey, but very pretty.

Make Your Own Vulva Art

Leslie Olin, *Yoni Shields,* http://www.yoni.com/sheilds/index.shtml.

Make Your Own Pussy Coin Purse

Visit my friend Sarah's site, *All About My Vagina,* http://myvag.net/zine/2004summer/luckyvulva/.

Aphrodite and Eros Statues

Mythic Images, http://www.mythicimages.com.

Chakras

Eastern Body, Western Mind, by Anodea Judith (Berkeley, CA: Celestial Arts, 2004).

Chakras, http://www.zaalberg.freeserve.co.uk/chakras.htm.

Eclectic Energies, http://www.eclecticenergies.com/chakras/differences.php.

Chapter Two: I Love Me, I Love Me Not, I Love Me!

The Great Weight Debate

The Obesity Myth: Why America's Obsession with Weight is Hazardous to Your Health, by Paul Campos (New York: Gotham Books, 2004).

Big Fat Lies: The Truth About Your Weight and Your Health, by Glenn A. Gaesser (Carlsbad, CA: Gürze Books, 2002).

Just the Weigh You Are: How to Be Fit and Healthy, Whatever Your Size, by Steven Jonas and Linda Konner (Shelburne, VT: Chapters Pub., 1997).

The Size Acceptance Movement

Revolting Bodies? The Struggle to Redefine Fat Identity, by Kathleen LeBesco (Amherst, MA: Univ. of Mass. Press, 2004).

The National Association to Advance Fat Acceptance

http://www.naafa.org/.

"Millions of fat Americans, as well as individuals from around the world, constitute a group that exists in a society geared toward slimness as an ideal. They therefore constitute a minority group with many of the attributes of other minority groups: poor self-image, guilt feelings, employment discrimination, exploitation by commercial interests, and being the subject of ridicule.

...It is the aim of this organization to help people all sizes of large deal more effectively with these and other problems and to promote more tolerance and understanding from society."

—From the NAAFA Constitution.

Lookism

Anti-Lookism Is Not Extreme, http://www.amnation.com/vfr/archives/000619.html.

Lookism: How It Affects Us, http://www.geocities.com/s_cullars/lookism.htm.

Charted Institute of Personnel and Development, "Getting Under the Skin of 'Lookism,'" http://www.cipd.co.uk/press/ResourceArea/FeatureArticles/Getting+under+the+skin+of +lookism.htm.

Learn About the Media Influence on Your Self-Image

About-Face, http://about-face.org.

"About-Face promotes positive self-esteem in girls and women of all ages, sizes, races and backgrounds through a spirited approach to media education, outreach and activism."

—From the About-Face mission statement.

Adbusters Magazine, http://www.adbusters.org/home/.

Gender Equality

United Nations Population Fund, http://www.unfpa.org/gender/faq_gender.htm.

"UNFPA...helps governments in the world's poorest countries, and in other countries in need, to formulate population policies and strategies in support of sustainable development. All UNFPA-funded programmes promote women's equality."

—From the UNFPA website.

Dress Reform Today: Top Freedom

Legal Freedom, "Ten Women Sue for Topfree Rights in Federal Court," http://www.legal-freedom.com/topfree/.

"Scientific studies show that forcing women to wear tops while men enjoy topfree-dom causes a psychological phenomenon called 'objectification.' Objectification contributes to social problems of sexual assault, domestic violence, and sexual harassment. The requirement for women to wear shirts where men do not creates a badge of second-class citizenship for women."

—Excerpt from the Legal Freedom website.

Women's Choice, "Topfree Action," http://www.geocities.com/womens_choice_org/topfreedom.html.

"What we are fighting for? We are fighting . . . for women's right to be topless WHERE EVER men can . . .

What we want to explain to society is that a topless woman is NOT a nude woman—just like a man without a t-shirt is not a nude man."

—Excerpt from the Women's Choice website.

Gender Bending

My Gender Workbook: How to Become a Real Man, a Real Woman, the Real You, or Something Else Entirely, by Kate Bornstein (New York: Routledge, 1998).

The Chicago Kings, http://www.chicagokings.com/.

DC Drag Kings, http://www.dckings.com/.

San Diego Kings Club, http://www.sdkingsclub.com/.

Drag King Magazine, http://drag.lesbiru.com/eng/.

The Drag King Book, by Del LaGrace Volcano and Judith "Jack" Halberstam (New York: Serpent's Tail, 1999).

Ms. Direction Zine, http://www.zinethug.com/.

Chapter Three: Pussy Power!

This Is Your Pussy!

Pretty Pussies!

Petals, by Nick Karras (San Diego, CA: Crystal River Publishing, 2004).

Snatch Styling

It's Your Snatch, Style It if You Want!

Gusto, http://www.dailygusto.com/columns/bitchslap/index-102103.html.

A Condemnation of the Hairless Craze

Nerve, http://www.nerve.com/Dispatches/Featherstone/shockingFuzz/main.asp.

A Brief History of Pubic Coiffure

World of the Nudest Nudist, http://www.wnn.nu/UK/History/historyhair.html.

Know Your Parts!

Female Anatomy 640, http://daphne.palomar.edu/psycsoc125/HSClass/anatomy_ts/pages/F_Anat.html.

Get Your Specula Here!

Medical Toys.com, http://www.medicaltoys.com/speculum.htm.

Let the Fabulous Dr. Annie Sprinkle Tutor You in Viewing Your Own Cervix!

http://www.anniesprinkle.org/html/writings/self_exam.html.

Clitical Information

The-Clitoris.com, http://www.the-clitoris.com/f_html/fr_index.htm.

Clit-Pumping Good Times

The Village Voice, "Pump Up Your Clit," by Tristan Taormino, http://www.villagevoice.com/issues/0049/taormino.php.

The Goddess-Spot

Find Your G Spot

Tantra at Tahoe, http://www.tantraattahoe.com/g-spot/where-the-g-spot.htm.

G Marks the Spot: An Interview with Female Ejaculation Expert Deborah Sundahl

Toys in Babeland, http://www.babeland.com/sexinfo/features/sundahl-gspot-interview.

Anal Play

Good for Her, http://www.goodforher.com/info/anal.html.

TheSite.org, http://www.thesite.org/sexandrelationships/havingsex/styles/analplay.

The Ultimate Guide to Anal Sex for Women (book or movie), Tristan Taormino, (San Francisco, CA: Cleis Press, 1998).

Nina Hartley's Guide to Anal Sex, CD (Adam & Eve Productions, 1995).

Vulva and Woman Worship Through the Ages

The Venus of Willendorf, http://witcombe.sbc.edu/willendorf/willendorfname.html.

Yogini Ashram.net, http://www.yoginiashram.net/HISTORY/body_history.html.

Sheela-na-gigs, http://www.whitedragon.org.uk/articles/sheela.htm.

Chapter Four: Carnal Knowledge: Masturbation, Menstruation, Matrices

Menstruation

The Centre for Menstruation Cycle and Ovulation Research, http://www.cemcor.ubc.ca/.
    "The Centre for Menstrual Cycle and Ovulation Research is an accessible research centre with a mandate to distribute information directly to women about changes through the life cycle, from adolescence to menopause.
    ". . . It is the only centre in North America that focuses on ovulation and the causes for and consequences of ovulation disturbances."
    —Excerpt from the CeMCOR website.

Museum of Menstruation and Women's Health, http://www.mum.org/.
    "Discover the rich history of menstruation and women's health on this Web site— MUM for short—devoted to menstruation and selected topics of women's health!"
    —Excerpt from the MUM website.

Blood Art

Vanessa Tiegs Blood Art, http://www.vanessatiegs.com/paintings/pgs/statement.html.

"Between September 2000 and September 2003, I completed a series of 80 paintings using the medium that could best express my experience of the monthly presence of blood. I was inspired by the desire to affirm the bright red cycle—the hidden forbidden monthly renewal process."

—Excerpt from the Vanessa Tiegs website.

Eeew! Bodily Fluids! http://buggeroff.org/bloodart.html.

Radical Menstruation

Tampaction Radical Menstruation Movement, http://www.seac.org/tampons/.

"The Tampaction Campaign aims to eradicate the use of unhealthy, unsustainable tampons and pads, institutionalize sustainable alternatives into our schools and communities, and infuse healthy attitudes surrounding menstruation into our culture's consciousness. We're letting the world know that bleedin' can be everyone's issue. In doing so, we work to destroy patriarchal taboos, end environmental degradation caused by disposable tampons and pads, and promote vaginal and menstrual health."

—Excerpt from the Tampaction Mission Statement.

The Blood Sisters Project, http://bloodsisters.org/bloodsisters/.

Menarchy! http://www.menarchy.com/.

Eco- and Body-Friendly Menstrual Products

Urban Armor, http://urban-armor.org/urban-armor/rant/index.html.

"Urban Armor is a cool handmade project that is dedicated to building safer, more comfortable and even fun protection for that time of the month. It is an act of resistance to corporate powers when you choose your Urban Armor. It is time to take our own protection into our own hands!"

—From the Urban Armor Rant.

The DivaCup™, http://www.divacup.com/.

" . . . The DivaCup™ is reusable, it is very economical. As well, you can feel confident that you are doing your part in environmental conservation. Landfill and pollution problems are on the rise and continue to be a worldwide concern. In 1998, 7 billion tampons and 13 billion sanitary pads and their packaging made their way into landfills and sewage systems in the USA alone!"

—From the DivaCup™ website.

The Keeper™ Menstrual Cup, http://www.thekeeperinc.com/.

"On the market for over sixteen years, The Keeper™ Reusable Menstrual Cup is the environment-friendly alternative women's health product that saves you money every month!

". . . Economical, comfortable, environment-friendly, The Keeper™ is an attractive alternative to sanitary pads and tampons, and—when cared for properly . . . it has a life expectancy of *at least 10 years.*"

—Excerpted from The Keeper™ website.

Bleed Freely

All About My Vagina, http://www.myvag.net/blood/free/.

Chapter Five: Coming to Our Senses

I (Heart) Health

The Institute of HeartMath, http://www.heartmath.org/.

Nonverbal Communication, http://members.aol.com/nonverbal2/nvcom.htm.

Gratitude in Action

Quality of Life Website, http://www.has.vcu.edu/psy/QOL/page8.html.

The Happy Guy.com, http://www.thehappyguy.com/gratitude-journal-happiness.html. A beautiful, Christian-community gratitude website.

Hearing

The Ear, http://faculty.washington.edu/chudler/bigear.html.

Seeing

Serendip, "Tricks of the Eye, Wisdom of the Brain," http://serendip.brynmawr.edu/bb/latinhib.html.

This site has some great exercises that will help you comprehend just how interactive the process of vision is. It's also quick, fun, and easy.

Smelling

Odors

Howard Hughes Medical Institute, "The Mystery of Smell: The Vivid World of Odors," http://www.hhmi.org/senses/d110.html.

Pheromones

Howard Hughes Medical Institute, "A Secret Scent in the Human Nose: Sniffing Out Social and Sexual Signals," http://www.hhmi.org/senses/d210.html.

Touching and Feeling

The Sense of Touch, http://whalonlab.msu.edu/Student_Webpages/Babies/The%20Sense%20of%20Touch.htm.

Hillendale Webquest, "Sense of Touch," http://hes.ucf.k12.pa.us/gclaypo/senses/touch.html.

Tasting

The Sense of Taste, http://users.rcn.com/jkimball.ma.ultranet/BiologyPages/T/Taste.html.

Sensational Sensuality

Discovery Health Channel, "Sensuality Test—Abridged," http://discoveryhealth.queendom.com/sensuality_abridged_access.html.

Sensuality, http://www.urban4est.net/406.htm.

Shanti Mayi, Eastern Spirituality and The Senses, "Spirituality: The Ultimate Sensuality," http://www.shantimayi.com/ch1/sensuality1.html.

Chapter Six: Myth Making and Mentors: Witch Power Rising!

Creation Myths

The Aboriginal Dreamtime Myth, http://www.didge.nl/trans/trans_dreamtime2.html.

Karen Finley: The Ultimate Black Sheep, http://www.geocities.com/WestHollywood/2399/KAREN.HTML.

Karen Finley fucking rocks!

Chapter Seven: The Seventh Initiation: The Mirror and the Path

Vow of the Bodhisattva

The Bodhisattva Vow, http://www.katinkahesselink.net/tibet/bodhisatva.htm.

Bodhisattva Vows, http://www.intrex.net/chzg/pat6.htm.

What Is Bodhisattva? http://kyky.essortment.com/whatisbodhisat_rfld.htm.

The Tibetan Goddess Tara

Green Tara the Bodhisattva, http://www.uwec.edu/greider/Buddha/Buddhism.Course/student.culturetexts.'01/MaackJM@Tara/bodhisattva.htm.

Free Catalog

Get the latest information on our body, mind, and spirit products! To receive a **free** copy of Llewellyn's consumer catalog, *New Worlds of Mind & Spirit,* simply call 1-877-NEW-WRLD or visit our website at www.llewellyn.com and click on *New Worlds.*

LLEWELLYN ORDERING INFORMATION

Order Online:

Visit our website at www.llewellyn.com, select your books, and order them on our secure server.

Order by Phone:

- Call toll-free within the U.S. at 1-877-NEW-WRLD (1-877-639-9753). Call toll-free within Canada at 1-866-NEW-WRLD (1-866-639-9753)
- We accept VISA, MasterCard, and American Express

Order by Mail:

Send the full price of your order (MN residents add 6.875% sales tax) in U.S. funds, plus postage & handling to:

Llewellyn Worldwide
2143 Wooddale Drive
Woodbury, MN 55125-2989

Postage & Handling:

Standard (U.S., Mexico & Canada). If your order is:
$24.99 and under, add $4.00
$25.00 and over, FREE STANDARD SHIPPING

AK, HI, PR: $16.00 for one book plus $2.00 for each additional book.

International Orders (airmail only):
$16.00 for one book plus $3.00 for each additional book

Orders are processed within 2 business days.
Please allow for normal shipping time. Postage and handling rates subject to change.